UNFINISHED
AGENDA

UNFINISHED AGENDA

An Autobiography

Lesslie Newbigin

GRAND RAPIDS, MICHIGAN
WILLIAM B. EERDMANS PUBLISHING COMPANY

First published 1985 by SPCK, London
This edition published through special arrangement with SPCK by
Wm. B. Eerdmans Publishing Company, 255 Jefferson S.E.,
Grand Rapids, Mich. 49503

Library of Congress Cataloging in Publication Data

Newbigin, Lesslie.
  Unfinished agenda.

  Bibliography: p.
  Includes index.
  1. Newbigin, Lesslie.   2. Church of South India —
Bishops — Biography.   3. Ecumenical movement — Biography.
I. Title.
BX7066.5.Z8N498   1985   285'.232'0924 [B]   85-10144

ISBN 0-8028-0091-2

Contents

Foreword

'In war', said Launcelot Andrewes, 'there is a note of charge fitted to action, and a note of recall whereby stragglers are called back. So the human mind, like as in the morning it must be awakened, so at eventide as it were by a note of recall it must be called back to itself and to its Captain, by scrutiny and inquisition or examination, by prayers and thanksgivings.' It was this sense of the need to reconsider the way that I had come – or, rather, been brought over the past seventy-five years, that led me to write these memoirs. They have helped me both to contrition and to thanksgiving. If they help others, I shall be glad. I hope also that they may prove acceptable as a small offering of gratitude to those who – as the following pages try to tell – have shown me the way and helped me along it: innumerable friends, my own dear family and, above all, my beloved wife without whom my life would have been a poor thing. And with these I must add my gratitude to my friend Verleigh Cant, who has once again put me in her debt by converting my illegible scrawl into a lucid type-script for the printer.

IT IS NOT FINISHED

It is not finished, Lord.
There is not one thing done;
There is no battle of my life
That I have really won.

And now I come to tell Thee
How I fought to fail.
My human, all too human, tale
Of weakness and futility.

And yet there is a faith in me
That Thou wilt find in it
One word that Thou canst take
And make
The centre of a sentence
In Thy book of poetry.

I cannot read the writing of the years,
My eyes are full of tears,
It gets all blurred and won't make sense;
It's full of contradictions
Like the scribblings of a child.

I can but hand it in, and hope
That Thy great mind, which reads
The writings of so many lives,
Wilt understand this scrawl
And what it strives to say – but leaves unsaid.
I cannot write it over, the stars are coming out,
My body needs its bed.
I have no strength for more,
So it must stand or fall – dear Lord,
That's all.

G. A. Studdert Kennedy.

1
Northumbrian Beginnings

My earliest memories are almost all very happy ones: picnics in the heather of the Northumberland moors or on the Borrowdale fells; trips with Daddy in the side-car of his motor-cycle to the village of Kenton (now part of the urban sprawl of Newcastle) and buying acid-drops at the village shop; collecting shells on the beach at Cullercoats or flowers in the meadows for the annual school competition; lying in bed and listening to Mother playing a Chopin sonata, the music flowing all round me like a fountain of beauty.

As I look back, and go through my father's papers, I realize what a remarkable person he was. His roots were entirely Northumbrian for as far back as they can be traced – and 'Newbigin' is of course a very common name, meaning 'new building'. He was born in 1863, his father being proprietor of a chemist's shop in Narrowgate, Alnwick, which continued to trade under the same name until 1980. Daddy came fourth in a family of eleven, and their father, a staunch Conservative, seems to have ruled his family with a very firm hand. In one respect, however, he was unusual: while the four sons were sent out at the age of fifteen to fend for themselves, the daughters were given the best education money could buy and two of them (Marion the geographer and Maude who became principal of a training college) were among the first women to graduate from Edinburgh University.

Daddy was sent for one very happy year to live with a Lutheran pastor at Cremen near Berlin. His diary of that period gives a wonderful picture of a very lively and intelligent boy who enjoys every moment of life and misses nothing. There are detailed descriptions of everything he sees – mountains, birds, waterfalls, complicated German clocks, glass-cutters and cannon-founders – altogether a vivid picture of life in Germany a hundred years ago. There followed seventeen hard and unhappy years of employment in a colliery office, a period of which he did not like to say much. But during those years he must have been

1

building up a reputation on the Quayside as an able and trustworthy businessman, for when he decided in 1895 to launch out on his own he was able quickly to build up a good business and soon to have his own shipping company. At the same time he was reading widely, with an astonishing catholicity of interest. During the coal strike of 1885, when there was no work to be done but he had to attend the office daily, he read the whole of Gibbon's *Decline and Fall of the Roman Empire*, and he was reading and commenting on Plato, Dante, Schopenhauer and Browning. When war came, he was asked by the Government to take responsibility for managing captured German shipping and at the height of this period he was in charge of ninety-six German ships in addition to his own little fleet. As Chairman of the North of England Shipowners Federation for 1922 he was much involved in national political issues, but unlike most of his business associates he was a vigorous and highly articulate radical. J. A. Hobson was his friend and – on economic questions – his guru. He was constantly engaged in political activity on behalf of the Liberal Party, but as he grew older he moved more and more towards a socialist position on many issues.

The oldest of his many political papers which I have is an address given in 1904 to celebrate the centenary of Richard Cobden's birth. It shows Daddy in the thick of the political battles of the day 'against tyranny of every kind, against monopoly and against militarism'. He saw the things that had been happening – the Boer War (essentially fought for the sake of people like Cecil Rhodes), the campaign of Joseph Chamberlain for protection, the growth of expenditure on armaments and the importation of Chinese labourers to provide for the South African mines – as parts of a single moral issue. Two quotations will illustrate the way he applied the basic ideas. 'What kind of consideration for trade unionism may we expect from men whose one idea of labour is that of human machinery for the production of dividends?' And then, near the end of the paper, 'The question we must answer during the next year or two is: are we really fit to govern ourselves? Or are we content to be governed by those who think they know what is most profitable for us, and certainly know what is most profitable for themselves?' And right at the end of his life, when he insisted on continuing to trade with the legitimate Spanish government, and his ships were being harassed and bombed on the high seas by Franco's forces, he staked all that he had against the ruling powers in England which referred to the Government as 'the reds' and – openly or covertly – supported Franco.

With all this Daddy was a devout and deeply thoughtful Christian. To the end he never failed to take time for prayer in the morning, humbly kneeling by his bedside before he went out to work. As his papers show, he was always struggling with the question of how to apply his Christian faith to the day-to-day issues of business and politics.

Obviously, this remarkably vigorous and effective public life was not what I perceived as a child. My memories are of his immense delight in everything that could interest a child: his knowledge of flowers, shells and stones, his love for mountain- and rock-climbing, and the gusto with which he entered into our games and charades, and the liveliness of his conversation on every subject that came up.

I have mentioned Mother's music. She was an exquisite pianist, having studied music in Germany. She also had a well-stocked and lively mind, but she was in many respects different from Daddy. Her roots were in Scotland and her mother's old family home – St John's Kirk on the slopes of Tinto – was always her own special paradise. In contrast to the Newbigin sisters who were formidable feminists ahead of their time, Mother was a gentle and vulnerable person, always ready to blame herself if anything was not perfect. She was totally loyal to Daddy in all his interests and commitments but in her innermost self I think she felt happiest in the rather more 'county' atmosphere that hung around some of her Scottish relatives. To her children she was the most loving and devoted mother that one could wish for. As I look back I feel ashamed that I took so much of that love for granted. I realize that, in a sense, I still live by its strength and constancy.

From the age of five to seven I was sent to the kindergarten of the girls' school where my elder sister Nancy was a pupil, and then for the next five years to a preparatory school. My memories of this are not bright. Most of our time was devoted to Latin. For history we memorized lists of dates and for geography the rivers, capes, cities and other features of England. I can still recite without thinking the cotton towns of Lancashire, the towns on the Thames from Oxford to Woolwich, and a selection of the capes around the coast. Perhaps this was more important than it seems now. There was Swedish drill, which I enjoyed, and of course there were the joys of holidays – more rock-climbing on the Simonsides and exploration of the Cheviots, and longer and more adventurous cycle rides. There was also a growing enjoyment of the things that could be done in the workshop where Daddy and I spent many hours together. I learned to enjoy woodwork, the use of the lathe and the making or assembling of model engines of various kinds.

The next stage was – as the convention of the time required – a boarding school. My father loathed militarism and was determined to find a school with no Officers Training Corps. This, I suspect, was the main reason for choosing Leighton Park, the Quaker public school in Reading. I was to be there until just past my eighteenth birthday.

My father took several days off to take me for the first time to London. It was a thrilling time for me, right up to the moment when he said goodbye at the school gates and disappeared in the bus for Reading station. I was totally unprepared for the sudden, overwhelming, desolating knowledge that I was alone. Never before, and never again afterwards, have I known such utter desolation. As I remember it now, I wonder how I survived it, and how countless other children can go through and survive that desolation. There is no way of describing it, for it is just darkness with no light at all.

Somehow I did survive and I began slowly to accept the new situation. The traditional 'ragging' of new boys added to the pain, but I began to make friends. Looking back, and reading the school history, I realize that this was not one of the better periods of its life. Discipline was, as I realize now, in a poor state. Near riots and the most outrageous practical jokes were rewarded with the mildest of punishments. I remember Julian Bell, whose desk was next to mine, filling it with newspaper and setting it alight just as the master entered the room. The only response was (as I remember) the agonized but ineffective bellowing of H. A. Davies, in his strong Welsh accent: 'Bell, you damned old goose! It was the act of a lunatic' – and that closed the affair. But the other side of this laxity was a great deal of freedom to develop one's own interests and ideas. Leighton Park made much of

4

hobbies and it is of my exploits in these fields that I have the most enduring memories: woodwork, poultry-keeping, meteorology, music and long explorations, on a bicycle, of the lovely Berkshire countryside. I did not much enjoy games except for fives, which I loved and played with modest competence. There was also plenty of political debate in which I espoused the Liberal cause. The school encouraged the art of public speaking, especially through the annual event in which the speaker was heckled by a large audience of parents and friends of the pupils. This kind of training was to be useful later.

I remember very little of the work which no doubt I was required to do, except for the geography. In that rather low period of the school's history there was one man who was a genius. S. W. Brown taught geography. But for the generations of boys who went through his classes he taught infinitely more. He created a capacity to think, to break out of stereotypes, to explore new ideas and to question old ones. He taught us to read voraciously and to get to the heart of the argument of a big book so that we could expound and defend it in debate. He made learning a thrilling exercise. And at the end of it he made you laugh at yourself.

In spite of Bill Brown I think I still took myself too seriously. I had the ambition to be a sort of Renaissance man with interests in all directions, and consequently refused to specialize in any field. For my final Higher Certificate papers I took geography, chemistry, Latin and German, thus trying to keep a foot in all possible camps. Perhaps it would have been better to aim at real competence in a smaller field, but I do not altogether regret this ambition.

I finished up as senior prefect in spite of the headmaster's wholly justified opinion that I was not good at maintaining discipline. Somehow I coped. I shall always be grateful that he was willing to take the risk, and for the advice he gave me: 'Don't over-rate opposition, and don't take it as directed against yourself.'

In the matter of religious belief I had, by the end of schooldays, abandoned the Christian assumptions of my home and childhood. Quaker meetings were not the best way for a schoolboy to come to a grasp of the Christian faith, though they gave me an experience of quiet, humble and attentive waiting upon God which is very precious. Scripture lessons were in general utterly boring. From my chemistry teacher I learned that 'life is a disease of matter', and from much of my reading in historical geography (though not from Bill Brown himself) I imbibed a broadly deterministic view of history. The distribution of Catholics and Protestants in Europe could be satisfactorily correlated with the climatic conditions of its different parts. 'God' was no longer a tenable hypothesis.

Positively the strongest impact on my thinking in my last year at school was made by a book called *The Living Past*, by F. S. Marvin. I have not looked at it for more than fifty years but it gave me a belief in the human story as an upward striving towards growing mastery over all that stands in the way of man's full humanity. I joined lustily in a hymn which was often sung in the school Assembly. It invited us to

> . . . spill no drop of blood, but dare
> all that may plant man's lordship firm
> on earth and fire and sea and air.

I saw myself as part of that noble campaign.

And yet that is not the whole story. I continued to wonder whether belief in God was possible. Among my father's books I had noticed an odd title, *The Will to Believe*. One day while I was working at the lathe this title came into my mind. Its absurdity amazed me: How could a wish to believe be anything but a recipe for self-delusion? I went to the shelf and took out the book and read William James's essay. I was not persuaded, but I saw that he had made a reasonable case for belief. At about the same time it happened that Herbert Gray, a well-known and loved Presbyterian minister, stayed with my parents for an Assembly meeting, Hearing that they had a son at school he left behind a book of his own as a gift for me. When I came home I read it – a lucid and reasonable exposition of the faith. Again I was not persuaded but I saw that Christian faith was not irrational.

It had been decided that I should go to Cambridge. The necessary exams were passed and I gained entrance to Queens' for autumn 1928. For the first seven months of that year I was an office boy in my father's firm. The office was on the Quay between the Swing Bridge and the High Level Bridge of Robert Stephenson. The new bridge, a pilot project for the one over

Sydney Harbour, was being built during these months. Like most small shipowners at the time, my father was struggling to remain in business. There were losses more often than profits. Some of the work was dull and depressing – especially going from office to office to try to persuade equally struggling debtors to pay their overdue bills. Some was more exciting. The shipping trade was a jungle of fierce competition between small firms. Each day merchants and shippers mingled on the floor of the Newcastle Exchange to pick up orders and seek contracts. Very quick decisions had to be made. A Northumberland colliery has 3000 tons of coal to ship to Hamburg. Another colliery needs a cargo of pit props shipped from Sweden to the Tyne. What rates can you offer for the round trip to each of these parties? How quickly can you get the tender coded and despatched by cable to Hamburg and Stockholm? Will you get your telegram on to the wire before your rival? It was classical capitalism in action, and when I came later to read Marshall's *Principles of Economics* I understood what was meant by 'the higgling of the market'. It was fierce but exciting. Many companies, including ours, were only just able to survive. Indelibly fixed in my memory is the day when, by very rapid and accurate work, we secured an order ahead of our rivals and – a day or two later – learned that for the colliery which had lost the order this was the final blow. It closed, and hundreds of miners were thrown on to the street. Our small triumph was their colossal disaster. I began to see the reality of what I later learned to call 'structural sin'.

During this period I continued to take singing lessons and to seize every opportunity for a day of fell-walking or rock-climbing. I went with a friend in one of the company's little ships to Hamburg and had a week exploring the Harz Mountains. And finally, the last weekend before leaving for Cambridge was a glorious spell of rock-climbing in the Lake District with the Fell and Rock Climbing Club of which my father had been an early member.

2

Cambridge

I wonder if it is true that one is more tempted to cling to the past in the days of youth than in later life. My first feelings about Cambridge were that it was dull and flat compared to the world I knew and loved. I wrote home with some contempt to say that I was planning to climb all the peaks above five feet. Only slowly did the beauty of the place begin to capture me and the enchantment of its history and its present greatness. That winter the Cam froze and there was skating on the river and on great stretches of flooded fenland. There was the special beauty of the river above Grantchester, the great open skies and the glow of newly formed friendships around the fire in college rooms.

In that first year I did almost everything except work. I was to do the first part of the Geography Tripos – a two-year programme – but I soon found that the work was well below the standard of what I had been doing with Bill Brown at Leighton Park. It was really unnecessary to do any work at all.

There were plenty of other things to do. The University Mountaineering Club provided wonderful opportunities for hearing at first-hand about recent exploits in the Himalayas and I went with fellow-members for climbing holidays at Easter in the Lake District and in summer in the Austrian Tyrol. A group of us in Queens' and Newnham formed a company to sing Elizabethan music, primarily for our own joy but also, on a number of occasions, to give recitals. And then there were the Union debates into which I threw myself with enthusiasm. It was customary for the motion to be proposed and opposed by undergraduates, with distinguished political leaders as their seconders. My most vivid memory is of a debate when I had Anthony Eden as my seconder and George Lansbury on the other side. Eden was then at the height of his popularity but it was Lansbury who captured my heart. My liberal principles began to shake a little, and I wondered if socialism was not the real way forward. Some time later I was asked by Liberal Party headquarters if I would be prepared to stand as a candidate for Parliament after I had finished at Cambridge, but by then my course was set in another direction. There was – as is now only too well known – a group of dedicated Marxists in Cambridge at that time. Some of them were my old school friends such as Julian Bell and Jan Gillett. Maurice Dobb and John Cornford were, as I remember, the leading gurus in this circle. Soviet Russia was already as near as possible to paradise on earth, and the redoubtable Dean of Canterbury, Hewlett Johnson, returned from his frequent visits there to report on its glories. I was drawn to the kind of socialism represented by George Lansbury but repelled by the intellectual style of the Marxists. Julian Bell was to die soon afterwards in the war to defend the Spanish Government against the Fascists. It was in one of his last letters that he wrote the words which I have often had cause to remember in later years: 'Revolution is the opiate of the intellectual.'

I occasionally went to the Friends' Meeting on Sunday mornings and through this became involved in an undertaking which was known to its clients as the 'Appy 'Our. It was an attempt to do something for the hundreds of boys who roamed the streets of Cambridge on Sunday evenings with nothing to do but get into trouble. They were invited to come into the warmth of the Quaker premises in Jesus Lane, where tea and biscuits were available and efforts were made to offer some improving form of programme. Pandemonium was liable to break loose at any moment, but at least it was chaos within a limited space. To devise a programme which would capture and hold their attention was almost impossible. I remember persuading Professor Debenham, hero of Antarctic exploration, to come and tell them of his adventures with Shackleton in the polar regions, but even he was unable to make them listen. However, it was not all wasted effort and it led to friendships with some of these boys which I hope were fruitful for them as they were for me.

If I was not working seriously at geography I was thinking seriously about other things. Queens' was a small college and it was easy to form friendships. There was a lively branch of the Student Christian Movement and several of its members became my friends. I found their company very attractive. They were committed to their faith and ready to talk about it, but also open to difficult questions and ready to take me as I was – interested but sceptical and basically unconvinced. I never felt that they were trying to 'get at' me, as I did about the 'evangelical' group. I began to think again about William James and his *Will to Believe*. Certainly there was something very appealing about this belief. I was more and more drawn into the company of the SCM, and in that company I *did* want to believe. I asked one of them (T. H. Sutcliffe): 'If I wanted to be a Christian, how would I begin?' Without a moment of hesitation he replied: 'Buy an alarm clock.' I knew what he meant. The 'morning watch' was still a living tradition carried on from the formative years of the Student Volunteer Movement. I began to get up earlier in the morning to read the Bible and to pray. I did not know whether God existed. I did know there were many things with which I could not cope. And with William James to support me I knew that I was not being irrational in seeking the help of One of whose existence there was no proof.

More than anyone else it was Arthur Watkins who drew me into a personal faith. He was several years older than most of us, captain of the college rugby team, leading member of the 'Cherubs' (a group which the rest of us were tempted to regard as brainless toughs) and with an extraordinary gift of friendship for every sort of person. As I came to know him I realized that the centre of his life was a profound devotion to Christ. Prayer was his deepest being, and he made me want to learn to pray. With it all there went an inexhaustible fund of laughter. He was the most vivid example I know of the fact that the grace of God is so overwhelmingly absurd that one can only laugh and sing.

By the end of my first year I was committed to the SCM and had become one of the college representatives. But I still had other compelling interests. I did not accede to the pressure to attend the summer conference at Swanwick but spent the long vacation in a Quaker service centre in South Wales and with the Mountaineering Club in Austria. The latter activity ended disastrously with a forty-feet fall in which I narrowly escaped death and had to return home in bad shape. The former had a more far-reaching sequel.

In those depressed and despairing years one of the blackest spots was the Rhondda Valley in South Wales, where miners had been rotting for years in hopeless unemployment and destitution. The Society of Friends, always ready to respond where others prefer to forget, had started a centre at Maes-yr-haf to bring some kind of comfort and hope to this apparently Godforsaken community. Through contacts with Cambridge Friends I was interested in this programme. It sounded like a brave attempt to do something in a hopeless situation. Jim Cottle and I decided to offer our services for several weeks of the long vacation. He was a friend from Leighton Park days, now at Queens' and, like me, being drawn to the SCM. As soon as the summer term ended we set off on our bicycles and travelled by easy stages through some of the loveliest country in England, sleeping on the hay of hospitable farmers and taking our time over the journey.

Our destination was Trealaw, where we were to help in the local programme – primarily with a men's recreation club. Anything in the way of religion was excluded from the programme. One could understand the anxiety not to use the helplessness of these men as an opportunity for proselytizing. And yet, as the weeks went by, I became less and less convinced that we were dealing with the real issues. From one point of view the real issues were political: national and international. Everyone must work for a more rational economic order. But that was a hope for the future. Now, at that moment, these men needed some kind of faith that would fortify them for today and tomorrow against apathy and despair. Draughts and pingpong could not provide this. They needed the Christian faith that was beginning to draw me.

For the last week of our stay we took about sixty of the men to camp under canvas near the sea at Llantwit Major. Things did not go well. One night the men managed to get a lot of strong drink into the camp, and before long they were roaring drunk and fighting with each other. I did not begin to know how to cope. When at a late hour we got some peace I went to my tent with the feeling of total defeat. I had nothing to contribute to the situation. As I lay awake a vision came to my mind, perhaps arising from something I had read a few weeks before by William Temple. It was a vision of the cross, but it was the cross spanning the space between heaven and earth, between ideals and present realities, and with arms that embraced the whole world. I saw it as something which reached down to the most hopeless and sordid of human misery and yet promised life and victory. I was sure that night, in a way I had never been before, that this was the clue that I must follow if I were to make any kind of sense of the world. From that moment I would always know how to take bearings when I was lost. I would know where to begin again when I had come to the end of all my own resources of understanding or courage.

That new certainty was strengthened soon after by the experience of sharing in the Cambridge Evangelistic Campaign to Preston. These campaigns took place every year under the leadership of the Vicar of Holy Trinity Church and Dr Alex Wood, a senior don at Emmanuel, who combined a first-class scientific intelligence, an active political life as a Socialist, an uncompromising commitment to pacifism, and an infectious gift for laughter. A group of a hundred or so undergraduates gathered under this leadership each year for a preaching campaign in one of the industrial towns of the Midlands and the North. The main programme was open-air preaching and visits to factories during lunchbreaks. It called for the ability to speak effectively from a soapbox in a crowded street, to stand up to heckling, and to meet the serious questions of working men and women. I do not know that any great impact was made on the towns visited. I do know that for the campaigners it was an enormously fruitful, if sometimes frightening, exercise.

I had been drawn into this good company before I could honestly say that I had something to give. But by the time we gathered in Preston in September I knew that I could at least point to the cross of Jesus as the ground of hope for every human being. One experience of that week has always remained in my mind. As the result of a street conversation after one of our preachings I visited a tenement where three families had to live in a single small flat, and at least one of the men was dying of tuberculosis. When I struggled to find words for that situation I knew once and for all that a merely humanistic hope was not enough. At that point my talk about a new social order was impertinent nonsense.

I went back to Cambridge at the end of that vacation a committed Christian, and threw myself with enthusiasm into the work of the SCM. I now had rooms in college – a lovely panelled room in Old Court looking across to the famous sundial. I could entertain people in my room and I hired a piano, so that there could be plenty of music.

Great men and women from many parts of the Christian world were willing to come to Cambridge at the invitation of the SCM and some of them were giants whose visits left unforgettable impressions. John R. Mott answered the questions of sceptical undergraduates with a quiet certainty which somehow could not be gainsaid. Jack Winslow from India was the first to awaken my interest in that country with which no one in our family had ever had any connection. With his black beard and his piercing eyes and his accounts of the work of the Poona Ashram he gave me my first taste of the most attractive elements of Indian spirituality. And there are many other memories: William Temple in the pulpit of St Mary's telling us 'it is possible to be comparatively religious but there is no such thing as comparative religion', and John Mackay of Lima and Princeton whose only remembered phrase was about 'concrete palpitating personalities' but who nevertheless impressed me profoundly with the vision of Christian discipleship which he had gained through his long ministry in Latin America. I was beginning to have a thrilling sense of sharing in a worldwide Christian enterprise which was commanding the devotion of men and women whose sheer intellectual and spiritual power was unmistakable. I became, even as a second-year undergraduate, a reader of the *International Review of Missions*, and the Christian faith into which I was growing was ecumenical from the beginning.

There were other visitors too. One of them was Frank Buchman, whose 'First Century Christian Fellowship' had recently acquired the title 'Oxford Group' and was later to become 'Moral Rearmament'. Many of us in the SCM were strongly challenged by the uncompromising claim for absolute standards. I had one long session with Buchman himself, whom I found less attractive than his disciples. I think most of us in the SCM were both disturbed and attracted by 'the Groups', as they were called, and I had many occasions then and in later years to be grateful for their witness. But I could not accept their view of

Christian faith and life as adequate and I never committed myself to them.

During that second year I began to go to Evensong in the college chapel. The services of the Book of Common Prayer were strange to me and not, at first, very attractive. But I came to love and cherish that quiet half-hour at the end of the daylight hours when we could share in a corporate act which, unlike the typical Free Church service, gave one both the ease and the freedom of a well-known and well-beloved song. It was the only place where the SCM and the CICCU could pray together, for the official evangelical view was that the SCM members were unbelievers. Even there, however, our divisions were published, for at the words 'I believe' the SCM turned obediently towards the East while the CICCU stood firmly and resolutely facing one another across the chapel. It punctuated each act of worship with a moment of absurdity.

We were deeply devoted to the cause of Christian unity. I was a member of a society called the Madingley Group, committed to regular prayer for unity, whose members walked to the village of Madingley on each Ascension Day to pray there in the parish church for the unity of all Christians. But it was a very strong principle in the SCM that one could not truly share in the ecumenical experience of Christianity without being a fully committed church member, and as I was now regularly attending St Columba's Presbyterian Church I joined the confirmation class there and was duly received into membership by its much loved minister George Barclay. I can honestly say that worship there Sunday by Sunday was a joy and a refreshment.

One thing in the SCM troubled me. It seemed that almost everybody who took his religion seriously was headed for ordination. I was not. I was preparing to follow my father in his business and I knew from all that I had seen in him that to be a Christian in the world of commerce was a difficult thing. I did not hear the SCM putting to its members the challenge to consider this calling. There were frequent references to the call to foreign missionary service, and the Student Volunteer Missionary Union was still a living and active part of the SCM in Cambridge as elsewhere. But where was the call to this very tough and unglamorous field – the world of industry and commerce? I got

14

together a few like-minded members of the SCM and we formed a society for Christians *not* intending to be ordained. We had a number of very good meetings, for one of which my father came to speak. I wish I could say that the society continued to flourish, but my connection with it was terminated by events which I had not anticipated.

As my second undergraduate year came to an end I had to make some decisions. I was asked by the President of the Union to let him nominate me for the committee, which would have meant giving a lot of time to its debates during the rest of my time at Cambridge. I was also invited to join the Mountaineering Club in the Alps, on dates which clashed with the SCM Swanwick conference. I did not find the decisions easy, but in the end I felt that the SCM must have priority. I turned down both – and went to Swanwick. Each of the two 'General Swanwicks' brought together about 600 students for a week in the summer. The men lived under canvas, the women in the hostel. Meetings were held in a big tent and there were innumerable smaller groups on particular issues. That first Swanwick opened up a new world for me. It is hard to describe now how thrilling it was. I can only say that I was lifted up into the heights. The excitement of being able to share new ideas and insights with many different people of my own age but of different background; the sheer high spirits bubbling up in all kinds of fantastic performances, such as Alfred Sadd's re-enactment of Exodus in which Pharaoh's hosts were duly drowned in the lake; the early morning times of quiet prayer; and, above all, the addresses in the big tent, all added up to a kind of transfiguration experience. We saw Jesus in his glory, and like the disciples we just wanted to stay. Very important for me were the nights when I took my bedding out into the field and slept under the open sky. R. O. Hall had the same idea and there were nights when we talked together long after 'lights out' and something of the spirit of that great man was communicated to my still searching mind.

There was a tent set aside for prayer. On an afternoon near the end of the week I went into it to pray. No one else was there. While I was praying something happened which I find it hard to describe. I suddenly knew that I had been told that I must offer for ordination. I had not been thinking about this. But I knew

15

that I had been ordered and that it was settled and that I could not escape.

I was in real distress. How could I possibly face my father? I was his only son and he was looking to me to join him and to take over from him the business which he had created and nurtured with such skill and Christian commitment. I knew that it was a strain financially for him to keep me at the University. How could I possibly go to him and tell him that I would not be coming into the firm and that I needed money for a three-year theological training? And what about the vocation to be a Christian in business, and the group of fellow-students at Cambridge whom I had encouraged to accept this calling?

Eventually I came out into the afternoon sun, feeling dizzy with all the questions that now had to be faced, but clear about one thing. I would seek a job as soon as I left Cambridge and earn enough for a theological training. That at least I could do, and I must. Only with that certainty could I tell Daddy of what had happened.

I went for tea. Willie Tindal, the national Study-Secretary of the SCM, told me he wanted to talk. We sat down in the 'Vinery', which still exists in the portico of the big house, and he started. It took me some time to discover what was on his mind, but suddenly I realized that he was making tentative soundings to see if I would be interested to serve on the SCM staff. The moment this dawned on me I cut in and said: 'You don't need to talk further. The matter is settled. I'm coming.' If I had been more pious than I am, I would have said, 'The thing comes from the Lord: you cannot speak to me good or bad.' As far as I was concerned, this was an overwhelming confirmation of what had happened. There was no place for discussion. The matter was settled. Willie was, understandably, taken aback and started telling me that this was a serious matter which should not be decided on the nod but needed prayerful thought. I told him that neither prayer nor thought was needed. In my own mind, the matter was settled. I would be available for service wherever I was needed from summer 1931. I could now break the news to Daddy and the task would be at least a little easier.

When I got home from Swanwick I told my parents what had

happened. I still find it hard to imagine what it must have felt like, especially for Daddy. But there was not a moment of hesitation in his response. I must do what God had called me to do. There was not the faintest hint of disappointment or reproach. He would be as wholly with me in this as he would have been if I had come with him into the business. It is only from the perspective of old age that one can begin to appreciate what that decision meant to a man of nearly seventy. It was made without a moment's hesitation. And, in the good providence of God, it was the son of my father's partner, Edward Haslam, who in due course took over the management of the business. He was and is a much better businessman than I ever could have been.

There was still a further problem: what about my advocacy of the calling to Christian service in industry and commerce? I wrote to John R. Mott. He was a layman. More than anyone I had met he embodied the worldwide Christian cause. I think it was a very confused letter, because I was trying to clear my own mind. I received a reply which was typical of Mott, both in the trenchancy of its language and in the care with which that man with six continents in his parish found time to write a long letter to an unknown student. The Christian ministry, he assured me, was 'the most highly multiplying form of Christian service'. I was to go ahead without hesitation. With or without Mott I had to go ahead anyway, but his letter cheered me. I am ashamed, however, that the 'Christians in Business' society wilted and – as far as I know – did not survive. It is a matter on which I have often pondered.

For my last year at Cambridge I was to read Economics. Part I of the Tripos was a two-year course, but I was to do it in one. The subject was completely new to me. I would, for the first time at Cambridge, have to work really hard. During the long vacation I struggled to master Marshall's *Principles of Economics* and during the whole of the following year everything else had to take second place. It was a good time to read the subject at Cambridge. J. M. Keynes was working on his new theory of money, and the running battle with the conservatives of the London School of Economics provided spice for the lectures. But I was now a member of the University SCM Committee, with Oliver Tomkins as Chairman, and I had responsibility for a group of about six college branches. I was also occasionally involved in national SCM events.

Meanwhile at SCM headquarters discussion was going on about where I might be employed as a secretary. I believe that Manchester and Liverpool were considered, but eventually Robert Mackie suggested that I might go to Glasgow. The Scottish Executive of the SCM was invited to interview me. There was some understandable anxiety about importing a foreigner, but Robert had drawn attention to my Scots grand-mother and the Committee agreed to have a look at me. On a cold winter day I met them in a basement of Edinburgh's old George Square. Their style was very different from Cambridge but I was impressed by the freshness and vigour of their thinking. They were all greatly influenced by John Macmurray, and his vision of the Christian life was the one that constantly came through.

The outcome of the meeting was that they were willing to take me on. But for me the meeting had a far more important consequence. One of the members of the Committee was Helen Henderson, then in her first year as a staff secretary for Glasgow, Dundee and Aberdeen. She did not say much and I did not say much to her. All I can say is that I fell in love with her there and then and I made up my mind that whether or not the whole Committee decided to take me on I would try to ensure that she did. It was – in the event – to be nearly six years before we could be married, but from that moment my life would have a new joy in it. And when I knew that I was in fact to be appointed to Glasgow, and that Helen would be my colleague there, I felt that the cup of happiness was running over.

On my last night at Queens' I sat late on the steps that lead down into the President's Court, drinking in the beauty of the half-timbered buildings in the light of the moon. I heard the midnight chimes of the distant Catholic church, those rather strange notes that had been the background of my first year in lodgings in Panton Street. And then came the now-familiar chimes of the nearby college clock. In the coming together of these two sounds the three years that were now ending came together: their beginning when I was still an unbeliever with no centre or shape to my life; the years of growing commitment to Jesus; and now the moment when I could look forward to the full-time service of my beloved SCM with my beloved Helen as a colleague. I knew with an overwhelming certainty that my life was in God's hands, that he and not I had the direction of it, and that I would be free of all doubt and anxiety. At that moment I did not just believe: I knew.

3

Glasgow

I filled in the interval between the end of Cambridge term and the graduation with a leisurely solo journey on my bicycle through some of the loveliest country in England, sleeping out of doors and using my raincoat as a tent when it rained at night. Travelling alone meant being caught up in all sorts of invitations and meetings which made the brief holiday even more delightful. Daddy and Mother brought the family car to Cambridge for my graduation and then we all drove home. The summer was filled with a variety of joys: climbing in North Wales with Cambridge friends and in Austria with a party from Leighton Park; the SCM conferences at Swanwick; and the Cambridge Evangelistic Campaign in Huddersfield. And so to Glasgow to begin the next chapter.

Archie Craig, then Chaplain to the University, invited me to stay with him until I could find a place of my own. That was to be the beginning of a friendship to which I owe more than I can ever say. Though I was a committed believer, mine was very much a faith seeking understanding. I had a thousand questions with which I was always wrestling. Archie was willing to set aside long hours in his study helping me to see things more clearly, to distinguish essentials from the rest, and to recognize the elements of mystery which must always remain for any honest mind. He himself combined a deep and firm rooting in the best strengths of Scottish divinity with a finely tuned intelligence, always questioning and always open to new possibilities. He was faithful to the best insights of the liberal theology of the time and at the same time listening seriously but critically to the new and strange voice of Karl Barth. Perhaps (I do not know) it was Barth's influence that caused him to hang the famous Grünewald altarpiece over his study mantelpiece; our conversations constantly returned to that picture and to the finger of John the Baptist pointing to the Crucified. Even after I had found lodgings of my own, a few yards from the Students' Union, I continued to visit Archie almost every day that I was in Glasgow and to receive from him a kind of theological training which was, I think, more significant than anything before or after.

The job of an SCM secretary was, and is, difficult to define. I was 'Intercollegiate Secretary' with responsibility for the men students of the University, the two Technical Colleges of Glasgow and Paisley and the Agricultural Training College. Helen had a parallel responsibility for the women. In each of these there was an SCM branch with its own officers, though in some cases it was more on paper than in reality. Our job was to stimulate, encourage and help but not to manage. Much the biggest part of the job, at least as I tried to do it, was simply sitting around in the Students' Union ready for any conversation that might turn up. I found that Glasgow students were at least as lively and as passionately interested in everything as my former Cambridge friends, but the accent was different. It was at once more metaphysical and more political. A. A. Bowman was then the Professor of Moral Philosophy and every Arts student was required to attend his lectures several times a week. His influence was enormous. When the SCM invited him to speak there would be an audience of up to 800. His lectures stimulated passionate discussion, and the large room of the Union would be filled with groups of students gathered with their coffee cups round the tables and arguing about what he had said in the previous lecture. It was right in the midst of these discussions that the SCM obviously had its real existence, and that was where I was happy to be. There is always a temptation for a Christian group to withdraw into a safe place. It was something I wanted to resist and it was a great asset that the SCM had at that time no room of its own. There was no 'Chaplaincy Centre' or anything of that kind. The SCM had to be part of the life of the Students' Union.

This was important from another point of view. With others of my contemporaries I was very much exercised about what a university ought to be. It ought not, I was convinced, to be a place where students were simply fed information or indoctrinated with the accepted ideas of society. It ought to be a place where radical questions were asked, and accepted wisdom tested, so that the student could come to his own convictions about what mattered. For this reason I saw the debates in the Union coffee room as a vital part of what a university ought to be. And it was

21

important that the SCM should be fully involved because their job was to be the place where the Christian message was made present in the form proper to such a community of students, that is to say, as something open for question and discussion.

But of course there were SCM study groups, weekend conferences and other events of all kinds. Often I would take a group of students away for a weekend somewhere in the country or – once – on a houseboat on Loch Lomond. George McLeod was then the parish minister of Govan, making a deep impression on the life of the Church through the early development of the ideas which were later to be embodied in the Iona Community. My first major conference was organized with his help at the Pierce Institute in Govan, where we tried to expose the students to the situation of the Clyde workers and workless and to George's vision of the Church's response. There were also bigger all-Scotland events, including a national conference at Dalhousie for which Helen and I had the main organizational responsibility. Some of these big events were such as to lift the heart; much of the day-to-day struggle was discouraging. In the Technical and Agricultural Colleges it was very difficult to make the SCM a reality. The Christian Union could operate effectively, but the kind of restless questioning that characterized the SCM fitted a university better than a technical college. There religion had to be clear and definite, or it was nowhere.

At that stage in my thinking the Sermon on the Mount was very much the centre of the Christian message. I was a pacifist, and believed that the consistent application of the teachings of Jesus would solve national and international problems. One particular relationship forced me to think through the meaning of the Sermon more deeply. One night I was accosted in the street by a beggar who asked for money for a night's lodging. He named a sum. As laid down in the Sermon, I gave him twice the amount. After he had walked a few yards and had had time to recover from the shock, he came back and asked for a much larger sum. I did not have that amount, much less double the amount, on my person. But the teaching of the Sermon on the Mount was clear. I gave him my address and told him to call next day. He did, and that was the beginning of a relationship with George King which was to last until he died long after I had gone to India. My letters of the next two years are full of my struggles to find out how to be faithful to the teaching of Jesus in a single relationship of that kind. I am sure I did many foolish things. I know that my good landlady was very puzzled when she found that two people were using the bed she had provided for one. But I knew that through that long-sustained relationship I was forced to think through the meaning of the Sermon on the Mount and its relation to the Christian message as a whole, and that through this I was prepared to receive and understand the teaching of Reinhold Niebuhr when it came across my mental horizon.

At the beginning of the 1930s Britain was in the appalling state of recession and paralysis that had followed the Wall Street crash of 1929. The misery of the unemployed was a constant darkness, and yet it did not create among the comfortable class to which I belonged the sense of moral outrage that it does today. To those who were politically alert it seemed that the capitalist system was collapsing. Socialism of various hues had a powerful attraction. Soviet Russia and Communism posed a challenge which it was impossible to ignore – not a threat but a hope and a promise. Internationally the League of Nations was still the centre of hope for Christian people. The memories of the senseless slaughter of the 1914–18 War were still such a strong factor in the mental atmosphere that people clung with a pathetic hope even to such toothless agreements as the Kellogg Pact of 1928. And the long-drawn-out preparations for the Disarmament Conference of 1932 kept alive flickering hopes for a world without war.

My time in Glasgow began almost on the day of the 'Mukden Incident' which triggered the Japanese invasion of Manchuria. We did not know, of course, but that was to be the beginning of the end of the League of Nations. Japan was to be the first to prove that the League's armoury of sanctions would be useless when the interests of a great power were involved. The successful aggression against China would lead through the Rhineland, Abyssinia, Austria and Czechoslovakia to the Second World War.

We did not know that, but we were passionately involved in the effort to rouse opinion against the aggressor. The SCM organized a meeting in the Union to protest against the fact that Scottish armament manufacturers were selling arms to Japan.

We asked the Vice-Chancellor to preside. When he refused, Helen and I went to Bowman. Bowman rose in wrath from his chair and paced up and down the room muttering 'The man's a coward'. Needless to say he accepted our invitation and delivered a blistering attack on the Glasgow arms salesmen which provided headlines for the newspapers and much of which I can still quote from memory.

National and international politics, the rise of Italian and German Fascism, the question of Indian independence and the ever-present reality of unemployment and destitution among the Clyde shipyard workers – these were the living issues in relation to which we tried to understand and articulate the Christian faith. The Glasgow International Club, presided over by a beloved Tamil Christian, Appadurai Aaron, was a place where I spent a great deal of time and where I formed many Indian and African friendships. The vision of Christianity as essentially a worldwide affair, the vision which the Cambridge SCM had given me, was still strong. I acquired the complete eight-volume report of the Jerusalem Conference of 1928 and studied it all with enthusiasm. The world was, emphatically, the context for discipleship.

Of one aspect of my international interests I am not very proud. Edwin Barker of the SCM national staff and I were selected to represent the British SCM at an Anglo-German conference organized by International Student Service at Giessen in Germany. The two delegations included politicians, academics and representatives of various walks of life. Ours was led by the Cambridge economist Professor Guillebaud, and included a rather pathetic ex-Cabinet minister whom Edwin and I had to take under our wing because he spoke no word of German. Predictably the meeting was dominated by the German situation. The dissolution of the Reichstag by Hindenburg took place while we were in session. The National Socialists were by far the most impressive among the German student delegation. They seemed to represent something fresh, a breakaway from the sickness of European capitalism. They were full of idealism, and of the conviction that God was at work in a new way in Germany. I was so much impressed that I arranged for a couple of young National Socialists to be invited to the forthcoming Quadrennial Conference in Edinburgh. I also addressed the SCM General Committee on the subject, and wrote in *The Student Movement* that what was happening in Germany was far more important than English people realized. In a sense I was right, but I was also very naive. Nothing then seemed to presage the demonic character that was later to become so obvious. I was taken in by the freshness and the vitality. That experience has made me inclined to be sceptical ever since, when I hear that what looks like the new wave is 'God at work in the world'.

Helen and I had become close colleagues, sharing our pastoral and administrative problems and helping each other out in our still carefully segregated fields of work. We must have been amazingly discreet, for when we announced our engagement it seemed to come as a total surprise. It was on a lovely Saturday in May, when we had gone for a walk in the woods beyond Milngavie, carpeted with bluebells as far as the eye could see, that I put the question and received the answer for which I had so much longed. That was a day of joy beyond anything before and it has been followed through the years with days and years of deepening joy and thankfulness as we have learned what it means (to quote a phrase we often used) 'to be completely known and all forgiven', and at the same time tried to learn 'to love each other only in God' so that love would always hold us to the best and never condone mediocrity.

Helen's parents had been missionaries of the Irish Presbyterian Church in Gujarat. Her father had died in a drowning accident while she was still a schoolgirl. His published biography shows him to have been a truly great missionary, full of love, of zeal and of a boundless sense of fun. She had left India at the age of seven and her deepest roots were in her old school, Walthamstow Hall in Sevenoaks, and in the home of her mother's remarkable family of sisters in Tralee, County Kerry. She had had a fine record at Edinburgh University and at the Moray House Training College: an able student, a first-class hockey player and one of the most dynamic figures in the Edinburgh SCM. I was to come to know and love her mother and her family in the months that followed.

One of the things that were settled that day among the bluebells of Milngavie was that we would go to India. Helen was already committed to missionary service there. I was committed to the ministry but, rooted as I was in the SCM, I had never thought of ministry except in a world context. I had already come to know and cherish many Indian friends both at Cambridge and in Glasgow. And Helen and I, who represented the SCM on the Candidates Committee of the Church of Scotland Foreign Mission Committee, already knew something of the needs of the eight Indian mission fields for which the Church of Scotland was responsible. We knew that if I were to take a full theological course it would be four years before we could be married, but Helen was willing to wait. We knew that the Church had a foolish rule which forbade marriage until the missionary had had two years abroad. Apparently the official view was that a wife was an encumbrance not to be taken on board until language study was completed. We were determined that in our case the rule would be waived!

The greatest event of my second year of service in the SCM was the Edinburgh Quadrennial of January 1933. Like its predecessors in the series of such meetings, it brought together a couple of thousand students from nearly fifty nations to put before them the call to world mission. Unlike its predecessors it was dominated not by the needs of the traditional mission fields but by the crisis within the old Christendom. Germany had a very big place in the thinking of the conference. Hanns Lilje, General Secretary of the German SCM, spoke powerfully of the challenge of Communism to the Christian conscience, but his address contained no hint of the existence of the growing Fascist alternative. Yet Hitler was to become Chancellor within that month. What was striking in Lilje's address was the repeated reference to the falsification of Christianity which had made it 'a mere appendage of bourgeois thought'. And J. H. Oldham, in a profound and prophetic address, spoke of the radical departure of Europe from the Christian faith when it followed Descartes and the pioneers of the Enlightenment. In other words – though it was not said so bluntly – the mission field was here in the 'Christian world'. It was not surprising that in the following days there were indignant letters in the *Scotsman* from representatives of the Edinburgh bourgeoisie who had thought they were hosting a missionary conference and had discovered a nest of saboteurs. From a perspective of nearly half a century later I would dare to say that missionary thinking in Europe and North America has not yet met the challenge which Edinburgh gave to develop a genuinely missionary encounter with post-Enlightenment European civilization.

It fell to me, as the newest recruit to the Student Volunteer Mission Union, to give the traditional call to foreign missionary service. I took as the text for my apologia the 'Message' of Jerusalem 1928. Later I was to see how many weaknesses that had. And in any case the call to foreign service was no longer the central issue that the new generation had to face.

The Conference was, of course, a good hunting ground for missionary societies seeking recruits. At the meeting organized by the Church of Scotland Helen and I introduced ourselves to the great Donald Fraser, now heading the Foreign Mission Committee staff after an heroic career in Central Africa. We presented ourselves as a couple offering for service in India and made our point so successfully that he introduced us to his colleagues as Mr and Mrs Newbigin. We let it pass. Half the battle was won!

For the last few months of my service I had to move to Edinburgh and serve the movement there and in Dundee, St Andrews and Aberdeen. I found the going much harder. St Andrews had more the atmosphere of an upper-class public school than the vigour of Glasgow University. It needed almost vicious prodding to awaken students to the realities of the world beyond that delectable place. Dundee was dour and unresponsive. But, just to prove that God works in his own mysterious way, I was to discover more than twenty-five years later that one of the students who had found something to nourish him in my seemingly unfruitful labour was Sir Francis Akan Ibiam, the beloved physician and churchman whose guest I was to be thirty years later when he was Governor of Eastern Nigeria. Aberdeen had some great student leaders: Albert Craig, later of Kalimpong; Willie Watson, later of Nyasaland; Horace Walker; Eric Duncan – to name only a few. But the greatest joy was getting to know D. S. Cairns, that splendid, craggy theologian whose own faith was a victorious battle against doubt and who did so much to enable generations of students to meet the onslaught of a pseudo-scientific positivism.

I had to begin preparing for the next chapter. It would have been natural to do ministerial training in one of the Scottish colleges with which I had become familiar. But there were strong reasons for preferring Westminster College. Cambridge still held my love. John Oman, the Principal, was a very old family friend from the days of his long ministry in Alnwick. And there was a good possibility of receiving one of the Lewis and Gibson scholarships which would cover most of the cost. I applied to the Newcastle Presbytery as a candidate for ordination, was accepted after a very cursory interview, and in due course accepted for Westminster subject to entrance examination.

Oman did not encourage prospective students to cumber the virgin ground with any preliminary theological reading. To one who asked for advice he replied on a postcard: 'Read Shakespeare and Milton.' But entrants were required to pass fairly stiff tests in Greek, Hebrew and philosophy – of all of which I was wholly innocent. For Greek I took a correspondence course which could be fitted into my SCM schedule. Hebrew I acquired from the books. For philosophy I borrowed the lecture notes of our SCM colleague Mary Macdonald Smith, who had studied the subject in Edinburgh. Apparently I made the grade and was rewarded by congratulations from the examiner of my philosophy papers who asked me where I had studied philosophy. He seemed to recognize a disciple of Kemp Smith! I was fortunate enough to be awarded a generous scholarship.

Summer 1933 was memorable for one of those glorious holidays at Rothbury which still provide a large part of the permanent scenery of my mind. There were days in the garden with its steep rocky outcrops and the tennis court at the top with heather all round; days by the sea at Embleton and Craster and Dunstanburgh Castle; expeditions to examine some newly discovered cup-marked rocks or ancient trackways; days spent with a rope climbing in the Simonside Crags. And, above all, there were glorious days in the Cheviots – a long tramp up the Salters Way or the Clennell Street to one of the streams where smooth porphyritic rock held deep, cool pools for bathing. A picnic lunch and then up to the Scots border at Windy Ghyle or some other point. Then down to one of the friendly shepherds' homes for tea and freshly baked scones. And then the long walk back to Alwynton or Linbrig while the lengthening sun lit up every fold of the hills and the baa-ing of sheep sounded everywhere from the hill-slopes. And yet, even in those lovely valleys, the distant rumble of a coming storm could be heard. I remember a night when Archie Craig and I stayed in the home of the Armstrongs – for many generations shepherds at High Bleakhope in the Breamish Valley. He tuned in the nine o'clock news and we heard a recording of the harsh and violent voice of the German Chancellor. When it was over Armstrong crossed the room, switched off the set, returned to his seat and said: 'Thon Hitler: he'll want watching.' He was more shrewd than those who were directing the nation.

4

Cambridge Again

At the beginning of October 1933 I went back to Cambridge to begin the three-year course of training at Westminster College, while Helen went to St Colm's Missionary College in Edinburgh for the statutory year of training. For her it was like being put into a small cage after having enjoyed the freedom of the wide air. From the responsibilities of national secretary for the SCM in Scotland, she had to come down to a status only a little higher than that of a schoolgirl. Needless to say she continued to find ways of being herself, but it was a difficult year.

For me it was a sheer delight to be back in Cambridge. It was natural to take up again the interests and friendships that had meant so much, and I never allowed the walls of Westminster College to limit my world. Nevertheless the years at the College profoundly changed and deepened my understanding of the Christian faith. I was expected, as a scholarship holder, to read for the University Tripos. However, with a brashness which I cannot now regret, I decided that it was too academic for the kind of work I hoped to do, and that I wanted freedom during the coming three years to do my own exploration of the faith. I unearthed an ancient university statute which excluded me from the Tripos, and having thus checkmated the authorities I was free to do a great deal of reading on my own.

The years in the SCM had filled my mind with questions to which I did not see the answers. I wanted to find out what I could believe. I decided that the Letter to the Romans was probably the most complete and condensed statement of the Gospel and I therefore spent several months wrestling with the Greek text of Romans, surrounded by half a dozen of the major commentaries. That was a turning point in my theological journey. I began the study as a typical liberal. I ended it with a strong conviction about 'the finished work of Christ', about the centrality and objectivity of the atonement accomplished on Calvary. The decisive agent in this shift was James Denney. His commentary on Romans carried the day as far as I was concerned. Barth I found incomprehensible. C. H. Dodd seemed to have made the Epistle palatable by removing its toughest parts – the parts where I found strong meat. His 'demythologizing' of the wrath of God seemed to me effectively to remove the love of God, for if 'wrath' was only an anthropomorphic way of describing the consequences of sin, then 'love' would have to be explained along the same lines. At the end of the exercise I was much more of an evangelical than a liberal. I had the opportunity of developing these ideas when I was given as my major Old Testament exegesis a passage concerning the Hebrew concept of atonement, and also when I had to give a paper to the College Theological Society.

But this shift in no way implied a lessening of commitment to political and social issues. I was in fairly frequent touch with Joseph Oldham and his work in preparation for the Oxford Conference on 'Church, Community and State', and in my last year led a study on 'The Kingdom of God and History' in which I tried to get leaders of the University political societies involved. This became the focus of my most passionate theological interest towards the end of the course. In fact, Robin Woods and I had an ambitious project, aided and abetted by Oldham and Temple, to get a selected group of Cambridge dons to Bishopthorpe for a prolonged exposure to these two prophets, but we failed.

John Oman was near the end of his teaching career. His lectures were obscure to the point of opacity, but his writings and, above all, his occasional utterances in chapel, were full of profound insight. Every student had to face, twice a year, the ordeal of preaching in chapel and of then having his sermon criticized by the professors. These were, for me, among the most memorable events in the course. When Oman criticized a sermon, he could be devastating; but when he went on to say how he would have expounded the text, he would produce gems of exposition that I could never forget.

In my last year Oman was succeeded by Herbert Farmer. He was a devoted disciple of Oman, but had brought to theology a degree of lucidity and brilliance which made his lectures an intellectual and spiritual delight. And he was always ready to give time for face-to-face theological discussion, so that I enjoyed the freedom of being able to take my half-developed ideas to him and have them thoroughly examined and refined in vigorous argument.

One of the changes which came with Farmer was the introduction of a quiet day when we were encouraged to take time for meditation and prayer. Coming from the life of an SCM secretary into the life of a theological college, I had been surprised and shocked to find that the whole area of the interior life, of the struggle to find and keep a steady discipline of prayer, meditation and contemplation, was – apparently – ignored. I had been accustomed to discussing these things with students and to struggling with my own repeated failures and humiliations in this realm. I had imagined that a theological college would be a place of learning in this regard. I found the subject seemed to be almost forbidden. A few of us who had an SCM background tried to help each other, but it did not seem to be a matter about which our teachers were troubled. The new initiative that came with Farmer was therefore a special encouragement, but I have often reflected since upon this weakness in the Reformed tradition of ministerial training which was so obvious then.

A big part of my time during these three years was given to the York Street Mission of St Columba's Presbyterian Church. York Street was situated in one of the poor areas of Cambridge and the Mission was run by that great and generous-hearted man Alex Wood, who combined in a marvellous unity the roles of scientist, evangelist, social reformer and politician. For almost the whole of the three years I worked under him as superintendent of the Sunday School and it was a very uphill and often discouraging task. But it was good for a theological student to learn how to talk to children and for a future missionary to learn how to cope with what seemed like continuous failure.

But there was another commitment which occupied at least as much of my attention in those years as everything else put together, and that was the SCM. It was inevitable that I should be drawn into the life of the Movement in the University and I was more than happy to become involved again. I was asked to be secretary of the Cambridge branch of the SVMU and I tried to kindle interest in foreign missions. Then came the request to take on the job of president of the SCM for the year 1934–5. I knew it would mean a huge commitment of time, but I decided I must do it and I shall always be glad that I did. The situation as I saw it was that the SCM could still put on an impressive series of university meetings, but it was weak in the colleges, was under pressure from the desire of denominational chaplains to look after their own, and was losing ground to the Christian Union. I tried to counter these trends by putting all the stress on work in each college and on developing a vigorous programme of Bible study groups to encourage the kind of free and open study which would interest the unbeliever. I had each of the college representatives to tea at regular intervals to discuss on a one-to-one basis the problems of each college. And I made a great drive to get a strong delegation to Swanwick. I was much disappointed that only sixty Cambridge men turned up at the first Swanwick of 1935 (there were always two each summer), but as this was three times the figure of the previous year I suppose I could have been encouraged. It was often my job to meet with denominational clergy to plead the case for the distinctive style of the SCM as a proper way of evangelism among undergraduates. And one of my bitter disappointments came when Robert Wilder visited Cambridge in 1935 to celebrate the jubilee of the 'Cambridge Seven', the famous group whose offer for missionary service had triggered off the formation of the SVMU. I pleaded with the President of CICCU that the SCM might be allowed to join in these celebrations and in welcoming Wilder, but was met with adamant refusal. The SCM was regarded as no legitimate part of the Christian scene.

But the Cambridge SCM was privileged to be the host of a great succession of Christian leaders and it was my joy to receive and entertain them. In this way I came to know such men as Mott, Temple, Kraemer, Hanns Lilje, C. F. Andrews, John Groser, Leslie Weatherhead, Nath Micklem, Nicholas Zernov, H. G. Wood. One who made frequent visits was J. H. Oldham and, as already indicated, I was drawn into enthusiastic involvement in the ideas he was developing about Church, community and state. Among all of them it was William Temple who most powerfully influenced the students of that generation. He visited Cambridge several times during this period and, with a generosity which was typical of him, he invited me to stay at Bishopthorpe and gave me a whole long evening of his time discussing theological issues and unfolding his vision for the future of the Ecumenical Movement. It was from him that I heard of the plans for some kind of world organization of the churches to follow the Oxford and Edinburgh meetings of 1937.

I was also very much involved with the work of the SCM at the national level. From 1933 to 1934 I was a member of a Commission on the Life and Work of the Movement and I had some part in shaping the report which it issued on 'The Movement and its Leadership'. The report emphasized the victory of Jesus on the cross and defined the Movement as 'a fellowship of men and women who share in that victory and who seek to give that message to the world'. At the same time it stressed the place of study as the way through which members could have 'their minds stretched' and their faith made more 'adequate to the facts of life'. It resolved to re-establish the Executive of the SVMU as a separate committee and to divide the General Committee into two sections dealing respectively with policy and message. For the next two years I was to be chairman of the 'Message Commission' which had the special duty of developing the ideas of the Report on evangelism and study. This was an exciting and deeply rewarding assignment.

All our thinking in these years had as its background the possibility of war. At the meeting of the General Committee in April 1934, when the Report of the Commission was adopted, we also adopted a long statement on international peace which was drafted by Arnold Nash and me. It asked students 'to face squarely the possibility – even probability – of war, and then, having faced the worst, to give (themselves) to that reconciling purpose which is God's and therefore must prevail'. It affirmed that there cannot be peace without justice, and then went on:

Like the Communist worker for peace, who recognizes the social cost of peace, and who also sees in the Soviet republic an adumbration of the new world to which he is looking, we have also, faintly adumbrated yet real and unquestionable, a foretaste of the new world for which we look: it is the Church. The Church is deeply divided by barriers of belief, of race and of class: nevertheless it is in a real, if partial sense, a supranational centre of unity and loyalty. This unity does not consist in similarity of opinion, of programme or of temperament: it is the unity born of God's act of love in Christ received and answered in its members. Apart from that relationship to God there is no Church and therefore no kind of unity. But where it exists there is a bond which can bind together men and women of vastly different belief and practice, race and class. 'We speak that we do know.' In that bond lies the hope of peace and the meaning of peace.

These were brave words. They were surprising then. They read strangely now. But they were an early adumbration of that ecumenical vision which would be captured later at the Tambaram Conference and in Temple's famous phrase about 'the great new fact of our time', and in the missiology of the 1950s.

My summers were much occupied with the study for which the weeks in Cambridge left too little time, and also with conferences and campaigns. I had a share in the Evangelistic Campaign to Warrington in 1934 when we had a tremendous response and where I chaired a final meeting which packed the Town Hall to capacity. I was also involved as a speaker at the Scottish National Conference at Glenalmond in 1935. At Swanwick I chaired the Officers' Conference in 1933 and was Camp Manager in 1934. In 1935 I also shared in the first of the combined work camps and evangelistic campaigns which were largely the brainchild of Arnold Nash, later carried on by Ronald Preston. There was, as always, a certain tension between those who were keen on direct evangelism and those who were concerned about social justice. It was a brilliant idea to bring them together in a combined operation. In July 1935 a substantial group of students, led by Robert Mackie, laboured with pick and shovel to provide a playground for children in a village near Swanwick, and each evening addressed street meetings about the Gospel. It was very hard work. We started each day at 5.30, did eight hours of hard labour, and preached, argued and answered hecklers for a couple of hours each night. We dealt with trade unions, the local ILP and the churches. We lived on one shilling (5p) per day. The women in the team did the cooking and the washing and shared in the speaking. At the end our hands were blistered and our throats were hoarse. But sceptics and critics had become friends and we ourselves had learned a lot both about the world and about the Gospel. Probably all of us were changed by that experience.

My own mind was certainly changing in respect of political ideas. I was a pacifist and a socialist of the kind who looked to G. D. H. Cole and the Left Book Club. Abhorrence of war was a universal feeling among students. I am ashamed to say that retired military men, who had no doubt served with great bravery, were regarded as fit targets for ridicule. We marched with demonstrators and attended peace rallies. I had a considerable part in organizing the Christian Peace Society in the University, for which we had the powerful backing of Charles Raven, Alex Wood and 'Polly' Carter (the Revd H. C. Carter of Emmanuel Church). We worked for the great 'Peace Ballot' which secured twelve million signatures. And Oxford undergraduates announced their intention not to fight for King and country.

Yet we were not blind to the fact that peace without justice was impossible. There was, first, the injustice inflicted upon Germany by the Versailles Treaty. Could there be peace unless this was righted? There was secondly, the endemic injustice of the capitalist system. Tawney had made me see that there was an inescapable contradiction between Christianity and capitalism. Soviet Russia (we half believed) had created a more just economic order. Could Christianity show a way to have both peace and justice? I was active in promoting study groups which sought to involve the University political societies in this quest.

The background of all these questionings was the steady rise of German militarism, the long-drawn-out failure of the Disarmament Conference, the re-militarization of the Rhineland, and the Italian attack upon Abyssinia and the Hoare–Laval Pact of December 1935. It was these last events which called my pacifism into question. For it seemed that when pacifism was translated into the terms of actual politics it meant simply a free field for the most ruthless aggressor. When I heard my revered friends in the leadership of the pacifist movement say: 'After all, Mussolini is only doing what all imperial powers have done', and when I heard exactly the same words from militaristic conservatives like L. S. Amery, I began to ask exactly where pacifism was leading. I remember very vividly a conversation with my beloved and revered guru Alex Wood on the subject of Government proposals for civil defence against air attack. His comment, as I remember it, was: 'If we are going to be asked to crawl into underground shelters, I think it is time to wash our hands of the whole business.' Did pacifism, I began to wonder, really lead in the end to that kind of escapism?

Meanwhile Helen and I were eagerly counting the months and

days till we could be married and set off for our work in India, about which we were constantly thinking and planning. Helen spent the year 1934-5 on the staff at Walthamstow Hall, and during 1935-6 did some work on Tamil at the School of Oriental Studies in London. In December 1935 I was summoned to Edinburgh to meet the Foreign Mission Committee and told that our offer of service was accepted and that we were assigned to the Madras Mission. In May 1936 we spent a few memorable days in Edinburgh and were formally received and commissioned by the General Assembly. That was an occasion which no one who shared in it could forget. The General Assembly of the Church of Scotland can be a very infuriating body, but it can also be magnificent on a big occasion. We were sent out with an overwhelming sense of the love, the prayers and the good wishes of the whole Church.

Helen came to be with me in Cambridge for the College Commemoration Day and the final ceremonies to mark the conclusion of the course. On the last evening after supper we took a punt right up to Grantchester and then came slowly back, enjoying the magical beauty of a still June evening. At ten o'clock we were among the colleges and as we glided slowly under each of the bridges we watched the familiar sights disappear one by one, and I said my farewell to a place which had been for me so filled with blessing.

Later in June I was 'licensed to preach the Gospel' by the Presbytery of Newcastle after a trial sermon in the little church of Bellingham in Northumberland. My theme was the Widow's Mite and it was unfortunate that at the evening service I lost my collection money and had to borrow from the minister's wife - to the entertainment of the whole congregation.

On 12 July I was ordained by the Presbytery of Edinburgh for service as a foreign missionary. I stayed with that grand old man W. P. Paterson; and Arthur Watkins came up to Edinburgh to be with me for the occasion. On 20 August Helen and I were married in the lovely little church of St Oswald's in Edinburgh. Our honeymoon was spent in the Lake District whither we were pursued by J. H. Oldham, who was still determined to dissuade me from going to India so that I might join him in the preparatory work for the Oxford Conference on Church, Community and State. Joe was a master of the art of arm-twisting in the service of the Kingdom and he had caused a number of very distinguished people to write letters telling me how indispensable I was for this particular enterprise. I had an enormous love and respect for him and a deep conviction about what he was doing. Consequently we both felt that even at this late date we must give serious thought to his so-often-pressed invitation. However, after a visit to Edinburgh for discussion I wrote to Joe with a firm refusal which he most generously accepted, and we sailed for Madras from Liverpool on the *City of Cairo* at 5.0 p.m. on 26 September. In our cabin to greet us was a note from Nicol Macnicol in which he said: 'My prayer for you is that you may have verandah grace.' I was to learn in later years just what he meant.

5

India: There and Back Again

The *City of Cairo* was a slow one-class boat which took four weeks
for the journey from Liverpool to Madras. We quickly learned
that the Brahmins of the Raj – the ICS officers – travelled P. and
O. Our company, except for four missionaries and half-a-dozen
tourists, consisted of people working in offices and plantations,
with a few army families. We were in a community where
Indians were 'wogs'. For the first two weeks we were not
conscious of this, but once we had stopped at Port Said and
bought our pith helmets at Simon Artz we suddenly realized
that, east of Suez, a white man was a sahib and a man who did not
wear a topee was a cad. It was all very odd and rather frightening.
Helen and I attended the fancy-dress dance dressed as 'the
missionary of fiction and his wife', a successful essay in poking
fun at the ideas of a missionary entertained by our fellow-
travellers. We got the prize but our success was slightly blunted
when we saw our future colleagues lined up to meet us on the
quayside in Madras; one of them (who came to be a very much
loved friend) looked rather like our caricature.

A good part of my time on board was taken up with the writing
of a book, *Christian Freedom in the Modern World*. It was in part a
criticism of the writings of John Macmurray which were
enormously influential among my SCM friends. I had been
myself greatly helped by Macmurray's writings but had also been
repelled by the conclusions which Christians were drawing from
them. Going back to read Macmurray more critically I concluded
that the crux of the problem was at the point which had become
so central to my thinking: the necessity for an atonement
provided by God, without which real freedom was impossible. I
had already started work on the theme and the long voyage gave
time to finish it. In due course it was published and, to my
surprise, it had its most appreciative reviews not from Free
Church critics but from Anglicans and Roman Catholics. I was to
learn more than thirty years later that it had played some part in

the early development of the theological ideas of a young layman of the Mar Thoma Church, M. M. Thomas.

We docked at Madras on 22 October and were immediately driven by car thirty-six miles to the small country town of Chingleput which was to be our first home. That first taste of India was so vivid that it could never be forgotten – the soft, cool evening air, the lines of brightly lit stalls as we slipped out of Madras by the trunk road, the glint of light on polished brass water-pots, the graceful movement of women in their beautiful saris, and then the open country with the paddy fields and the big leafy trees fringing the road. On the way we had to stop because of a puncture and there was a chance to stand still in the darkness, smell the strange and delicious scents, listen to the symphony of the cicadas everywhere and watch the slow rhythm of the bullock-carts going by patiently, endlessly, through the night.

When at last we arrived we were astonished to find what looked to our eyes like a spacious palace: broad steps fringed by potted plants, lights at the top, glimpses of spacious rooms within, and a line of white-clad figures standing in an attitude which combined welcome, dignity and complete subordination. We had not reckoned that the word 'bungalow' meant anything so palatial. It was as though we had stepped out of the life of the twentieth-century student into that of an eighteenth-century country gentleman. And that feeling was renewed when we were awakened next morning by a servant with a tray of breakfast, and found ourselves looking out over a scene of breathtaking beauty – green grass and leafy trees in the foreground, a beautiful lake fringed by palmyra palms in the middle distance, and a background of low hills covered with wild jungle.

We had never expected to find such beauty in the country which was to be our home. In the weeks and years following we were to come to love it more and more, very specially in the magic hours of sunrise and sunset when all the colours were at their most delicate. Of course we would learn later how harsh and cruel the country could be, especially in the scorching days of May and June. But now it was the season of the north-east monsoon when Tamilnadu gets rain and there is an infinite variety of colours among the wild vegetation of the jungle and of shades of green from the paddy at its various stages of growth.

During the next few days we were taken by our colleagues to visit various places of work in the villages and in the town of Chingleput. If our first shock came from the beauty of the country, our second came from what we saw of the relations between missionaries and their Indian colleagues. One of the pieces of advice which Nicol Macnicol had given us was to keep a very private diary of our first impressions formed during the early days when we would necessarily have to keep our mouths shut and our ears and eyes open. I have always been grateful for that advice and have passed it on to others. Some first impressions prove to have been mistaken. Some are valid, but if one merely suppresses them one is in danger of gradually coming to accept what at first was (rightly) shocking. One passage from my diary of those early days will serve as a sample of how I was feeling:

I must say I couldn't help being horrified by the sort of relation that seems to exist between the missionaries and the people. It seems so utterly remote from the New Testament. There seems to be no question of getting alongside them and sharing their troubles and helping them spiritually. There never seems to be a word of encouragement. We drive up like lords in a car, soaking everybody else with mud on the way, and then carry on a sort of inspection, finding all the faults we can, putting everyone through their paces. They all sort of stand at attention and say 'Sir'. It's *awful*. And yet I know how easily tired I get and how much I need the help of things like motor cars and electric fans, etc. There's a sore thing to be tackled here. But one thing is as sure as death: surely they won't stand this sort of thing from the white man much longer.

Some of what we saw of the work of Mission and Church impressed us very much but we soon became aware of deep tensions and of quarrels that were always breaking out from under the surface. It was clear that the fundamental problem was the unwillingness of missionaries to entrust full responsibility to the Indian leaders whom they had trained. To quote my diary once again:

> Everywhere the same gulf between Indian and missionary, the conviction that Indians are not fit for responsibility, and corresponding irresponsibility on the other side. More and more I feel the test of our sincerity must be: Are we putting the training of Indians in responsibility above the efficient running of the machine? After all, that is what one had to do as an SCM secretary. One could always have run the machine more efficiently than the committee. What was required was the ability to stand aside and give responsibility to others – putting their growth in Christian leadership as the first criterion of success. I am sure this is not being done here. Partly, I suppose, it is the tragedy of overwork and under-staffing. But all the time one is aware of the missionary circle as quite clearly exclusive of the Indians from real intimacy.

This matter of 'devolution', as it was called, would be a dominating issue for the next ten years. And of course it was tied up with the much bigger question of the Raj and the Indian National Congress. Within a few days of our arrival I noted in my diary that one of our senior missionaries had told me that her husband had been called to an 'Internal Security Conference' with the Collector.

> She thinks this means arrangements for taking us all to St Thomas Mount in case of troubles during the elections. If so, this raises an important issue. I don't think I could either accept this kind of relation with the army, or put myself in this way on the side of the British Raj if there is going to be a clash. Pray God this may not happen till we have been here long enough to speak for ourselves.

But our main business in Chingleput was to learn Tamil and we soon got into a steady routine of eight hours of hard study each day. It was a struggle but we made progress and by early March I was able to risk chairing a meeting and giving a very short address. The shattering problem was the vast gulf between the literary Tamil of our teacher and the ordinary language of the street and the shop. One had to learn both, and sometimes they seemed different languages.

On Sundays I helped with the English services in the leprosy colony where 800 patients lived and where our colleague Bob Cochrane was making the pioneer discoveries that would ensure that leprosy could be cured. We shared in social events with the patients and learned not to be afraid of the disease. I also took over the leadership of a Young Men's Fellowship. This was a great joy and some of its members were to be beloved fellow-workers thirty years later.

At the end of March we were sent up to Kodaikanal to do four months of concentrated language study in the cool of those lovely hills, and to take the language exams which were conducted there. This was our introduction to a new and enchanting world. During the next forty years the Kodai hills were to become for us the best-loved part of earth, next only to Rothbury and the Cheviots. Kodaikanal began as a summer retreat opened up by the missionaries of the American Madura Mission, a place of refuge from the extreme heat and the malaria of the plains. It lies about 7000 feet above sea level and its houses are scattered among the trees around a small lake. In former days it could only be reached on foot and the climb of 6000 feet up the old 'coolie ghat' is one that I have done several times and which has a thrill of its own. But the normal approach now is by a thirty-mile road which carries you in easy stages from the blazing heat and the scorched earth of the plains, through great leafy jungles to the place where you hear the splash of running streams and feel the exhilarating freshness of mountain air. To this heavenly spot missionaries from all over India would come each year, normally in May, for three or four weeks of holiday. There was refreshment for body, mind and spirit - times for Bible study and for spiritual renewal, conferences on various problems of missions, concerts, plays and operettas into which we threw ourselves with enormous vigour and which often reached a high standard. There were long treks over the vast area of the Palni hills, sleeping out at nights in the huts built for the use of the staff of the Forest Department. There was bathing in the mountain stream, singing around the campfire at night and the long quiet moments when one could look out over the miles of ancient impenetrable forest and hear only the cry of the wild animals echoing through the silence.

For the next four months we were to live among these beckoning joys, firmly anchored, however, to our schedule of eight hours of Tamil every day, and leaving only the Saturdays and Sundays free. We secured the services of the most successful Tamil teacher available, a redoubtable and colourful Brahmin named Ragavachariar. He was a brilliant teacher with a great love for the language and a very delicate ear for the precise nuance of meaning conveyed by a word or phrase. He helped us not only to read and speak Tamil but to see things through the eyes of a Hindu.

At the end of June I passed the first language exams and we began to plan for our first spell of proper duty. It was understood that we should be sent to Kanchipuram. I was eager to break out of the existing pattern and to find ways of closer contact with village congregations and therefore to return to the old missionary practice of camping out in the villages. Above all, I wanted to give priority to direct evangelism. I petitioned the Mission authorities to allow me to be my own driver and to use the money allotted in the budget for a driver's salary to pay for an Indian colleague who could be both Tamil teacher and evangelistic colleague. The person I had in mind was our Chingleput teacher who was a member of the Oxford Group (later known as 'Moral Rearmament') and very willing to accept the plan. Horrifying visions were conjured up of the sahib, covered with grease, lying on his back under a car stranded on a country road but, in spite of these, the permission was given and we were eager to begin.

But God had other plans and it was to be more than two years before we would see Kanchipuram. I had heard much about the rapid growth of the Church in the Dharapuram area under the leadership of J. J. Ellis, a Methodist missionary who was also, I understood, involved with the Oxford Group. I was eager to see how this kind of direct evangelism could happen among outcaste villagers – a milieu so remote from that in which the Groups had had their birth. I arranged to pay a visit to Dharapuram. Helen had had to undergo surgery to clear up the consequences of a bungled operation during her schooldays. When she was well enough to be left, I set off on a rather complicated bus and train journey. At Palni I boarded an old country bus for Dharapuram. It was the normal vehicle of the time, a row of benches mounted on a chassis with no protecting sides. As it left the railway yard in the darkness, a heavy iron gate swung in and caught the bench in front, smashing such legs as were conveniently located – one of mine and two of the conductor's. Pandemonium ensued. The driver absconded, fearing the wrath of the passengers. Eventually I got the bus driven to a small Government clinic where the conductor and I could be attended to. My small resources of Tamil were stretched to the limit! After a rather unsuccessful attempt to set the leg, in the light of a small hurricane lamp, I was despatched next day to the splendid Mission Hospital in Madura and thence, after some weeks, to the General Hospital in Madras. At each point the work of the previous surgeon was held to have been defective and so I had a series of painful and inconclusive operations. Finally, the Mission decided that we should be returned to Edinburgh for treatment. Sorrowfully we left Madras on 5 October and on 14 November I had the tenth operation, in Edinburgh, which consisted in re-breaking the left leg, taking a sliver of bone out of the right and screwing it into the left with ox-bone screws. I hoped that the sanctity of this bone graft might do the trick, but it didn't. Osteomyelitis set in and there was a period when amputation seemed probable.

At this point I had a visit from Denzil Patrick, then working in Geneva for the embryonic World Council of Churches. He said: 'Is this being prayed about as it should be?' Helen and I took his words to heart and wrote to ten of our friends, explaining the situation and asking them to pray daily for a fortnight that God might give healing. Shortly after the expiry of that time the surgeon opened the plaster and found that healing had begun. At the end of February I was released from bed and by the end of May I was free to move around on crutches, a means of locomotion which is exhilaratingly rapid and effective once your muscles are attuned to it! I was told, however, that it would be at least another year before I would be out of the doctors' hands and it was decided that for that period I should have a full-time job as Candidates Secretary for the Foreign Missions Committee of the Church.

The long period in bed had been by no means without profit. Apart from learning a little embroidery, my main work was still at Tamil. Ragavachariar kept me supplied by airmail with reading matter suitable to my powers of comprehension, and I sent him compositions and answers to his written questions. These months gave us an opportunity to press ahead with work on the language which few missionaries are given.

It was also a time for reflection about many things, especially about my political convictions. The radio news each day provided much food for thought. More and more the central question seemed to be: How can the family of nations restrain the ruthless aggressor? My pacifism seemed increasingly untenable. On that night of February 1938 when the evening news announced the resignation of Anthony Eden over the issue of resistance to German threats to Austria, I lay awake for hours thinking through the implications of my total sympathy with Eden. The outcome was that I could no longer count myself a pacifist.

I was also reading Indian history and seeing more vividly than I had done before the elements of sheer greed and violence which had marked the rise of British power in India. I could see that Japan and Italy were not morally inferior to us in their imperialistic adventures. But the unfolding events in Europe and the Far East convinced me that neither justice nor peace was possible if there was not force at the disposal of the League of Nations to curb the aggressor.

The long period of enforced inactivity, marked with periods of considerable pain, was fruitful in other ways. In any case a new missionary has to accept a kind of drastic diminishment. To learn the language and the culture of another people he must again become a child. In a letter to my younger sister Frances during that period I expressed my feelings as follows:

I have been thinking about this specially lately, because I think it is one of the things which God in His wisdom is teaching me by this long inactivity just at a time when I most want to be active. I have been naturally so full of thoughts of what I am going to do, and screwing myself up each day to the job of learning Tamil and so on. All this weakness has rubbed in the lesson that even if I never managed to do a hand's turn of missionary work, God is still my Saviour and I can give myself to Him and trust Him for everything.

INDIA: THERE AND BACK AGAIN (1936-9)

Not long after the accident an Indian pastor had, of his kindness, come to visit me. I vividly remember him sitting on my bed and saying: 'It is the will of God', and my stubbornly replying, 'No, it is the stupidity of that driver'. Perhaps there was truth on both sides, but if I meet that dear pastor in heaven I shall confess to him that my truth was a very trivial one compared to his. God did indeed turn that accident into a source of manifold blessing for which I cannot cease to give thanks.

From June 1938 till July 1939 I was in full-time work as Candidates Secretary. Till near the end of the time I was on crutches, my leg in plaster with a tea-cosy at the end to keep the toes from freezing. The infection in the leg had destroyed some of the tendons in the foot and it was considered essential to keep the toes free for inspection but also desirable to preserve them from freezing. With a clerical collar at the top, a bright red tea-cosy at the bottom, and a pair of crutches which enabled me to cover the ground much faster than an ordinary pedestrian, I was, no doubt, an entertaining spectacle for the citizens of Edinburgh. Work in the office at 121 George Street was made happy by the friendship of splendid colleagues, especially Alex Kydd, with whom I spent many hours, since we always took a snack lunch together in his room. He was the director of the Church's Foreign Mission enterprise – a very wise, humane and experienced missionary.

Much of my time was spent in travelling. We had decided to make 1938-9 a 'Youth Missionary Year' throughout the Church. A small team of outstanding young missionaries on furlough was set aside for visits in all the presbyteries. It was my job, along with my colleague W. M. (Mickie) Dempster in the Youth Department to activate the Youth and Foreign Missions Committees of the presbyteries to brief the team, and generally to oversee the whole campaign. With the help of Dempster's car we travelled all over Scotland.

I was also responsible for efforts to recruit missionaries in the Universities and the Divinity Halls, to deal with offers of service, and to 'process' these offers through the various committees. The hardest part was to deal faithfully and creatively with offers of service from young men and women who had to be judged unsuitable for acceptance. I hope those whom I had to advise have forgiven me for the blunders which I am sure were made.

I was troubled by the fact that there was no specifically missionary training for the men who were sent out. All women had to take a one-year course at St Colm's, but there was nothing at all for men. Digging into records I unearthed a number of funds which had been given to provide bursaries for precisely this purpose but had become merged with general funds. Not without some conflict I was able to get hold of this money and use it to organize a brief but intensive period of orientation for those going abroad in 1939. This single effort was small in itself but it paved the way for the systematic provision of training which later became accepted as necessary.

The job of Candidates Secretary was open-ended and could have taken more than all the time available. But I was also asked to help with literary work. My first job in this area was to go through the annual reports of several hundred missionaries and compile a popular report for the General Assembly and for sale in the Church. I called it *Things not Shaken*. Because it was anonymous it was quickly given the name of the head of the Home Organization Department of the Foreign Missions Committee and became known as 'Leslie Duncan's Cocktail'. The following year's report, which I also wrote, was titled *Living Epistles* and did not acquire such a felicitous sub-title. I also planned and began a series of 'Sketches of the Fields' – booklets giving a popular account of each of the eighteen mission fields of the Church, and a booklet on 'Missionary Education in a Congregation'. And I was still working at Tamil.

During this period I was again in touch with J. H. Oldham. He had convened a group of able thinkers to reflect upon the human situation from a Christian and predominantly lay perspective. This 'Moot' has since become famous, but at the time its privacy and confidentiality were closely guarded. It included T. S. Eliot, Middleton Murry, Karl Mannheim, Walter Moberly, Gilbert Shaw, H. A. Hodges, John Baillie, Alec Vidler, Eric Fenn and Bill Paton. Oldham wrote to invite me to a meeting as he wished to have a contribution from the younger generation. A paper had been prepared for the meeting of September 1938 by Middleton Murry, and the members were asked to send critical reactions. Mine were evidently not pleasing to Oldham. I had a rather tough session with him at the Athenaeum and we then proceeded to the meeting. My diary records that the evening session was occupied by 'a long and very fine paper by Murry largely concerned with my criticisms', but in the plenary discussion next morning 'it was clear that Oldham did not want my viewpoint and it seemed best to keep silent and not interfere with the discussion. But I had some very fruitful talks with individuals, especially Hodges, Vidler and Paton.' The final session, I record, 'was taken by Murry and was deeply and searchingly honest. He is a great man. The imminence of war set the tone of the meeting.'

War did, indeed, seem immediately imminent. My father continued to send his ships to ports held by the lawful Spanish Government. When they were bombed at sea by Franco's Italian aides he protested to the Foreign Office, but it was made clear that he would get no help in his efforts to support 'the Reds'. The morning after Chamberlain came back from Munich with 'peace in our time' I had to lead worship at St Colm's. I took as my text the grim words of Isaiah 22, 'What do you mean that you have gone up all of you to the housetops, you who are full of shoutings, exultant town?'. The chapter as a whole could have been written, it seemed, for the occasion. But the exultant shout soon turned again to anxiety and foreboding as the intentions of Hitler became more and more apparent.

Nevertheless this was a happy time for Helen and me. After I was discharged from the nursing home we were given a furnished flat in Comely Bank Avenue, and this was really our first home after two years of living in other people's houses. We had many friends in Edinburgh. We were able to entertain members of the family as guests. And we had the great happiness of being able to look forward to the birth of our first child. In the spring of 1939 I was allowed to put my foot to the ground and had to learn very painfully and slowly how to walk again without crutches. By the summer I was fully recovered. Margaret, our first daughter, duly arrived in June and was a vigorous and happy baby from the first day. In August we left Edinburgh for a final spell at Rothbury. We were booked to sail for India at the end of that month but when war became certain the sailing was cancelled. We were in Newcastle when war was declared, uncertain what the next step would be. A day or two later we were offered a sailing for India and accepted it. On 15 September we left Newcastle. As the family stood on the platform and the train pulled out I saw how old and tired my father looked. He was erect and alert as always, but I knew in my heart that I would not see him again.

On 18 October we arrived at Kanchipuram, which would be our home for the next seven years.

6
Kanchi: The City

Kanchipuram is one of the seven cities counted most sacred in all India by all denominations of Hindus. It is referred to in the literature of the second century BC as already a holy place. Buddhist tradition affirms that the Buddha himself preached there and gained converts, and it was for many centuries dominated by that faith. The Chinese Buddhist traveller Huien Tsian, who visited the city in AD 640 reported that there were 10,000 priests of 'the great Vessel' (Mahayana). From the fourth to the ninth centuries it was the capital of the great Pallava Empire with Mahabalipuram as its seaport, and its commercial and cultural influence reached as far as the 'Golden Isles' (Java, Sumatra and Bali). From this time forward Buddhism was gradually eliminated and the Jains became a very small minority. Both the Saivite and the Vaishnava forms of Hinduism were to dominate the future. Here the great Vaishnava philosopher Ramanuja lived till he was over thirty and here the most ancient temple buildings in all southern India still stand. And hither come thousands of pilgrims each year from every part of India to visit the hundreds of temples, to join in their festivals, and to sit at the feet of great Hindu scholars. When we came to live there it was a city of about 70,000 inhabitants, all – except for tiny communities of Moslems and Christians – Hindus. And the vast temples, the largest covering twenty-five acres and with a tower rising to 188 feet, dominated the life of the whole community.

The first, and up to the time of our arrival, the only attempt to establish a Christian presence in Kanchipuram was made by the pioneer missionary of the Church of Scotland, John Anderson, who established a school there in 1839. This was one of a chain of schools established on the same principles. One of them has grown into what is now Madras Christian College. One has become the Voorhees College, Vellore. The rest flourish today as high schools. Anderson followed the missionary principles of Alexander Duff in Calcutta. He believed that a western, English education in which the Bible was an integral part would undermine and

51

destroy the power of heathen religion. Even though the teachers were all Hindus, it was believed that the teaching of the Bible in itself would have this effect. As John Anderson sat alone in Kanchi in the sweltering heat of a June day in 1839, he wrote to his friend and colleague:

> Could I only set before you what I have seen here in this stronghold of Satan, your spirit would be stirred in you like Paul's to see the city wholly given to idolatry. Details are perfectly useless; you would require to *see* the masses of votaries, the pagodas, and the idols, to receive the true impression. It is my duty to wait, though I had only ten to teach; the ignorance is so great and the chances of light so small. There may be people even here to be saved through the light which we bring. You see I am sound and well, and full of sober hope; by no means so *sanguine* as some of my friends would have it, and, at the same time, not so *cautious* as to blight the hopes of success. The thing is in God's hands, and to Him we must lift up our eyes.

No evangelistic missionary lived in Kanchi itself until J. H. Maclean came there early in the present century, and the real impact of the Gospel upon the city must be dated from his time. He was one of a famous class at Trinity College, Glasgow, which included James Moffatt and Harry Miller. He claimed to be the first person in Great Britain to sign the SVMU declaration: 'It is my purpose, if God permit, to become a foreign missionary.' He was one of ten students from Britain invited to the Northfield Conference of 1888, where he met John R. Mott, and he was one of the four at Keswick in 1895 who drew up the first draft of a constitution for the World's Student Christian Federation.

For forty years he had laboured in and around Kanchipuram, raising the school to a level which gave it a premier place among the high schools of the district, supervising village schools and churches and, above all, tirelessly preaching the Gospel in the streets of the city. He was jeered at and sometimes attacked but he came to be revered even by the most orthodox Hindus as a man of God. Of course, many of the leading citizens were his former pupils and that gave him a tremendous standing. But it was much more than this. Even those who rejected his message could not withhold from him the reverence due to a holy man. I vividly remember the awe with which a Saivite ascetic recounted to me how he had seen Maclean submitted to the most outrageous humiliation. While he was preaching in the street a schoolboy was sent up to the first-floor verandah above to urinate on the preacher's head. Maclean had merely looked up and then, very quietly, said: *'Thambi* (little brother), don't do that again.'

It had been intended that I should directly follow him. The interval caused by my accident was nobly filled by my colleague Ellis Shaw. But it was Maclean's shadow within which I had to work. I well remember my first visit to one of the villages at a time when the rain had failed and morale was low. The villagers were standing in a forlorn and despondent group. They did not know that I had learned some Tamil and as I came towards them I heard one of them say: 'If it had been Maclean the rain would have been falling by now.' It was a formidable business to stand in the shadow of so powerful and holy a man. But it was also an enormous privilege.

As missionary colleagues throughout our years there we had the two ladies in charge of girls' schools and the work of Biblewomen, and the doctor in charge of the Mission Hospital, with his family.

There was a vast amount of learning to be done. Many hours a day had to be given to Tamil. I was in charge of a district and every day there were people who came to pour out their problems in very colloquial village Tamil. Somehow or other I had to find out what was wrong and do something about it. And one does not just 'pick up' a language like Tamil: it requires very hard work for several years. Fortunately Ragavachariar was willing to come from Madras several times a week. I also took to visiting Hindu homes where no English at all was spoken or understood and got their help in correcting my pronunciation and drilling my tongue in the strange contortions which the palatal consonants require. As I progressed I realized that Ragavachariar's noble Brahmin Tamil was being replaced among the younger generation by a new style of language which sought to eliminate all traces of Sanskrit and to use only pure Dravidian roots. This anti-Brahmin cultural movement which was, thirty years later, to sweep Congress out of power had as its leader the brilliant young citizen of Kanchipuram, C. N. Annadurai, later to become Chief Minister of Madras. One could not ignore the movement, and I was able to get a young non-Brahmin Hindu to help me to master the new style. One had to learn to speak and write in both styles, and to know when to do which.

Meanwhile, as the 'district missionary' I constantly found myself being required to deal with all sorts of problems, great and small. Agitated villagers would arrive at early dawn with a tale of woe that had to be poured out in a cataract of high-speed colloquial Tamil which I struggled to understand. If asked to say it again the visitor would draw a deep breath and repeat the tale at even greater volume and velocity. Sometimes it was real disaster: fire in a village, floods, an outbreak of cholera, or a fatal accident by snakebite or drowning in a well. Often it was one of those village quarrels which blow up with the force of a hurricane and then mysteriously disappear. As I groped my way through a barrage of half-understood words it was a struggle to find out what was really the matter.

But there was one thing I could do immediately and that was to teach in the High School, where English was the medium of instruction. This opened up relationships for which I was very grateful. Indian schoolboys are eager to learn and seem to have a deeply felt respect for any teacher who obviously cares for them. These boys were among the sharpest and cleverest one could meet anywhere. They quickly found out my weak points, especially the fact that I was very vague about the finer points of English grammar, but many of them gave me their friendship and came regularly to the house to talk. Correcting forty English compositions each week was a painful job but it had one useful side-effect. By noticing the constantly repeated mistakes of grammar and syntax I was able to get the feel of the way a Tamil sentence is constructed and this was enormously helpful. The hardest thing was to get past the mere repetition of stock phrases to some original thinking. When I complained that there was no originality in a composition, the boy would be completely unable to see what I wanted. If a thing is true it has been said before. If it has not been said before it is almost certainly not true. What on earth, then, is this thing called 'originality'? It was hard to explain. And even harder to teach from a textbook which would introduce a passage for study as follows: 'This is a humorous poem and should be studied with a view to enjoying the joke.'

Scripture teaching, which was part of the syllabus, raised other problems. How to make the Bible come alive to Hindu schoolboys with very sharp intelligence and coming from orthodox homes? How to communicate its message in a way which did not arouse antagonism and break trust? I do not think I found the right answers, but I do look back with gratitude on the contacts this gave me. I was able to start an annual schoolboys' camp, at a pleasant spot ten miles from the city, where Hindu and Christian boys shared in a few days of fellowship and teaching.

Street preaching had been a vital part of Maclean's ministry and I continued it. Each month we went out, a group of a dozen or so, to preach and to discuss with those who wanted to ask further. There were always people ready to listen, sometimes to heckle, sometimes to stay for serious talk. And each year at the great festival in May and June, when hundreds of thousands of pilgrims came from all over India, there was a special effort to reach them through preaching and the distribution of Gospels. For this it was customary for outstanding speakers to come from other parts of the country to give their help. The season was the hottest of the year with temperatures well over 100° and the work was exhausting. In a letter home I described

the seething crowds, the dust, the heat, the intense excitement with which the crowds respond to the glamour and pageantry of the festival, of light and music, of the rhythmic drone of prayers intoned by processions of Brahmins, and of the idols proudly carried on the shoulders of hundreds of sweating men – all this as a background to long and close arguments and sharp encounters with questioners generally hostile, often very able, and always backed by a crowd ready at any moment to flare up in resentment and anger when it seems that the ancient faith is being attacked. Such experiences test as with fire those views which first took intellectual shape in friendly battles round college coffee cups, test and also sharpen one's missionary convictions. The way lies along a knife edge; on the one hand the kind of words that lay one open justly to the charge of embittering India's already bitter inter-religious tensions; on the other the kind of words that will allow the crowd to disperse happily reassured that no fundamental conversion is necessary, peace restored and the cause decisively betrayed.

In my early years there was often hostility, but towards the end of my time I was writing:

Everyone who has taken part in this work over a long period testifies to the amazing change which has taken place in the attitude of the people to Gospel preaching. Not many years ago the public proclamation of the Gospel was an invitation to abuse or even assault. Now we find that we can give the most direct and challenging presentation of the message and be sure of a steady and respectful hearing and a substantial sale of scriptures at the end. Here above all it is true that other men have laboured and we are entered into their labours.

The value of this street preaching may be questioned. The answer which I gave in my own mind was that the people listening to us knew that we were also the people who taught their boys and girls in the schools and who cared for their sick in the Mission Hospital, so that the preaching was not disembodied words but had some flesh on it. In the same letter I wrote:

I do not think that the street preaching of wandering strangers is likely to bear much fruit in a place like this: but when men have earned their right to be heard by their service to the city in a school or hospital, their public testimony will carry weight, especially with those who have themselves learned the story of Jesus in a Mission school. Thus the institutional work gives weight to the preaching, and the preaching gives point to the institutional work.

What matters is that word and deed are not separated. What matters more is that they are seen to flow from a centre where Jesus Christ is confessed and worshipped. Apart from the schools and hospital there was only one Christian building in Kanchipuram, the church which Maclean had built in 1922. It had no need of a denominational name for no other Christian body worked in Kanchi. It was a very simple building with open door and broad verandahs, so that an interested person could sit outside in the cool shade without actually entering the building, and yet hear everything. There were many who were sufficiently interested by what they had experienced in school, in hospital, in listening to a street preacher or in reading a Gospel, to want to come and listen in the place where it all had its centre. And there were a few, not many, who took the further step and came inside. That usually meant total excommunication from home, family and inheritance. So there were not many, but there were some.

Kanchipuram was and is a strong centre of traditional Hindu learning, and I was privileged to enjoy the welcoming friendship of the scholars who gathered in the *math* or monastery of the Ramakrishna Mission. Along with the head of that community I shared in the leadership of a weekly study group in which we studied alternately the Svetasvara Upanishad and St John's Gospel. We sat, Indian fashion, cross-legged on the floor and the leader in each case read the Scripture in the original language – Sanskrit or Greek – and expounded it, after which there would be an hour or more of questioning and discussion. These sessions were extremely rewarding for me. I would like to think that they also had some value for my Hindu friends. Certainly none of them became a Christian and I did not become a Hindu, though I learned to see the profound rationality of the world-view of the Vedanta. I well remember how I astonished the Swami by saying that if it could be shown that Jesus had never lived and died and risen again I would have no alternative but to become a Hindu. He thought that only a lunatic would allow his ultimate destiny to hang upon a questionable fact of history which – even if it could be proved – belonged to the world of *maya*.

The Ramakrishna Mission follows in general the school of Vedanta, but one member of the group was a respected teacher in the school of Visishtadvaita, the theistic form of belief which stems from the teaching of Ramanuja. This has been called 'India's Religion of Grace' and has many close parallels with evangelical Christianity which had been explained in Rudolf Otto's book with that title. This scholar was kind enough to give many hours of his time to initiating me into the teachings of this school. At the end I had to confess (contrary to my expectations) that Hendrik Kraemer's criticism of Otto's assessment was justified (*The Christian Message in a Non-Christian World*, pp. 168–73). Even this profoundly moving and gracious form of religious devotion had its roots and its only support in the human need for salvation, not in a divine act of redemption within the real history of which this human life is a part.

I am bound to say that as I reflected on these long discussions on religious subjects with gracious and helpful Hindu friends, I became more and more sure that the 'point of contact' for the Gospel is rather in the ordinary secular experiences of human life than in the sphere of religion. I had not then read Karl Barth and did not know that 'religion is unbelief', but I was certainly beginning to see that religion can be a way of protecting oneself from reality.

Throughout the time of our stay in Kanchipuram, petrol was severely rationed. My ambition to do without a driver had been granted, but I used the car only for village visits and went about the city on foot or on my bicycle. Needless to say this made it very much easier to establish contact, even if only fleeting, with all sorts of people. Especially in the atmosphere of growing tension as the freedom struggle gathered force and as the long and repeated disappointment of popular hope led to increasing resentment against the white rulers, it was very important to be able to walk or cycle everywhere among the streets and lanes of the city and to be available for personal contact. Only once was there any occasion for anxiety about personal safety when a riot took place and the High School boys were under intense pressure to join in. The last Governor of Madras, Sir Archibald Nye, had a name which was, unfortunately, the Tamil word for 'dog'. This gave rise to a very handy slogan which could be chanted on all occasions: 'Vellai nay, vellie po' ('White dog, get out'). But one could walk into a crowd of schoolboys shouting this slogan and they would courteously explain: 'Of course we don't mean you!'

I fitted a wooden box to the back of my bike and stocked it with cheap paperback copies of the Gospels which could be sold for one anna. Every now and then I would stop, prop up the bike, open the box and take out a Gospel to read. At once a small crowd would collect and within the next ten minutes some friendly conversations would have ensued and a dozen Gospels been sold. It was a good, simple way of communicating.

Obviously our closest friendships were with our Christian colleagues in the Church and on the staff of the High School. We very much enjoyed the hospitality of their homes and the opportunity to entertain them in ours. The pastor in charge when we came was a very senior man whom we greatly respected but who had been schooled in the traditional relation between missionaries and their Indian colleagues. In 1942 a young pastor, the Revd J. S. Subramaniam, came to take charge and from that time he and his wife Kamala were to become our very close and beloved friends. It was an enormous strength to be able to share all our problems and to spend time in prayer together seeking God's help at the many points where we felt helpless. More often than not these were the points at which faction and strife within the Church had erupted into open quarrelling. At first I found these quarrels as incomprehensible as they were heart-breaking. Their bitterness seemed to be out of all proportion to any real issues. It was only after some time that my eyes were opened to the reality – namely that the apparent issues were only a screen for the real one, which was caste.

The official view of missionaries was that caste does not exist in the Indian Church. A question about the caste affiliation of a Christian was absolutely inadmissible. When I made discreet inquires from the greatly respected Indian headmaster of the High School he put me firmly in my place: 'There is no such thing as caste among Christians.' It was some time before I realized that this was a comfortable rationalization of the fact that all major posts in the Mission institutions and all the places in the governing bodies of the Church were held by people of one caste only: the Nadars of Tinnevelley. The spectacular growth of this community under missionary leadership in the nineteenth century had produced an abundance of educated men and women who were available for service in the (later) missionary work of other churches in the rest of Tamil Nadu. They had great gifts of intelligence and hard work, and they were also a close-knit community of families interlocked by marriage. It was easy and natural for them to monopolize all the higher posts and to create an atmosphere of accepted opinion that the local Christian products of more recent evangelism among the outcaste communities were 'not yet fitted' for higher responsibility. The resulting resentment among Christians from other castes was the source from which these otherwise inexplicable quarrels burst forth. My missionary colleagues generally did not question the accepted wisdom. In spite of the fact that the Church of Scotland was the parent mission of the Madras Christian College

- the most prestigious educational institution in the whole of India - not one single boy from the villages of the Kanchipuram area had been sent to college. They were judged unfit. It was only when, after my father's death, I had a substantial sum of my own money, that I could finance the sending of some of our village boys to college. I later had the joy of seeing them filling posts of great responsibility in the Church, and one of them is now a bishop.

7
Kanchi: The Villages

These quarrels in Kanchipuram heightened my feelings of relief
and happiness when I could escape to the work in the villages. It
had been the practice of earlier missionaries, before the days of
the motor car, to spend long periods camping (in, it must be
admitted, somewhat elaborate style). As the fruit of this work
there were Christian congregations in a score or so of villages,
normally under the immediate pastoral care of a teacher who also
ran the elementary school. With the use of a car missionaries
could easily visit distant villages for an hour or two and return
for the next meal. I was sure that much had been lost in this way
and from the beginning made it a practice to spend longer times
in the villages, including overnight stay. This gave time for
leisurely talk, for enjoying the hospitality of the village teacher's
home and, above all, for visits to a great many villages where
there were as yet no Christians. Very often there was a verbal
message from a village hitherto unvisited that a group of families
wanted to hear about the Gospel. Often it was because of a
contact made in the Mission Hospital. And so a group of us would
set off through the darkness, following winding tracks through
the jungle or balancing on the narrow 'bund' between the flooded
paddy fields, with a paraffin lantern to light the way and sticks to
deal with snakes. These times were full of rich joys – the kind of
free-flowing conversation that happens when you are sharing a
task and a journey, the marvellous beauty of the star-studded sky
and the sounds of the tropical night all around. Often there
would be times of silence and then my mind inevitably flew back
to Europe where the terrible events of the war were unfolding.
Hitler's armies were over-running the whole continent and the
world I had known seemed to be coming to an end. In one of my
earliest letters home I wrote:

> I wish that I could convey more effectively the interest and
> hopefulness of this work here, especially to you who are in the
> midst of the life-and-death struggle of the old Christendom.

During these evenings in the villages, watching the faces of the eager listeners who squat in a circle round the Petromax lamp, my mind has wandered back and forth between this little world, bounded by the dim outlines of thatch and the jagged silhouette of palm trees, and that world in which the one reality seems to be the monster of universal war. And again and again I have reminded myself that it is upon these people, the inarticulate and exploited millions whose labour keeps the world going, that that other world is built. And if the dynamic power of the Gospel is at work among these, it will ultimately revolutionize the other also.

The people who used to gather round the Petromax lamp to listen and to question were indeed among the poorest in the world. In the same letter I described the villages that I was coming to know and love:

They are settlements of crude mud and thatch huts, separated from the ordinary caste villages, and inhabited by the people who are variously called Adi-Dravidas, Untouchables and Harijans. As most people know, they are a very much exploited group of people, excluded by traditional Hindu law from all participation in the social and religious life of the nation, and even from the use of the streets and wells used by their masters. Economically their position is that of casual labourers, working for hire in the fields of the caste Hindus. It is very rarely that they have land of their own. The rate of wages current in the villages is 3d–4d per day for a man and 2d for a woman. When it is remembered that this is casual labour, and that there are long stretches of unemployment, the level of poverty can be imagined.

It should be added that very few of these villages were near any road. Bus services had not developed as they would do later. Except for the schools run by the Mission very few had schools. The village was an island, living its own life, to be reached only on foot or, perhaps, in a bullock cart.

I came to have a deep respect for the people who lived under these conditions, who laboured day after day and year after year for a pittance, who were subject to systematic humiliation at every point and who yet retained a dignity and a courge that often put me to shame. During the following years I was to be involved in numerous efforts to help them improve their economic position by the introduction of high-yielding poultry and of village school gardens where tomatoes and other useful crops could be grown within the village area. I do not think any of these made much difference. What did make a difference was the Gospel. One could not fail to see that the Gospel was doing what it has always done, making it possible for those who were formerly 'no people' to become 'God's people'. That is, of course, the meaning of the name Gandhi coined for them: 'Harijan'. The reality which that name was intended to carry was being actually experienced and enjoyed by those who had been enabled through Jesus to look up and say 'Father'.

In these days I was reminded over and over again of the parable of the sower. There would be many long tramps in the dark, many village visits and many hours of talking which produced nothing at all. And then again there would be an astonishing harvest from a seed dropped into the ground, apparently by accident. Here is one incident, from a letter written in 1940:

Early in January two men came to our Mission Hospital here from a village of which we had not heard, named Thirupanamur. They said they had come on behalf of their village to ask us to send someone to tell them about Christianity. The Hospital Catechist promised that someone would come, and two or three days later three of us set off to look for the village. After many inquiries, and much wandering about in territory which was new to all of us, we arrived after dark at the village. In the middle of the village was a small, well-built temple. To our surprise, the temple was immediately opened, a lamp brought, and ourselves invited to sit down inside. In a few minutes a large crowd was gathered round the porch of the temple, and the leading man, having made us sit down, spoke to us in words that reminded me of Cornelius welcoming Peter. In effect, he said: 'We have invited you to come, and we are glad that you have come. Now here we are, and we know nothing about Christianity, but we want you to tell us all about it from the beginning.' The Catechist, whom by general agreement we had made our spokesman, replied by asking why they had invited us, and in particular how it came that they invited us into the temple. They answered that they had asked us because some of them had been in the Mission Hospital, and what they had heard and seen made them want to find out more about this Christian way. As for the temple, they were not using it, and they were wondering whether the idol was any use at all, or whether they should not go over entirely to the Christian way. So they asked us to tell them all about it.

It was wonderful to see the eagerness with which they listened. Here were people who were really in earnest, and their attention never wavered. The Catechist began from the idol in whose temple we were sitting, drawing from the people, by question and suggestion, their own admission of the futility of worshipping the work of their own hands. Then he went on to appeal to the sense in all of them of a supreme creator God, and to the common situation of guilt before Him. Then came the change from argument to announcement as he told them of Jesus, and of the life which He gives. When the meeting at last came to and end, the majority had expressed themselves as satisfied that this was the truth, and they wanted to be instructed further. They had responded to my suggestion of sending a teacher with the promise of house and food and welcome for him, and the unfettered use of the temple for Christian teaching and worship.

But the main burden of the work in the villages fell upon the people who were known as 'Mission agents' – the teachers in the village elementary schools, the catechists who travelled from village to village, and the Biblewomen who did the work of teaching and preaching among women. Apart from these last who were under the care of my women missionary colleagues, these 'agents' were under my supervision. Every month they came together for two days of meetings in which there were classes in Old and New Testaments, Christian doctrine and other subjects. Monthly salaries were paid, policy was discussed, and a thousand and one personal matters were settled. The preparation for and conduct of these meetings placed a severe strain on my Tamil in the early days but I came to value them enormously. Even more I came to appreciate and honour the men who were doing the work. Sometimes I had serious problems and once, very painfully, had to terminate the service of a village teacher. But my feelings about these men are expressed in a letter I wrote towards the end of our time in Kanchipuram:

It seems to be a common practice to regard the elementary teacher in a Mission village school as a contemptible sort of hack, doing his job for the sake of his pay. I confess that the longer I stay here the more I admire these men. The burden they carry is staggering. Here is the schedule of duties of the village teacher in our district: responsibility for 5½ hours teaching per day for 220 days per year, generally of several classes simultaneously, under the very strict rules of the Education Department, together with the maintenance of the multitudes of complicated registers and returns which it seems to be the chief function of Government to invent; maintenance of census returns for their village; conduct of two full services each Sunday, and morning and evening prayers each day; conduct, alternately with the Catechist, of classes for catechumens and young communicants; conduct of singing practice, Christian Endeavour, and Sunday School; general oversight of the discipline of the congregation, visiting of homes, convening the village elders' court, and leadership of regular evangelistic work. In addition they attend monthly meetings with the missionary and pastor for instruction in Old and New Testaments, sermon class, Tamil poetry, and for meetings of church courts, cooperative society and other meetings. They are expected to be, and generally are, the friends in need of all the people, Hindu and Christian, in their villages – settling quarrels, tending the sick, standing up against the oppressor and feeding the starving. And they contrive to do it on a salary that averages about £25 per year.

When one sits in the Mission office and the village teachers come in and bother one at awkward hours, one is apt to forget these things. The 'agents' become ledger entries which refuse to stay put. This ossification of the soul is the Devil's chief way of making a district missionary harmless to him. But when one can shake oneself loose from the office and spend days in the villages, living as the guests of the teachers and sharing to some extent in their work, one sees things in a different light. Indian hospitality is one of the best things in India, and if it be true that behind it is the old idea of winning the guest's blessing, I confess that, as I have sat outside the teacher's house enjoying a cup of coffee or a meal after an exhausting tramp across the hot fields or late at night after a long evening of street preaching, I have not had any mind to withhold the blessing.

By the time I wrote these words the position of the village teacher was changing. As India became more and more involved in the war effort, more and more of the village boys and girls were drawn into military and nursing services. In these occupations they could command salaries three or four times that of the village teacher who had previously been, on his small pittance, the richest man in the community. Food prices had soared, farmers were richer than ever before, and since the hire of farm labourers was usually paid in grain, they also benefited. Moreover, the families in our village congregations were getting substantial monthly remittances from their sons and daughters in military service. This made a big change in the position of the village teacher. And it also helped to raise the self-confidence of the village congregations previously so dependent on the goodwill and support of the Mission. It helped to shift the centre of gravity from Mission to Church, from the 'Mission agent', paid and supervised by the missionary, to the ordinary Christian in his lay vocation. This seemed to me a shift of enormous importance.

From my first contact with those village congregations I had been struck by the fact that they all saw themselves as dependencies of the Mission rather than as congregations of the holy catholic Church. They depended upon a teacher who in turn depended upon the missionary. The Indian pastor visited only occasionally and consequently the sacraments were not an integral part of their life but an extra brought from outside. There could hardly be any of the 'spontaneous expansion of the Church' which we see in the New Testament because it was assumed that a congregation required a teacher, a teacher required a salary and a salary had to come from a committee in Scotland which had firmly declined to sanction increases in the budget. The 'Great Commission' was, apparently, to be suspended *pro tem*.

I was sure that the only way forward was to develop a local

leadership within the village congregation, even though the vast majority of the members were illiterate. From my very first year in Kanchipuram I arranged a one-week gathering of these village leaders in the disused buildings at Walajabad during the extreme hot weather of May when there is no possibility of work in the fields. I lived with them for a week of relaxed meetings and we studied the Bible, sang Christian hymns, discussed village problems, and trekked off each morning to preach in some neighbouring village. These were uneducated men but they were shrewd, often wise, and generally devout. I was sure that they were capable of being real leaders of their congregations. In the places where there was no school they had freedom to develop. Where there was a resident teacher it would be much more difficult. But I took it for granted that before long Government would replace the foreign missionary as the provider of education for the 800,000 villages of India.

These small efforts received an enormous impetus from the development which I have already mentioned – the departure of hundreds of village boys to military service. At first it was a small trickle, clandestine because of the adamant opposition of parents. A lad of seventeen with perhaps a fourth-standard education, barely literate, with no experience of the world outside his village, would creep out of his hut in the middle of the night and make his way to the nearest recruiting station. Nothing would be heard of him for weeks. His parents would mourn as for the sudden death of a son. After some weeks notes scrawled with a pencil in atrociously mis-spelt Tamil would arrive from unknown military post offices. He might be in North Africa or Iraq or Italy. Nobody knew. And then one day the clatter of enormous boots on the verandah announces the arrival of our village boy. He has apparently grown a foot taller. His salute is of machine-like precision. He talks with immense confidence and enthusiasm. This lad who had never seen a railway train is now driving a military lorry in the African desert and facing cheerfully all the dangers of modern war.

But there was much more than this. Taken out of a position of dependence and given responsibility these boys were developing gifts of Christian leadership. As more and more of the young men left the village I worried more and more about their future. They were barely literate, their Christian training was minimal.

Hardly any had Bibles and there were no chaplains in most units of the Indian army. Would they not simply be lost to the Church? How could I help them?

I need not have worried. As the months went by my mail contained more and more letters from these boys in all the theatres of war, telling me that they wanted Bibles and other Christian books to help them in their evangelistic work. A typical letter, usually written in pencil on the back of an army form, would run: 'I am the only Christian in our unit. I have started a Bible class. All the others want to have Bibles. Please send me six Bibles and a lyric book.' Before long I was mailing Bible-reading notes to about 120 of these men all over the areas of war. What I had thought to be a pastoral problem was in fact a huge missionary opportunity. The story of Acts was being repeated. And of course when the young men would come back after the war it was clear that the village congregations and the Church as a whole could never again revert to a position of dependence on the Mission. It was a lesson which I was to have an opportunity of applying in a wider sphere later.

I was sure that the strengthening of local leadership in the villages was the key to future expansion. It was the same principle that I had learned in the Cambridge SCM, that the health of the whole depends upon the health of the smallest unit. So I started producing an annual 'Village Workers' Almanack', providing teaching suggestions and material for every Sunday in the year, of a kind which could be used by village leaders who had no theological training. Later on in Madurai I was to have an opportunity to develop this for wider use throughout the Tamil churches. And I also seized with joy on a booklet produced by Raymond Dudley – the *Madurai Moonlight Kummies*. There were verses telling the great stories of the Gospel in a form which could be sung to the dancing of traditional village folk-dances – Kummi and Kolattam. The choruses were very easily picked up and sung by any group of village people, and I found them a wonderful help both in teaching and in evangelism among village folk.

Although Helen obviously could not come with me on these village visits, we were able as a family to do a little visiting in the district. At Walajabad, ten miles from Kanchi, there was a bungalow which had originally been built for the use of British army officers and now stood vacant. On several occasions we went there for a few days of camp while I visited the surrounding villages. We all enjoyed these trips, and the children were endlessly inventive in producing new games and dramatic performances based on the varied experiences they were having.

8

Kanchi: Beyond the Villages

Inevitably in this fallen world I found that these delectable rural activities tended to be crowded out by administrative duties. As I gained more experience I was pushed into accepting responsibilities which kept me for more hours than I wished behind a desk. I did not think that the proper role of a foreign missionary was to sit at a desk and organize the work of Indian pastors and evangelists. I thought that he ought to be himself a pastor and evangelist sharing their joys and sorrows as a colleague. I contributed an eloquent plea to this effect to the *International Review of Missions* (January 1945). But I was not allowed to have my way. In the middle of the year the Mission Council was persuaded to hand over the work that I had carried to my colleague S. J. Subramaniam and I was able to insist that he should also have the car under his control. But I was not allowed to do what I asked, to take over one of the places usually held by an Indian pastor. Instead I was made chairman of a new body which took over from the Mission the responsibility it had had for village work, the actual day-to-day work being in the hands of Indians. Thus I was the victim of the process which has been so frustrating to so many missionaries. Instead of being allowed to move sideways into equal partnership with Indian colleagues, I was withdrawn upwards into a superior administrative post created for the purpose. The consequences of this policy were, of course, much more serious than the frustration of the desires of a few missionaries. The steady pursuit of this policy all over the world has built into the life of third-world churches the unacknowledged assumption that the work of preaching the Gospel, ministering the sacraments and building up the Body of Christ, is a relatively unimportant occupation compared to the work of administering a large organization. It has caused thousands of pastors to speak of their workplace as an office rather than a study, to cherish a drawer full of files as the symbol of a status higher than that denoted by a shelf full of books, and to see the office desk as the place of real power.

For my last year in Kanchipuram, therefore, I was travelling more widely than before, but having less continuous contact with the villages. I was also put in charge of the work in Madras City and came to know the congregations there. In a letter that year I wrote:

Madras is a field which has suffered tragically from a wrong policy with regard to the relations of Church and Mission. Pursuing the ideals of independence and self-support, and seeing that the Madras congregations comprised many people of wealth who could well support their own churches, missions have largely withdrawn from Madras except for the maintenance of certain large institutions. But if independence and self-support are interpreted too narrowly, they lead only to sterile introversion, the fruits of which are perpetual internal quarrels and the complete absence of evangelistic outreach. The unity of Church and Mission should have been secured and self-support gradually developed within that unity. That, at least, seems to be the moral to be drawn from the situation in Madras. The congregations are largely ineffective, repudiate any responsibility for or relation with the Mission, and spend their time in disgraceful quarrels.

When I wrote these words I never dreamed that, twenty years later, I would return to Madras as a bishop. Such a thought would have filled me with horror. But it was to be through a larger unity, under episcopal leadership, that these quarrelling congregations were to be brought into a real missionary engagement with the life of the city.

The churches which had been brought to birth through the mission of the Scottish Churches (the 'Auld Kirk' as well as the 'Free Kirk') formed part of the 'South India United Church', which had been set up in 1908 by a union of Congregationalists and Presbyterians. Much the strongest elements were those which looked to the London Missionary Society (in Travancore, Coimbatore, Salem, Erode and in the Telugu and Kanarese fields) and the American Board of Commissioners for Foreign Mission (in Madura and Jaffna). We were part of the Madras Church Council which included the work of the Arcot Mission of the Reformed Church in America as well as the Scottish work and two congregations in Madras founded by the LMS. Each year the Madras Church Council met for three or four days. The missionaries had their meals separately from the Indians. There was a lot of good fellowship, for the Dutch Americans were great characters. But it was a kind of fellowship in which Indians had no place.

We sat as members of the Council but there was also a somewhat shadowy entity called the Madras Presbytery of the Church of Scotland, which included the Scottish ministers of the Ecclesiastical Establishment of the Government of India. We were still ministers of the Church of Scotland and therefore, in matters ecclesiastical, subject to the jurisdiction of this Presbytery. At the very first meeting of the (SIUC) Madras Church Council which I attended an event occurred which raised for me a question of conscience. One of the Scottish missionaries brought charges of a serious kind against an Indian pastor. The latter defended himself by bringing counter-charges against his accuser. The missionary replied by saying: 'These charges cannot be made here. I am not under the jurisdiction of this Council. I am solely under the jurisdiction of the Presbytery of Madras, Church of Scotland.' To me this was intolerable and I found that the two ordained missionaries who were my contemporaries felt the same. Eventually we wrote a formal letter to Edinburgh requesting that our names be removed from the roll of ministers of the Church of Scotland so that we might be wholly and unambiguously responsible to the Indian Church.

When my next quarterly salary cheque arrived from Edinburgh there was a little note in the handwriting of the accountant: 'Your letter has been received; it will cause much scratching of bald pates.' It did. But, after two General Assemblies and several committee meetings we were informed that our request was granted and that, should we later wish to return to the Church of Scotland, 'the usual fee will be waived'. This has, of course, subsequently become the normal practice. But I have sometimes wondered what would have happened if, at the time when I was made a bishop, I had still been a minister of the Church of Scotland. I fear that heads might have not been merely scratched but broken.

One of the joys of being born into the Christian faith through the SCM was that one was from the beginning part of an ecumenical family. The SCM in South India enjoyed the brilliant

leadership of Malcolm Adesishiah, then a professor at the
Madras Christian College and later to be Deputy Director-
General of UNESCO. From the earliest days of our stay in
Kanchipuram he invited me to student conferences and brought
me into a continuous and happy relation with succeeding
generations of students. I wrote a study book for them on 'What
is the Gospel?' and took part in the founding of the India SVMU. I
was also invited to lecture at the United Theological College,
Bangalore, and took the opportunity to develop further the ideas
I had been working on during my last years at Westminster on
'The Kingdom of God and Progress'. This brought me into touch
with M. M. Thomas, who attended the lectures, and was the
beginning of a personal and theological friendship which has
lasted as a very pecious gift through the years. He in turn invited
me to share in the leadership of a conference in Kerala of the very
dynamic 'Kerala Youth Council of Action' and thereafter I was
frequently asked to speak at student conferences in Kerala.
These student contacts were very enriching to me and gave me
the privilege of a very wide circle of friends among the young
Indian leadership.

I was also asked to chair a committe under the auspices of the
National Christian Council, charged with the duty of implementing
for the Tamil area the intention of the Ranson Report to bring
into existence for each of the main language areas a single high-
grade institution for the training of the ministry in the mother
tongue. It was in 1942 that I was asked to take on this
responsibility; it took nearly thirty years to bring the dream to
fulfilment in the creation of the Tamilnadu Theological Seminary
at Arasaradi, Madurai.

Church union was not an immediate issue in Kanchipuram
because (until the end of the period) there was only one Christian
Church. But J. H. Maclean had been one of the architects of the
famous 'South India Scheme' and at each annual meeting of the
Madras Church Council the matter was on the agenda. Like the
SIUC as a whole, the Madras Council was very much divided.
The smaller Scottish section tended to support Maclean, but the
larger Arcot Mission group with its strong Dutch Reformed
background was generally against the proposals and viewed
episcopacy with profound suspicion. The very able secretary, Mr
G. V. Job, one of the group which produced *Rethinking Christianity*

in India, was an articulate and determined opponent. (He was later to be the first General Secretary of the Synod of the CSI!)

In the early 1940s the whole unity movement had reached something of an impasse. For more than twenty years discussions had been going on and the scheme revised again and again, to meet criticisms from one quarter or another. It seemed as if there could be no end to the process. Everybody could postpone decision indefinitely by asking for amendments. In 1942 the Joint Committee published what it hoped would be the final form of the scheme and made an urgent appeal to the three Churches to make up their minds for or against. It so happened also that around this period most of the great men who had fashioned and pressed for the scheme were leaving the stage. Three of the Anglican bishops mainly involved left India or died in the period 1938–44. Banninga, the SIUC leader, left in 1942 and Monahan the Methodist leader in 1940. Dr Maclean himself had retired and in 1942 I was elected to succeed him as convener of the Union Committee of the Council. In the following year I was elected convener of the Committee of the SIUC as a whole.

There was a great sense of weariness about the whole matter. It was twenty-four years since the proposals had been launched with immense power and passion at Tranquebar. Nearly a quarter of a century of talk seemed to be ending in paralysis, and the great pioneers were all leaving the scene. Some of my colleagues openly regarded the whole enterprise as a waste of time and a diversion of energy from the real business of a missionary.

As the three Churches tried to respond to the appeal of the Joint Committee it seemed as if one of these would be incapable of doing so. The Methodists gave final approval in 1943 and the Anglicans in 1945. Unfortunately, as will appear later, these votes were taken on the basis of mutually incompatible interpretations of one element in the scheme and therefore were not as final as they seemed. The SIUC, however, seemed incapable of making any decision at all. Its eight councils were only held together in a very loose federation. Its General Assembly could only act with the approval of at least six councils. Many of the councils were fluctuating in their votes according to the influence of powerful personalities in their meetings. And while six councils might at some time or other give an affirmative vote, it seemed utterly impossible to conceive of a moment in which six would do so at the same time. The two councils related to the American Board – Madura and Jaffna – were generally in favour. Three of the four related to the London Missionary Society – Travancore, North Tamil and Telugu – were against. The remaining three – Madras, Kannada and Malabar (related to the Basel Mission) – were uncertain. It seemed impossible that a decision could ever be reached.

As far as the Madras Council was concerned, I felt that one of the reasons for its uncertainty was that while the speeches by the proponents of union were in English, those of the opponents were in Tamil, and therefore much more effective. I took pains to argue the theological issues in Tamil and I think that this helped to swing the vote of that council in favour. For the wider debate in the SIUC as a whole I promoted the publication of a sixty-page booklet in which five of the leading participants in the debate could develop their arguments (for or against) at length for the whole Church, and this had a wide circulation.

My own contribution was titled 'The Church and the Gospel' and contained the results of a good deal of theological wrestling which was later to be expanded in *The Reunion of the Church*. I had serious difficulties with the scheme in so far as it involved acceptance of the so-called 'historic episcopate' as a necessary element in a united Church. The Church, as I understood it, was constituted by the Gospel, communicated in word and sacrament and evoking the response of faith. Ministerial order was therefore secondary and could never be put on the same level of importance as word and sacrament. On this I had some vigorous correspondence with my old Cambridge friend, Oliver Tomkins, who insisted that the apostolic ministry was part of that which was given and constitutive of the Church and not to be separated from word and sacrament. What changed my mind was the reading of Michael Ramsey's book *The Gospel and the Catholic Church*. I found there a doctrine of the ministry which did not contravene but rested upon the biblical doctrine of justification by grace through faith, and I saw that the historic episcopate could be gladly accepted as something given by the grace of God to be the means of unity. But this meant that one had to reject at the same time any way of interpreting the historic episcopate which made it a *conditio sine qua non* of the fullness of grace. That was what some Anglo-Catholic theologians seemed to be doing. This issue arose in a sharp and painful way shortly after I became convener. From time to time it had been proposed that the problem of Anglican recognition of Free Church ministries might be solved by some kind of reciprocal commissioning. The 'Lambeth Appeal of 1920' invited the Free Churches to bestow on Anglican ministers 'a form of commission or recognition which would commend our ministry to their congregations' and expressed the hope that the Free Churches would likewise be willing to accept 'a commission through episcopal ordination'. In his influential book *The Christian Sacraments* O. C. Quick had developed the idea that all ordinations in separated churches are defective in that they lack universal authorization and he therefore proposed a form of mutual authorization which would have a clearly sacramental character, would include prayer with the imposition of hands, but would at the same time recognize the reality (albeit defective) of the previous ordination. This proposal, often called 'supplemental ordination', was being discussed in Australia and in the USA. In August 1943 Bishop Azariah of Dornakal proposed that this should be adopted in South India in order to avoid the parallel existence of two classes of ministers in the united Church – those episcopally ordained and the rest. Azariah's initiative was enthusiastically supported by Bishops Palmer and Western, both now in retirement, and was commended by Bishop Hubback of Assam to the General Council of the CIBC in such moving terms that many felt it as a fresh wind of the Spirit breathing new life into the dead bones of the scheme. A number of leading theologians in the Methodist Church and in the SIUC also supported it as did, very surprisingly, the Inter-Church Relations Committee of the Church of Scotland. H. V. Martin, the redoubtable anti-union leader of the Telugu Church Council, was another unexpected convert to the idea.

The problem was that different people interpreted the proposal in different ways. To its Anglo-Catholic supporters its whole point was that it did convey episcopal ordination. To its supporters in the other Churches it was 'an extended commission'. The whole basis of Quick's argument had been the denial of a distinction between ordination and authorization, but those who discussed the proposal could not escape from this distinction.

I was asked to serve on a small group to discuss this and other matters involved in the inauguration of union. The others were Bishop Azariah himself, Paul Ramasesham (Methodist) and J. S. M. Hooper, Secretary of the Joint Committee. But before the group could meet, the SIUC General Assembly had its biennial meeting. It was my job first to chair the Union Committee in a day-long attempt to hammer out some sort of agreed proposals for the Assembly and then to pilot these through an intense two-day debate. In the end the Assembly adopted by an overwhelming majority a resolution to suspend the constitution so as to enable the 1946 Assembly to take final action whatever the state of voting in the constituent councils. This made possible the SIUC's acceptance of the scheme two years later. At the same time the Assembly decisively rejected the proposals for supplemental ordination with the result that when the small Committee met at Dornakal in the following month we proposed a first draft of the service of inauguration with a commissioning which could not be interpreted as ordination. In the following month the full Joint Committee met and after a long debate agreed to drop the proposal. I was much involved in the debates, which generated a good deal of emotion, for many of the Anglican proponents of supplemental ordination were deeply convinced that this was the way the Spirit was leading. The debate was to continue on a wider front for a very long time.

At this point the prospects for an early inauguration of the union seemed bright. In 1945 the General Council of the CIBC gave the final vote for acceptance. But immediately a new crisis arose over the interpretation of the clause in the scheme known as 'The Pledge'. This was an undertaking to respect the conscientious convictions of congregations regarding traditional forms of worship and ministry. Many Anglicans interpreted this to mean that in no circumstances would a minister not episcopally ordained be appointed to a formerly Anglican congregation. The Joint Committee had, however, in an official statement declared it to mean that such a ministry would not be *imposed* upon an ex-Anglican congregation. Owing to the death of Bishop Azariah on New Year's Day 1945, the General Council was not made aware of this official interpretation and the bishops later in the year declared that the Anglican acceptance of the scheme did not include acceptance of this interpretation. At this time intense pressure was being exerted in England against the scheme and it was almost impossible for the bishops to take any other position. For the other two Churches this meant that the Anglican acceptance was void. It looked as if the scheme was doomed after all, and when we left for furlough in May 1946 I thought that the prospects of union in my lifetime were almost non-existent. My faith was too small.

During all these years India was still under British rule. The Congress ministries which had governed in the States for two and a half years from 1937 to 1939 had been ordered by the Congress High Command to resign. Congress thus consigned itself to political irrelevance for the duration of the war and left a vacuum in which there were no alternatives except acquiescence or ineffective rebellion. In 1941 I wrote:

> Poverty is of course the problem that overshadows everything else. Christians tend to be rather aloof from the general political struggle in the country. About that struggle I feel very puzzled and bewildered, but I feel more and more deeply that the changes which India most clamantly needs are those which can only come when Government is based on popular support. Which boils down to the well-worn truism that if democracy is good for Britain, it is good for India too. One other thing that strikes me very much is that students, who are politically interested, so far as I have met them, have no use for any of the present political programmes and are pinning their faith wholly to Marxism and Soviet Russia. But most of the people I meet haven't heard of either.

Four months later came Pearl Harbor and within another four months the Japanese were shelling the Madras coast and invasion was expected at any moment. The mission of Stafford Cripps was a bold attempt by the British Government to break the deadlock and many Congress leaders were apparently ready to accept it, but it was rejected by Gandhi as 'a cheque on a failing bank'. It was only necessary to await the Japanese. Once more, Congress was consigned to futility. That great Congress statesman, the Madrassi Rajagopalachariar, was a political realist and argued for a serious recognition of the anxieties of the Moslems. But he was ejected from Congress and the British Government was left to hold the ring. The disaster of partition became inevitable. In August of the same year Gandhi launched his 'Quit India' campaign with the words 'Leave India in God's hands, or in modern parlance to anarchy'. The Government coped and the movement petered out, but the price of Gandhi's colossal misjudgement had to be paid in blood later. In my annual letter of October 1942 I could only say this:

> Present circumstances permit little news beyond what is suitable for transmission to the marines and other members of the forces. Let this at least be said, lest it be forgotten even in democratic Britain that in whatever respects they may disagree, Indians agree in this, that they love their own country, and that they do not relish any more than does any other proud and ancient race being governed by foreigners; and that hope deferred maketh the heart sick.

As India became more deeply involved in the war, with two million men in the army, and as the traditional supplies of rice from Burma were cut off, hunger and even famine became the overwhelming concern. My 1943 letter was full of the problems of hunger and pestilence in the villages, but I went on to say:

> To this gloomy picture add the accumulated despair produced by the political deadlock. The surface, since Rajagopalachariar's last efforts were extinguished, has the dead calm of a stony desert. The Government has naturally been severely criticized for its inability to handle the food situation, more severely by the European community than by anybody else. But the truth seems to be that so long as Government remains a vast corpulent organization of clerks engaged in passing files on to other clerks, and at no point answerable to public opinion, no amount of devotion and ability among the few at the top will enable it to tackle the work which the organization of a nation for war entails. The fantastic lengths to which government by clerks has gone was brought home to me this year when for the first time I had to sign the annual returns for the High School to the Education Department; this, in a year when Government is said to be exercising the most ruthless paper economy, involved the filling up and signing of about 370 separate sheets. It is sadly true that the task of Government fails to draw to itself the highest motives and the most vigilant

public opinion. That is partly because the sense of nation is, except among a few, much weaker than the sense of community or caste; and partly because, so long as the Government is foreign, those few will mainly be in the anti-Government camp. Community means to the average Indian what nation means to the average European, and good nationalists are perhaps as rare as 'good Europeans'. But surely, if we are pledged to India's freedom, it must be our greatest political task, now, in war-time, to foster all true nationalism that seeks to make India one.

A year later the strong hand of Wavell had brought a change of atmosphere. Food was available. Law and order reigned. The surface was calm and there was good money to be had. In October 1944 I wrote:

Here in this temple city life moves from festival to festival. In spite of the appalling conditions of travel pilgrims still throng the station platform, and mingle with the local crowds when the gods are carried round the temple precincts and the city streets. Brahmins still march down the streets behind and before the idols, chanting the ancient litanies of the Vedas and marching with the step of hereditary lords of heaven and earth; though sometimes one meets such odd situations as I saw one day outside the great wall of the temple of Vishnu, where a temple procession headed by an elephant was disputing the passage with an enormous tank. Our local Congress leader is in gaol, but was out for a few days and we had a chat about prison conditions, all very friendly and courteous. Moslems are too small a minority to take a hand in local politics, but the Brahmin–non-Brahmin split is everywhere. In one's cycnical moments one is inclined to feel that every one of the new civic ventures which from time to time sprout and wither away is just a new way of holding the ring for the old, old squabble. Meanwhile Government pursues its way, full of thoroughly sound ideals at the top, but somehow indescribably wooden, when not actually corrupt, in its contact with everyday life. Clerks are everywhere, and the way to get anything is to get on the right side of them. And meanwhile there is money to be had, money undreamed of a year or two ago. The High School boy who fails his final examination can walk into an army job with bigger pay than his headmaster. And the army contractor – well, if you are wise you will make hay while the sun shines and keep out of politics. Doubtless everything is ultimately an illusion; the time will come to remember that, though the West doesn't fully understand it – not yet. But meanwhile the sensible man will take what is going, without, however, giving any more loyalty than is strictly necessary to the order that provides it. Garlands are cheap and it doesn't much matter what peg you hang them on.

That kind of stagnant peace could hold only as long as the war lasted. As soon as it was over, the basic political issues re-emerged. In May 1946 I wrote:

The end of the war has brought a crop of local insecurities in addition to the vast insecurity of our whole civilization. First and basic is the question of India's political future. The present governmental structure was held together by the necessity of carrying on the war. Now no one any longer seems to have any belief in it, not the rulers, and very few of the ruled. Yet the alternatives of the Congress and the League are at present [6 May 1946] mutually contradictory. The elections have shown that the other parties count for nothing, except the Communists, who are, however, not yet strong enough to challenge the main parties. There is an air of utter unreality and irresponsibility about most political utterances, and there cannot be health until the present impasse is ended. Whether it will end in anarchy or in a reasonable compromise remains to be seen.

Four days after writing that I left India for furlough and was to be away from the scene of action through the great days that would bring India to the joy of freedom and the tragedy of partition.

Through all these years when the world was convulsed by war, our life as a family in Kanchipuram was so calm and peaceful as sometimes to make it hard to visualize what the rest of the world was suffering. Within nine months of our arrival we had word of my father's death. He had struggled on to the end, keeping his little fleet of ships trading with the Spanish ports in face of bombing and shelling, supporting and encouraging the captains and crews. The news of his death came along with the fall of

France and the apparently irresistible advance of Hitler's army. It seemed as if the world we knew was gone for ever. By contrast our little world in Kanchipuram seemed incredibly secure. The only occasion when real danger seemed to threaten was in April 1942 when a Japanese invasion of Madras was immediately expected. The Government of Madras panicked and ordered all 'whose presence was not essential' to leave the city. No further definition was given and there was a large exodus. Trains, buses and roads were crammed with pathetic groups fleeing with their small possessions. The United States authorities ordered all American missionaries to leave. As most of them had already gone to the Kodai hills for their summer holidays there was a cataract of missionaries down the ghat – an unedifying spectacle generally known among Indians as the 'Great White Flight'.

Kanchipuram is just off the Madras–Bangalore road and we concluded that it was not a good place for Helen and the children. On the other hand we were sure that it was my duty to stay with the Church. We decided that the family would go to Kodai, whence – if necessary – they might be able to find a way westwards to Bombay, and that I would put on Indian clothes and disappear into one of the village congregations. Thus it happened that while a flood of missionaries was coming down the ghat road from Kodai, we were on the way up and found an almost deserted hill station.

I went back at once to Kanchipuram and found that an army unit was camping just outside the town. Its commanding officer had no maps and was very vague about where he was. I was able to provide him with a map, and from that time onwards till the end of the war we had the privilege of entertaining successive companies of British troops camping in generally miserable conditions in the vicinity of the city. As the result of a long-drawn-out and complicated legal battle with the South India Railway Company regarding the accident in 1937, I had secured substantial compensation which we used to buy a Bluthner grand piano, secondhand but in marvellous condition. With this to help us we could have magnificent evenings of singing with the troops, and when we had a Welsh regiment stationed near us we almost raised the roof.

The piano was only one of the things that made our Kanchipuram home a lovely place for children to grow up in.

Margaret, of course, came with us in 1939 and we had two additions to the family – Alison, born in 1941 and Janet in 1944. The big airy bungalow with its wide verandahs was a grand place for children's games. There was always plenty of music and occasional picnics in the cool weather. Above all there was the annual holiday in Kodai with its glorious scenery and its cool, refreshing climate. When the children grew older Helen would take them to Kodai early in April and remain with them until July and I would take three or four weeks holiday during this period. These Kodai holidays were times of unforgettable joy filled with good fellowship, music and drama, long treks over the hills, camping in the forest huts, and worship in the lovely church of St Peter perched on the edge of the ghat and looking down to the plains scorching in the summer heat 6000 feet below. It was always hard to return to the plains again after those blissful days, but there was joy in returning to the friendship of Indian colleagues who were, in those days, practically excluded from the possibility of a hill holiday, but who were always so warm in their welcome and their friendship.

Helen always saw her first work as being to make and keep a loving and welcoming home and to care for her family. I have been more thankful for this than I can say. And of course this meant that Indian ladies were welcomed and that she gave a good deal of time to the Women's Fellowship. Towards the end of our time we had a good deal of anxiety over Janet who was very seriously ill and nearly died. In fact at the end we were all in poor health with mild attacks of malaria and amoebic dysentery. It was for this reason that we were afforded a fairly high priority in the long lists of people waiting to return to England when the war ended and passages became available. At the beginning of May 1946 we left Kanchipuram and moved to Madras to await word of a passage. In the middle of the month we got our call, took the mail train to Bombay and sailed for 'home'.

9
Unity: The Last Struggle

We were lucky to get a passage, but the voyage was not easy. The *Canton* was carrying four times its proper quota of passengers and Janet was ill for much of the time. We landed at Southampton on Whit Monday, 10 June, a perishingly cold day, and travelled straight to Newcastle. Our old home had been requisitioned early in the war. Most of it was now a school, but my sister had kept two bedrooms and we spent our first three days there. Alison and Janet were ill and utterly miserable. As soon as possible we moved to Rothbury, and then – for all of us – things began to look up.

It was a strange homecoming. My father had gone, and the cataclysm of war had changed everything. For us it was an entering into a new world. But Rothbury, the garden and the Cheviots were still the same, and their beauty was full of healing. For the next three months that was our home and we were able to introduce the children to all its joys.

For me there were only two substantial interruptions. One was a journey to London to spend two days with Joe Oldham and Archie Craig. The purpose was to persuade me to accept appointment as Secretary of the British Council of Churches in succession to Archie and in partnership with Alec Vidler. It was very good to have two days with these great and beloved men, but it did not take long to decide that this was not God's call for me. India held me fast. The other was a week in Iona for a conference led by Charles Raven, Hendrik Kraemer and, of course, George Macleod. I had long talks with Kraemer and was captivated by his strong yet open and flexible spirit. He had come through imprisonment and all the agony of Nazi occupation. Yet he was full of joy and the victory of Christ. Raven, on the other hand, from the serenity of a Cambridge college, seemed to be oppressed and overwhelmed by the darkness of the world, and the cross of which he spoke much seemed to have no resurrection beyond it. He appeared to regard Kraemer's theology as part of the world of darkness and I found myself clashing with him at many points. I am afraid that I did not bring any light into the scene for him.

With George, on the other hand, I had a lot of argument but no sense of estrangement. He was at that time full of 'the incarnational principle' which I thought needed correcting both from the side of creation and from the side of atonement. At the end of one of these tough but thoroughly cheerful arguments George suddenly said: 'Let's go round all the Divinity Halls together next winter and say to all the students, "It doesn't matter whether you go abroad or stay in Scotland; are you a missionary?"' 'Agreed,' said I, 'provided you don't mention the incarnational principle.' The result was that we did in fact travel round Scotland together to visit the four universities. At Aberdeen and St Andrews we were courteously received. At Glasgow we were informed that the students would be willing to meet one of us but not both, and on being further informed that I was the one they were willing to meet we both did a smart about-turn and left them. At New College, Edinburgh, the picture was solid; no one was willing to meet either of us!

From September until the following June our home was in a Church of Scotland furlough house in Morningside Park, Edinburgh. It was great fun to have a home of our own with the much more intimate kind of existence than was possible in India. We had a great many friends in and around Edinburgh, and rejoiced to be members of Morningside church where J. S. Stewart gave us every Sunday rich nourishment from the word of God. Margaret and Alison started school, and Janet began to enjoy really good health for the first time so that they all played happily together. After the perpetual heat of South India there was something exhilarating about the cold crisp air of Edinburgh, especially as the Braid and Pentland hills were close enough to enable us to have many excursions and picnics.

I was again working as Candidates Secretary for the Foreign Missions Committee, and spent many weekends visiting churches all over Scotland for the usual missionary deputation. I was also involved with visits to universities, with broadcasting, and in meetings – often joint – of episcopalian and presbyterian ministers to expound and discuss the 'South India Scheme'. There was also a good deal of correspondence – an attempt to organize the reunion of German missionary families tragically divided between internment camps in India and Japan, and a campaign launched by a letter I wrote to the *Scotsman* to get people in Scotland to share some of their food rations with starving pastors' families in Germany. The results of the appeal included both abuse and generous response, and I had grateful letters from the families of unknown pastors in Germany.

But as the months went on I became more and more deeply involved in defending the 'South India Scheme' against its critics in the Church of England. I had of course been aware of the existence of such criticism but I was not in touch with Anglican opinion and was unaware of its strength. During the visit to London in July, I went to a bookshop which stocked 'Catholic' publications and came away with an armful of books and pamphlets. I was staggered by the violence of their tone and by the misinterpretations of what was happening in South India. Most of them were published by a body called The Council for Defence of Church Principles, in which a leading role was being played by my old friend and colleague on the SCM staff, Michael Bruce. From August 1946 until my departure twelve months later I was involved in almost continuous correspondence and discussion with him. He combined many passionate affirmations of his total dedication to the cause of unity and his love and regard for all of us involved in the scheme, with repeated warnings that if the scheme were accepted by the Church of England disruption and prolonged litigation would follow. Never have dire threats been voiced in accents of such profound and affectionate regret! It was not easy to find the right way to respond.

Urged by Michael Bruce I arranged two residential meetings at the home of the Cowley Fathers in Oxford. At the insistence of Michael the representatives from South India were all non-Anglicans: Cyril Firth, Henry Lefevre, Marcus Ward and myself. The Anglicans were Gregory Dix of Nashdom, Fathers O'Brien and Fitch of the Cowley Fathers and Fathers Bruce, Bently and Blood of the CDCP. I had very great hesitation about undertaking these talks from which Anglicans who would have defended the scheme were excluded. However, I was assured that no harm would be done and some good might result from purely informal theological discussion designed simply for the clearing of misconceptions.

The first meeting was held in October. The discussions were

dominated by Dix whom I found charming, brilliant and totally unconvincing. We clashed vigorously at every session and afterwards he wrote me a charming letter and invited me to arrange the second meeting at Nashdom. In the end it also took place in Oxford and I was prevented at the last minute from attending, by illness in the family. These meetings were, I think, worth while, but the CDCP was not led to modify any of its views. From April 1947 onwards I was freed from work as Candidates Secretary and devoted the next three months mainly to writing a theological defence of the scheme which was published as *The Reunion of the Church*.

Meanwhile events were moving fast in India. In September 1946 the five Anglican bishops in South India issued on their own authority a statement of the way in which they understood the practical meaning of the 'Pledge'. In this they said:

> We agree that all who have the status of Presbyters in the United Church are capable of performing all the functions assigned to Presbyters in the United Church by the Constitution of that Church in every congregation of the United Church.
>
> We agree that no Presbyter of the United Church will exercise his ministry in a congregation where members conscientiously object to his ministrations.
>
> In all cases where no such conscientious objection arises within the congregation concerned, we shall act in accordance with the resolution of the Continuation Committee (1945), viz: It is understood that during the period of unification congregations will ordinarily continue to be served by the ministries to which they are accustomed, except where pastoral needs obviously demand other arrangements. The duly constituted authority within the United Church shall be the sole judge of the urgency of such pastoral needs.

This simple statement, made on the initiative of the Bishop of Madras, Michael Hollis, completely transformed the situation. It was clear and unambiguous and it evoked an instant response. A few days later the General Assembly of the South India United Church which had seemed for so long incapable of decision resolved by a majority of 90 per cent to enter the union, provided that the official interpretation of the Pledge was accepted by the Church of India, Burma and Ceylon. On 22 January the General

Council of that Church formally accepted the Joint Committee's interpretation by a majority of thirty-three to seven in the House of Laity, thirty to twenty-two in the House of Clergy and only seven to six in the House of Bishops. It was a very narrow majority but it was the decisive act which ensured that the union would take place. Michael Hollis wrote to me: 'One only regrets that so many people are so much upset by the idea of our saying "Yes". Still, we have said it.' It was one of those moments when decisions have to be made. Michael Hollis was the one among the bishops with the clarity of mind to know that the time for decision had come. It was his courage that removed the last block on the road to unity.

It soon became clear that while the bishops of the CIBC who had voted with the minority were doing all that they could to help the united Church to come into being and develop along the right lines, some Catholic critics of the scheme in England were threatening disruptive action. In April the SPG appointed an advisory group to consider the relationship of the society to the South India scheme. A majority of the group recommended that the society should continue to support missionaries and Indian workers hitherto dependent upon the society so long as they 'remain severally free and willing within the bounds of their own responsibility to profess and practise nothing prejudicial to Anglican formularies and standards'. A minority report, for which Michael Bruce was largely responsible, proposed that all such support should cease and that the possibility should be explored of 'the continuation of SPG's work in South India in friendly association and fellowship with the new body'. At a full meeting of the Standing Committee on 8 March, the minority proposal prevailed. All the missionaries and Indian workers in South India who had believed that they were loyally following the decisions of their Church were faced with the abrupt termination of their service on payment of an honorarium of one year's salary.

Michael Bruce followed this up with a seven-page letter to me pleading that the Joint Committee should invite the SPG to send out a bishop-commissary to initiate the new work in South India 'outside the union but in fellowship with it'. He was unable to believe that Anglicans in South India loyally supported the scheme and told me that if the majority report had prevailed, 'you

would have had in the Union people who were there with
hesitant and divided loyalties, looking over their shoulders all the
time and owing their effective allegiance to the SPG commissary
rather than to the bishop'. This was, of course, nonsense. As
regards the future support of the SPG missionaries and other
workers whose salaries were stopped, he advocated a separate
fund outside the SPG. A fund sponsored by the SPG itself would
be morally indefensible and would split the society. Michael was
confident of his ability to deliver the support of Catholics in the
Church of England. 'I know Gregory Dix would help and I think
we could swing Catholic opinion to an effective support of the
policy I am hoping for. Between us we know and have a great deal
of influence with all the people who matter. But it all depends on
your side being able to say "Welcome". I hope you can.'

I tried in my reply to make him see how disruptive his proposal
would be. It could only provide a cave of Adullam for anybody in
the SPG area who wanted to separate himself from the Church.
Already the tragic consequences of the society's action were
beginning to be felt in India. Those who had always looked to the
SPG as their parent in the faith, and who had done nothing
except follow the lawful decisions of the Church, found
themselves disowned and dismissed. The result was to be strife
and bitterness that lasted more than a quarter of a century and
which (in words said to me many years later by a high official of
Government) poisoned the whole life of the district. It was only
healed when the Christians of the Nandyal area were reunited as
one diocese within the CSI in the year 1975.

In June the Secretary of the SPG proposed that members of the
Joint Committee available in Britain should meet with him and
others, including Michael Bruce, to discuss this proposal. In
declining the invitation I wrote:

I must frankly say that the resolutions which you have sent do
not seem to me to provide a basis for any discussion in which I
could with a good conscience engage. I do feel deep sympathy
for the difficulties in which some members of the SPG are
placed. But I think you will understand that I could not feel it
right to take part in discussions, however informal and non-
committal, which were designed to discover ways by which
Anglicans in South India could be assisted, under threat of the

loss of their livelihood, to disobey and separate themselves from their provincial and diocesan authorities. If there were a group of Anglicans in South India who felt compelled upon conscientious grounds to take such action, I should respect their right to do so, and should desire to do all possible to deal with the resultant situation in a conciliatory spirit. But that is not the present situation as I understand it. As things now are I cannot feel it right to do otherwise than stand by the decision which has been made by proper ecclesiastical authority, and refrain even from discussing plans for the accomplishment of a disruption (in however friendly a spirit) of the work of the Anglican Communion in South India.

Within the next few days the position was changed by the intervention of the Archbishop of Canterbury who proposed and persuaded the Standing Committee of the SPG to agree to the opening of a special fund by the SPG itself. This would ensure that missionaries and Indian workers loyal to the Church would not be immediately sacked. Under these changed circumstances three of us who were to be bishops in the United Church – Michael Hollis, Arnold Legg and I – met with representatives of the SPG on 10 July. It was agreed that it would be appropriate for the CSI itself to invite the SPG to send a commission to South India to visit and confer with the Church on the clear understanding that they would not treat the entire CSI as excommunicate but would be willing to receive communion from episcopally ordained clergy of the Church.

The agreed Constitution for the new Church provided that bishops should be elected, both the Diocesan Council and the Synod of the whole Church having a voice in the matter. But there were as yet no councils or synod and it had been agreed that the first bishops should be chosen by a small body representative of the three Churches from lists of names presented by all of them. In February I learned that my name was proposed for inclusion in the list prepared by the SIUC. I knew that it was a long list and I agreed to allow my name to be included without much fear that I would be chosen. On 11 April I received a cable: 'You are appointed Bishop Church of South India Madura. We pray God's blessing.' The prayer was comforting but the news was shattering. Madura was widely known as a place where in-fighting within the Church and between Indians and missionaries was at its worst. I found it hard to sleep that night and the following weeks, while they brought many loving assurances of prayer, brought also many warnings of difficulties ahead.

The new diocese of Madura and Ramnad was to be formed by uniting about 50,000 Christians of the SIUC Madura Church Council – spiritual children of the American Board of Commissioners for Foreign Missions – with about 15,000 Anglicans, formerly part of Tinnevelley diocese, and including a solid SPG area at the eastern end of the diocese and a similar CMS area on its southern side. The Tinnevelley diocese was a very strong, stable and closely knit body. There was naturally considerable anxiety among the congregations in these areas at the prospect of being detached from their mother Church and plunged into the turbulence of Madura church politics. The Anglican congregations in Madura city were especially alarmed. On the SIUC side the most powerful leader was the Revd Paulraj Thomas who had been President of the General Assembly and was put forward as the sole nominee of the Madura Church Council for the position of bishop. The news of my appointment created an immediate crisis and there was a move to withdraw the Madura Church Council from the union. Much agitated correspondence ensued. But the wisdom and loyalty of Paulraj Thomas himself, the firm pressure of the American Board, and the wise counsel of Bishop G. T. Selwyn of Tinnevelley who visited all the churches in the area to reassure them, combined to calm the situation and I was assured that I would be cordially received. I was especially cheered and touched by the letters of welcome from the three SPG missionaries who were to receive me as their bishop.

I rapidly discovered that by the American missionaries my appointment was being greeted as the appearance of a *deus ex machina*. Some of them were in near despair about the state of things in the Church and in the big institutions and had cast me for the role of a super-administrator who would iron out all the problems. I had to write beseeching them not to expect the bishop to be that kind of person. They were anxious that all authority should immediately be vested in the Diocesan Council with me as its head. In my reply to the Mission Council I write:

As regards the question of constitution-making, I confess that I am in favour of proceeding pretty circumspectly. I wholeheartedly agree with the policy of Church-centred control which the Sangam and Mission advocate. I agree that the ultimate control should rest with the Diocesan Council. But I am very anxious to emphasize at the outset that I do not regard the Bishop as therefore mainly an administrator. You will remember that the Scheme is very clear about the functions of a bishop; he is to be a pastor, an evangelist, a teacher of the faith, and a leader in worship. I am holding on to that definition with both hands! He is not to be, I am convinced, a super-Circle Chairman! Nor should the Council be primarily concerned with the administration of institutional and similar work. I feel that we should aim at a series of Boards or Committees responsible to the Council for their general direction only, in order that that work may always serve the fundamental evangelistic purpose of the Church, but having a very large degree of autonomy as regards the routine of their work. I envisage the chairmen or secretaries of these boards as being the administrators. The Diocesan Council would thus be kept free to devote its main strength to its strictly ecclesiastical functions, while exercising supervision over the general policy of the manifold work carried on in its name. The Bishop, as chairman of the Council, would need to know the work – of course – but his relation to the workers *must* be that he is pastor to them as members of the Church, but not administrative 'boss' to them as its employees. That distinction I conceive to be absolutely vital, and I trust that it will govern both the way the Bishop behaves and the way the Church treats him! I trust also that the respecting of it will secure that the Diocesan Council is really kept free to give itself to attend to the main business of the Church's life – worship, evangelism, and pastoral care and discipline.

It would be a long struggle to keep these priorities clear in the years ahead.

Meanwhile our family life was marked both by the joy of seeing the girls growing up in every way and by the trials of illness. The winter of 1946–7 was intensely cold. There were frequent failures of electric power. Coal, like everything else, was strictly rationed and we had no stocks saved from the summer. At some times our only source of warmth was the gas-oven in the kitchen. The three girls all had measles and Helen was unwell. At the end of March we fled to Rothbury where at least we could be warm, though the girls took a long time to recover. Again in the summer all the children went down with whooping-cough and took a long time to get over it. Helen was expecting our fourth child in October and so we decided that I should go back to India alone in time for the inauguration of the union and that Helen and the children would go to her sister in Liverpool and travel out early in 1948. We had a few weeks of glorious holiday at Rothbury and then I sailed for Bombay on 21 August. Two of my closest SCM friends came to see me off – Jim Cottle and Davis McCaughey. I wrote in my diary: 'Jim wished me courage. I suggested that the wisdom to distinguish courage from foolhardiness might be better. But he stuck to it that sheer courage was the biggest need. I believe he is right; it is my biggest need.'

The *Empire Windrush* was inappropriately named. It took four weeks to reach Bombay, having apparently lost its steering gear outside Port Said when we lay becalmed for five sweltering days. The empire was, anyway, on the way out. India had become independent a week before. As we passed the Rock of Gibraltar I wondered how long it would be before the whole thing would be part of history. But the voyage gave time for some really concentrated reading on Hinduism, both in English and Tamil, and for completing a paper I had been asked to write for the forthcoming Amsterdam Assembly on 'The Duty and Authority of the Church to preach the Gospel'.

After very brief stops at Bombay and at Kanchipuram I finally arrived (in a rickshaw) at the Women's Christian College in Madras where all the fourteen bishops-designate were already gathered in silent retreat. For the next three days we were led by that great saint of God, Bishop Packenham Walsh, in a deeply searching and strengthening time of preparation. There then followed a two-day conference in which a great number of detailed questions were raised and settled. The final stage of decision-making had come so swiftly that dozens of questions remained unanswered. But we were of one heart and mind, and things that in other circumstances could have been the subject of long debate were settled in a few minutes. One small detail remains in my memory. As the youngest present I was appointed to record the minutes. At one point someone asked: 'What do we do about archdeacons, deans, canons and things like that?' There was a silence. I dutifully inscribed the appropriate heading in my notes and awaited the debate. After a moment someone said: 'Abolish them.' The chairman asked for other views. There were none. I wrote the one word 'Abolished', and we went on to the next business.

There was, however, one very sad matter before us. As the news of the SPG's decision became known among the churches in the Nandyal area it caused profound disturbance. Indian clergy who had given their assent to the union now discovered that they were repudiated by their parent society to which they felt a deep loyalty. As the date for the inauguration approached some of them withdrew the assent they had given. The issue was complicated by local rivalries and by the disappointment of those whose candidate for the bishop's office had not been chosen. We were faced with apparent disintegration of the Church in the Nandyal area. None of us had any desire to force the consciences of those who now wished at the last minute to withdraw, and we therefore agreed at once to cable the Metropolitan in Calcutta asking him to take pastoral charge of all those Anglican clergy and congregations who wished to withdraw.

From the college where we had stayed for the five days of retreat and conference we all went on the Saturday morning, 27 September, to St George's Cathedral for the services of inauguration and consecration. There was a heavy shower on the Friday night and Saturday was cool and bright. I quote from the letter I wrote at the time:

> The cathedral had seating for about 1500 and there were about 2000 in the pandal outside. Exactly as the clock was striking eight, the procession came into the cathedral and we began to sing 'O God, our help'. It was wonderful to see that great sea of faces, people from all over India, and representatives from other countries and other Churches. And the singing was just tremendous.
>
> Then we had prayer and the reading of John 17. Then a prayer of confession; I truly think we came to the central act

purged of any pride in our own achievements; it was a day when everyone spontaneously felt that it was to God we must give the glory, and there was no flattering of men. Then in turn a representative of each of the three uniting Churches went to the chancel steps, read out the resolution of the governing body of the Church accepting the union, turned and walked up to the altar, and laid on it a signed copy of the Scheme, and a book containing the signatures of all the ministers of his Church who had assented to the basis of union and accepted the constitution. Then there was a moment of silent prayer as the decision of each Church and its ministers was laid on the altar. Then we all joined in prayer for God's blessing on the union, and then the Bishop presiding (Jacob, of Travancore) went to the chancel steps and proclaimed that these three Churches were now become the Church of South India. Then came the greatest moment in the service, when the whole of that great congregation rose and burst into the Te Deum. It was as though all the agonizing fears and delays of these twenty-eight years had dammed up a flood that was now bursting through. I have never heard such singing, and I think there were very many like myself who found it hard to keep back tears of joy as one remembered all that had gone before and all that might lie ahead.

Then when we sat down, the six existing bishops went to the altar steps and stood there, while Weirenga as president of the SIUC Assembly, and Ramaseshan as chairman of the Methodist Synod, asked them to promise their assent and obedience to the basis of union and constitution. Then they knelt and were commissioned to have authority as bishops in the new Church and to exercise that authority in the congregations which had hitherto been parts of the South India United Church and the Methodist Church. Then prayer and another hymn and the Bishop presiding went back to the altar and commissioned all the presbyters of the three Churches similarly. Each group rose in their places and answered the questions and then knelt to be commissioned. Then prayer and praise, the offering, and the Lord's Prayer, and that was the end of the first part of the service.

I wish I could convey a sense of the unity of the whole congregation in the whole of the service. It was, after all, something quite new for which there were no precedents, and yet there was never a moment of stumbling or awkwardness. I could not help often thinking of those two days at Dornakal in 1944 when Azariah and Hooper and I drafted the order of service for the inauguration. At that time it sometimes seemed an academic exercise and one wondered if it would ever by more than something printed in the minutes of the Joint Committee. Yet here God had taken something lifeless in itself, and breathed life into it and it became the vehicle of a working of His Spirit that none of us will ever forget. It was unthinkably faithless now not to believe that just in the same way the scheme of union, which had been a paper document for so many years, will become the vehicle of the living Spirit.

After a short interval we returned to the cathedral for the consecration of nine new bishops. In my letter I wrote:

What struck me over and over again in it was that the two notes which are so often opposed – Catholic and Evangelical – were constantly and completely blended throughout. It is something we have so often talked about as an ideal, and yet here it was really happening, and they fitted as if they had always been made for each other – as indeed they had. I am sure everyone present, from all the Churches, felt that here the things believed from the bottom of his heart were being worthily expressed. I have talked to very many and I am sure that it is so. It made one so utterly sure that what we are doing is not patching things together, but being led by the Holy Spirit back to the fullness and simplicity of Gospel truth. As I knelt waiting my turn to be consecrated I had a sudden sickening sense of my utter incapacity, and then looked up and saw above the altar the carving of Christ rising from the tomb, and took it as the answer to my fears. Then it was my turn to kneel in front of the Bishop presiding, and he and the other eight, representing the three uniting Churches, laid hands upon me, and gave me the Bible and the staff.

The climax of the service was, of course, the communion. That was the other moment when I found it hard, and I'm sure others did, to keep back tears. I believe about 2500 people took the communion. A great company of ministers of all the three uniting Churches served them. As one saw them moving about, men who yesterday could not have shared communion together, but now all fellow-members of one Church; and as one saw the great multitude of people, so absolutely rapt and intent, and their faces so full of joy; and the servers moving about to see that all were served; the thought uppermost in my mind was: Never again will I say that a thing which I believe is God's will is impossible. Here we were at last, not a scheme of union, or a committee, but one Church really in being, and accepting one another as fellow-members. It sounds simple to say it in this way, but I am sure you can see what I mean. Then there were the post-communion prayers and the blessing, and then a great procession down the long nave of the cathedral - all the fifteen bishops and all the presbyters and laymen who had taken part in the service, to the tune of 'Thy hand, O God, has guided'.

In the evening there was a public meeting at which those who had come to represent our parent Churches brought their greetings. It was sad that the Church of England could not be officially represented but I think that even this was forgotten in the joy of that day. It was summed up in a phrase by the Irish missionary, George Wilson: 'The tide of the Spirit just rose and blotted out the old boundaries.'

From Madras I went back to Kanchipuram to bid farewell to the congregations there and to pack up our belongings for despatch to Madurai. And then the night train south to begin a new and uncharted journey.

10
Madurai: New Beginnings

The city of Madurai is usually regarded as the cultural centre of the Tamil country. Its ancient Pandyan dynasty was known to the Greeks and it appears on Ptolemy's map of the world. Numerous discoveries of Roman coins have testified to its commercial links with the Roman Empire and the Pandyan kingdom sent an embassy to the court of Augustus. More important and more ancient is the tradition of the Tamil Sangams – the company of poets and saints who created the classical Tamil literature. Its great temple, one of the most renowned in the whole of India, is dedicated to the goddess Meenakshi who, like Kamatchi of Kanchipuram, was undoubtedly a pre-Aryan mother goddess, but whose co-option into the Aryan religious world is re-enacted in the annual festival for which thousands of pilgrims come to celebrate her marriage with Siva. It has maintained an amazing continuity through more than two millenniums and the Pandyan dynasty which ruled there in the first century before Christ was still ruling when the British raj took over.

In 1947 Madurai was a city of about a quarter of a million people, its economic life dominated by the Scottish-owned cotton-spinning Madura Mills with a large labour force strongly influenced by Marxism. It was a place where politics was – as it still is – vigorous to the point of violence.

The American Board of Commissioners for Foreign Missions had been at work there for over a century. They had developed an impressive array of large institutions: schools, training colleges, a liberal arts college, two large hospitals and industrial schools for boys and girls. They had also been very successful in evangelizing the surrounding country. Their village congregations were not, like those I was used to, small groups of a score or so of Harijan families; they were often ten times that size, drawn from many different castes, and including relatively wealthy farmers owning land of their own. They had trained up Indian men and women to the highest levels. They had been anxious to transfer responsibility for the work of the Mission to Indian hands. By the time I arrived the full responsibility for all the village work, including elementary schools and boarding schools, had been taken over by the Madura Church Council of the SIUC. To handle the large institutions they had created an entity called the Sangam, which included a majority of Indian members.

Somehow these good intentions had run into deep difficulty. There was not mutual confidence between Indian and American colleagues. Politics in the Indian Church were passionate and complex. No one caste group could dominate the rest and the power struggle was carried on by means of constantly shifting coalitions. Of course the official view was that caste did not exist, and the political intrigue was made much more poisonous by being conducted under false pretences. The centre of the problem was the Sangam. This body commanded enormous patronage since it appointed the heads of all the big institutions. But it was responsible neither to the Indian Church nor to the American Board. Its members were free to pursue their sectional interests and they did so with vigour and astuteness. The college had its own governing council in which the same forces operated, but here the Board had retained residual powers in that the endowment funds were still held in the USA.

In this situation the missionaries as a body were in near despair. The secretary responsible for Indian affairs at the head office in Boston, Raymond Dudley, had only recently retired from the field. He knew the situation intimately and was also committed to the cause of union, having been my predecessor as the Convener of the SIUC Committee on Union. He confided to me the fact that he was being inundated with letters from the missionaries, and that he had never experienced such utter despair as these letters conveyed.

Into this tense and complex situation the announcement of my appointment had come as a bombshell. The dominant elements in the Church Council and the Sangam had been confident that their nominee would be the bishop and their first reaction was (as already recounted) an attempt to withdraw from the union. The missionaries saw my appointment as an answer to prayer. At the annual meeting on 21 August the move to withdraw had been countered and now, five weeks later, I was standing on Madurai station platform, obviously the object of very varied hopes and fears. The missionaries hoped that I would somehow solve their problems. The Indians were generously willing to welcome me and hoped that I would be an ally in their (mutually conflicting) causes. But no one knew what sort of an animal a bishop would be.

Meanwhile there were, of course, the Anglicans. There had been very little coming and going between the two communities. The large areas of village work, SPG and CMS, were situated more than fifty miles from Madurai to the east and the south respectively. They were not immediately threatened by Madurai church politics. But there was also an Anglican presence in the city itself. This had an interesting history. In the early days of British rule there had naturally been Anglican contacts. The great Schwartz had visited the city, the SPG had done some evangelistic work, and there were English services for the Government and army officers. But in the mid-nineteenth century the SPG and the American Board had made a 'comity' agreement by which the former withdrew and left the area to the latter. For some years, therefore, there were no Tamil Anglican services. However, within a very few years the local Tamil Anglicans, led by an enterprising lawyer from Tanjore, took the law into their own hands and started their own services. The Bishop of Madras tried to stand by the comity agreement but (as many bishops from Reginald Heber onwards have learned to their cost) Tamils are not easily coerced. The Madura congregation forced the bishop to recognize them and to give them a priest. They were Anglicans with a totally congregationalist, not to say independent, ethos.

When in the 1920s the separate SPG and CMS work in the area was brought into a single closely integrated diocese of Tinnevelley, Madura and Ramnad, the Madurai Anglicans demanded and obtained a special status which exempted them from many of the rules governing the rest of the diocese. Their bishop (and they could hardly refuse all episcopal contact and still be good Anglicans!) was now uncomfortably near – only 100 miles instead of 300 – but they could preserve their 'special status'. Now, however, in 1947 they were confronted by a bishop on their doorstep and the prospect of a diocese in which they were no longer on the periphery but at the centre. It was a situation which would require extreme circumspection. However, as they included among their members many of the leading lawyers in the city, of whom one was the Public Prosecutor, they were reasonably confident that they could ensure that the new bishop would be relatively harmless.

There were clearly some very complex administrative problems to solve. Three bodies – the Sangam, the Madura Church Council and the Tinnevelley Diocesan Council – were legally responsible to Government and to the public for the management of many hundreds of schools and other institutions. If the whole work were to be integrated into the new diocese and made fully responsible to it, these three would have to hand over their responsibilities. But this could not be done at once. The early life of the new diocese must not be crushed by the problem of these institutions. And it was by no means certain that the Sangam would be willing to accept euthanasia.

It was clear that the first contact of the bishop with the churches must be and must be seen to be that of an evangelist and pastor, not that of an administrator. I therefore immediately planned a series of tours to reach as many as possible of the 700 or so congregations in the area. But first the diocese had to be formally constituted, the bishop properly installed, and all the pastors commissioned for service in the united Church. The planning of the service had to be done in a few days but all went well and on 13 October we had a very large gathering culminating in a celebration of Holy Communion conducted according to the Reformed tradition in which 1100 people took communion. Everything was done in Tamil. There were, it must be admitted, a few last-minute crises when denominational *amour propre* seemed to be threatened. And there was the Anglican priest who rushed up to me and said, 'Are we to wear scarves or stoles?' to which I had to reply honestly that, up to that moment, I had not been aware that there was any difference. However, these shocks were overcome. We shared together the Body and Blood of our Saviour and therefore we were one body whatever might be the dangers ahead. And the same evening I was formally welcomed at a public meeting which is chiefly memorable for me on account of the fact that the (Anglican) Church band played incidental music which included the splendid lines (the words being, of course, unknown):

It won't be a stylish marriage,
We can't afford a carriage,
But you'll look sweet
Upon the seat
Of a bicycle made for two.

As I sat upon my improvised episcopal throne, trying to maintain a suitable appearance of dignity, I had to avert my eyes from the little group of English missionaries in the back row who alone knew the words. Anyway, the bicycle had started on its journey.

No car was provided for the bishop so my journeys were by bus, bicycle, bullock cart or on foot. In the first six weeks I visited the main centres in each of the seven 'local councils', and thereafter I set about visiting each of the forty or so pastorates, trying to spend about three days in each. It was like the old days in the villages around Kanchipuram except that it was on a much bigger scale. There were very large village congregations, often including fairly prosperous farmers. In many places there were Government officers or merchants who were Christians and were eager to give hospitality. My proposal had been to visit three or four congregations each day but in most cases the pastor was unable to refuse demands from other villages and consequently arranged impossible programmes which kept me fully stretched from five or six in the morning till after midnight. A typical visit began with an enormous and noisy reception complete with fireworks, bands, dancing and, of course, garlands and fruit; then a slow procession through the village, a service in church and a public meeting outside to which the whole village came. In each place I preached first to help the congregation to understand the meaning of the union and then to commend to the village as a whole the One who has promised by the power of his atonement to draw all peoples to himself. Ten preachings in one day with journeys between added up to a punishing programme but it was nothing when compared with the thrill of knowing that this promise was being fulfilled. Those were wonderful days even if exhausting. As I reflect upon them I am sure that they illustrated and, in a measure, justified the claim that the office of bishop could truly be seen as a focus of unity for divided Christians.

It must also be admitted that there were some for whom the arrival of a bishop was primarily an opportunity for the display of worldly pomp in the face of the heathen! In Palni, a staunchly Congregational centre, I was paraded through the town in the blazing sun for two hours behind the temple elephant borrowed for the occasion, and there were other similar absurdities. In some places I had to fight very hard to resist this idea of episcopacy. In one place I was adroitly checkmated. It was on my first visit to Ramnad, the headquarters of the SPG. I went with some trepidation, wondering whether there might be black flags. It was far otherwise. I was confronted with the following: an elephant, a brass band, an open landau drawn by two white horses (borrowed from the Raja's palace), a choir and a procession of the whole congregation. The landau was almost covered with roses. I was invited to step in. I tried to imagine what my Presbyterian friends would think. 'But I can't,' I said. 'Why not? Is there any problem?' was the courteous and worried reply. 'Well,' I said, 'when our Lord went in a procession he rode on a donkey.' There was an immediate relaxation of tension. 'Of course! He did that so that you could do this. Please get in.' I did.

These crowded visits did not, of course, give me the opportunity to enter in real depth into the life of the congregations. But I was learning new things all the time. I had to learn from the beginning the depth of the chasm which separated the SPG from the CMS. In my previous ignorance I had simply thought of them as 'Anglicans', but only the most sophisticated among them would have so identified themselves. In fact most Indian Christians at that time identified themselves by the name of the foreign mission to which they were attached rather than by the name of an Indian Church. It was only after 1947 that the ordinary church members began to identify themselves as 'CSI'. I can entirely believe the story of the Tinnevelley Christian who declined to attend worship in Westminster Abbey until he knew whether it was CMS or SPG. In the villages they almost looked like different religions: in the SPG area the most miserable mud-walled chapel had an altar decorated with ornaments, whereas in the CMS area a cross on the holy table meant a relapse into idolatry. But each had its own strength which I learned to respect.

In the much larger area covered by the American Board the

ethos was very different. Their missionaries came from the most liberal wing of American Protestantism. The village people were accustomed to seeing each new generation of missionaries arriving with a fresh set of enthusiasms. They were prepared to try anything (even episcopacy) but lacked the firm (perhaps too rigid) foundation of the Anglicans. Worship was experimental rather than devout and sometimes it was slovenly. In my visits I would find myself presented with an 'Order of Service' which began with 'Chairman's opening remarks' and ended with 'Vote of thanks' but had no place for a Bible reading. The Church sometimes seemed to be more of a community movement than a place of worship.

Moreover, the village work of the American Board had been devastated by the financial consequences of the Wall Street crash of 1929. In the 1930s the Board's income had collapsed and scores of village schools had been abruptly closed. The damage done by this had never been repaired. Hardworked pastors could not possibly cope with a score of large congregations most of which had no resident teacher-catechist. The level of pastoral care was inevitably low. There was clearly a very big job for a bishop to do.

But there was also much to enjoy. In the years at Kanchipuram I had learned to love the richly varied beauties of a small patch of the South Indian plain. Now I had the freedom of a much bigger and even more varied world of natural beauty. Some of our congregations were among the toddy-tappers of the coast and after a strenuous day among them I would take my bedding roll down to the shore and go to sleep on the beach with the sound of the surf in my ears and the jagged outline of the palm trees etched against the spangled beauty of the night sky. A day or two later I would be in the Palni hills 7000 feet above sea-level, with the air full of the scent of the eucalyptus trees and the quiet of the forests broken only by the sound of jackals hunting. Between the mountains and the sea were 5000 square miles of country, broken by hills and dotted everywhere by villages each as distinct from the others as the islands of an archipelago, each having its own character, its own tragedies, its own triumphs. And in 700 of them were Christian communities deeply rooted in the life of that rural world. The challenge was to help each one of them to be a living sign and foretaste of the Kingdom. That is how I understood the job of a bishop. That was why I believed these long journeys to be of the first priority. They would help to make union a reality and help to establish the fact that a bishop is not first an administrator but first a minister of word, sacrament and pastoral care. And I was still convinced of the truth I had learned in the Cambridge SCM – that the health of the body depends upon the health of the smallest units.

But there were administrative tasks which could not be evaded. The scheme of union had provided a broad framework within which each diocese was free to determine its own constitution according to local traditions and circumstances. Before I arrived a temporary 'steering committee' had been set up by the two churches to handle the arrangements for inauguration, and from this we chose a small group to hammer out the details of a constitution. It was important to see that the three elements – episcopal, synodical and congregational – were in proper balance. The bishop must be neither an autocrat nor a puppet to be used by the local masters of the arts of politics. The administration of schools and other institutions must be so ordered that they are responsible to the Church as a whole but do not dominate the Church. The transition from the former managing bodies to the new diocese must be made without any disruption. And all this had to be done while bitter struggles for power were going on, struggles which centred on the control of the big institutions. I was the subject of slanderous allegations to Government by those who saw their ambitions thwarted by my presence. On 1 January I wrote in my diary: 'The New Year begins with responsibilities crowding in which I feel utterly incapable of bearing. Only if it is really true that God carries them and me can I go on. But it *is* true.'

Yet it was exciting work and I enjoyed it. We were creating something new, trying to embody in a coherent whole styles of church order which had been opposed to each other. The work was only possible because the two most powerful leaders gave their hearts and minds to the job. Paulraj Thomas had been chosen as the nominee of the Madura Church Council for bishop. It had been assumed that he would be appointed and he had been treated as bishop-designate. It would have been only human if he had been reluctant to play his full part. A few days after arriving in Madura I was received as guest in his home for a long weekend during which he gave me unstinted hospitality and we established a mutual confidence which was not to be lost. Canon John Asirvatham was priest-in-charge of the main Anglican church in Madurai. His churchmanship was Catholic and he had held high positions in Tinnevelley diocese. Coming into the CSI was not easy for him, but having made the decision he was completely loyal. These two men learned slowly to work together. There were times when mutual confidence seemed to be on the point of breaking. But it held and we were able to hammer out a constitution on the basis of which the first diocesan council could be held in the middle of January, an executive committee and other committees duly formed and the *ad hoc* 'steering committee' disbanded. On the following day the Sangam met for the last time and agreed to dissolve, handing over its responsibilities to a temporary body which would arrange for all its work to be devolved upon the appropriate diocesan boards on 31 March 1949. Meanwhile the continuation committee of the Madura Church Council had agreed to hand over legal responsibility for all the schools and boarding homes on 31 March 1948. Thereafter I went to the headquarters of Tinnevelley diocese in Palamcottah to arrange for the transfer of their schools and other institutions on the same dates. The complicated pieces of the puzzle were falling into shape.

Meanwhile similar things were happening in the other dioceses and by mid-March it was possible to hold a properly constituted meeting of the Synod composed of the elected representatives of all the fourteen dioceses. It was our great privilege in Madura to be hosts to this first meeting and it was a time of great joy and inspiration. While much time had to be given to the business of getting administrative processes into working order, the greater part of the whole period was given to the challenge to mission and to wider unity. An invitation was issued to all the other member Churches of the National Christian Council in South India to discuss the possibility of union. And a strong Board of Missions was set up to co-ordinate and encourage fresh missionary outreach throughout South India and to support the newly launched mission in Papua.

The whole of Sunday was given over to worship and to a missionary rally. We began, of course, with communion. As no moderator had yet been chosen, and as I was the local bishop, it was my privilege to preside. I used the liturgy of the Church of Scotland, and the ordering of the service was entirely according to the Reformed tradition. For at least half of the members it was the first time that they had ever participated in a Eucharist otherwise than in the Anglican order. Many of them told me that they had been surprised and deeply moved by an experience which was quite new and yet had touched their hearts. It was out of this experience that the demand arose to have a liturgy which could be used for meetings of the Synod. It was always basic to the scheme of union that existing orders of worship would not be disturbed. There had not been any suggestion that the united Church might attempt to develop its own liturgy. Even when the first Synod appointed a liturgical committee it was more to monitor liturgical developments in the dioceses than to produce fresh material for the whole Church. But it was now clear that, at least for our gatherings in Synod, we should have a liturgy common to all. The task given to the committee was, in the first instance, not to produce a liturgy for general use in congregations but simply to produce one for use at the next Synod. In the event, under the inspired leadership of its first convener, Leslie Brown, it was to do very much more. He has himself told something of that story in his own memoirs.[1] I was also a member and shared in the excitement of those early days. I remember the battle fought by Carl Keller of the Basel Mission to have the confession and absolution placed at the beginning of the service on the ground that we need cleansing to hear the word aright as well as rightly to receive the sacrament. I remember Leslie's excitement when he found the beautiful prayer 'Be present, be present, O Jesus, thou good High Priest, as thou wast in the midst of thy disciples', and rushed into my bedroom (where I was having a mild illness) to ask how we should end it, and my proposing 'and be made known to us in the breaking of the bread'. I remember the great debate which had to be held before we decided to introduce the giving of the peace – a custom which the Syrian Church had kept during the centuries when the Western Church lost it. We did not know in those exciting discussions that what we were doing would give a lead to changes in liturgy all over the world for several decades to come.

The first Synod gave me the convenorship of two committees which were to lead me into new duties in the ensuing year. One was the ministerial committee, responsible for all aspects of ministerial training and ordination. The other was the committee on 'lay deacons'. With the first of these hats on my head I was able to press forward the plans for a united theological seminary for the Tamil Church. Immediately following the Synod I called a meeting which led to the development of the theological college of the Tinnevelley diocese at Tirumaraiyur into a union college training for all the Tamil diocese. With Canon Sitther as its wise and able principal and with additional staff and resources drawn from the Methodist and Reformed traditions, it became a splendid place of training for the ministry of all the Tamil dioceses until the long-desired day came (fifteen years later) when, with Lutheran participation, it could become the new Tamilnadu Theological Seminary at Arasaradi in Madurai.

The other committee was appointed to study the whole question of the diaconate in view of the fact that we had inherited two different kinds of deacon: the Anglican deacon who was a clergyman on his way to the priesthood and the Reformed deacon who was regarded as a layman. The committee never found a solution to the problem, but its work was to lead out into fruitful work on the role of voluntary workers in the total ministry of the Church, especially in the villages.

On the wider political scene there was much to bring zest and excitement into life. India, newly independent, was full of plans for development. The style in which Mountbatten had carried through the final actions had wiped out the bitterness of earlier years and the British who remained in India basked in the sunshine of an unaccustomed popularity. Even the tragedy of partition brought one good gift: the challenge to Christians in the south to go to the north and help to cope with the terrible consequences of the murderous communal strife between Hindus and Moslems. The assassination of Gandhi by the hand of a Hindu zealot sent violent shock waves through the whole nation. It happened on a Friday and almost instantaneously people turned to Good Friday to find a framework in which to interpret it. On that Saturday I was accosted by a group of men who wanted me to tell them if it was really true that Jesus had risen from the dead on a Sunday after being killed on the Friday. And the oration broadcast on Sunday by the poet Sarojiru Naidu ended with the words: 'It is the third day; will you not rise again?'

Gandhi's memory did indeed remain a powerful force for a dozen years, but, sad to tell, did not endure to capture the next generation.

For five months I was on my own but had the immense joy of knowing that our son John had been safely born into the world at the very hour when I was being installed and the new diocese inaugurated. In mid-February I went to Bombay to meet Helen and the four children with May, her eldest sister. May had lost her husband ten years earlier. Two of her three fine boys had been killed in action within a few months of each other. Her third boy seemed well settled, so we had arranged for her to travel out with Helen and spend some months with us. But I had to give her at Bombay the terrible news that her only remaining son was dead. The courage which she brought to that moment, and the way in which her deep sorrow became the source from which she could in later years comfort others in their grief, have always been for us a shining proof of the power of the Gospel.

We had a month together in Madurai and then I took the family up to Kodai so that Margaret and Alison could rejoin the Kodai school and all of them could escape the scorching heat of April and May in Madurai. For most of May I had my office at Kodai and combined the work of the diocese with some glorious days in the hills, including a four-day trek around the forest huts, as well as giving the addresses for the annual Missionaries' Convention and conducting our first clergy conference for the diocese. In former days Kodai had always seemed to be part of a different world from the world of everyday work. Now it was part of my area of duty. Yet its magic was unspoiled and even a few days of its beauty were enough to make the world seem bright.

During our twelve years in Madurai there were to be many wonderful holidays in the Kodai hills. The school year was arranged so that the main vacation came in the cool weather from October to January. During this period we had the children with us in Madurai. There was also a short break in May so that they could be with us on holiday in Kodai. As the children grew they could enter more and more into the joy of those holidays – longer walks in the hills, camping in the forest huts, picnics by the mountain streams and outings by boat on the lake. I always knew that when I came to the end of the sixty-mile drive from the dry scorching heat of Madurai to the cool of the hills 7,000 feet above sea-level, there would be a rush of welcome from the children, shouts of joy and excitement, and a variety of pictures, poems or dramatic entertainments prepared to welcome me home. What joy is to be compared with that?

11

Lambeth, Geneva, Amsterdam: An Ecumenical Excursion

At the end of May I received, to my great surprise, an invitation to be a 'consultant' at the forthcoming Assembly in Amsterdam at which the World Council of Churches was to be formally constituted. The Church of South India had, at the first Synod, accepted the invitation to membership and had appointed Bishop C. K. Jacob as a delegate. As no funds seemed likely to be available to send more than one person I did not take the invitation very seriously. But Bishop Hollis suggested that both Jacob and I might also attend the Lambeth Conference so as to answer questions about the CSI. He said that he was able to find funds for my travel. The Archbishop of Canterbury signalled his cordial invitation and it was so arranged. It was also agreed that we should represent the CSI at the Assembly of the World Presbyterian Alliance in Geneva. And thus early in the morning of 9 July I found myself for the first time in a plane, looking down for a few brief moments on the little villages round Kanchipuram which I knew so well. It was an extraordinarily moving experience to see them from this different angle – the village well a round unseeing eye, the thatch roofs with their lines of palm tree and the village temple in the middle, so tiny, so fragile and yet so permanent compared to this noisy machine (a DC3) which was just plunging into the low clouds.

There were numerous misadventures before we were eventually deposited in Paris and left to find our way by train and ferry to London. I went to Eric and Kay Fenn for a very brief night and early next morning Jacob and I were duly ushered into the large hall at Lambeth Palace, where the committee on South India was meeting. It was a strange experience. The room was packed. Fifty-five of the bishops were present. The atmosphere was tense. The ark of God was in terrible peril. Those godly men were in what seemed to be an agony of anxiety. Jacob and I each spoke for a few minutes and then for three hours we had

111

questions fired at us. The underlying assumption of most of them was that the Church of South India was, if not already heretical, at least on the slippery slope that leads to the abyss. All the questions, as I remember, centred on matters of doctrine. What was the 'reasonable liberty of interpretation' which we claimed? Did it extend to the denial of the Virgin birth; of the resurrection? When I tried to say that we wanted bishops to be able to exercise a reasonable pastoral discretion in dealing with the intellectual scruples of ordinands I was asked if I could get a written confirmation from South India – perhaps by cable? – that this was what was meant!

One particular conversation remains in my memory. One of the English bishops put the following question to me: 'I see that you ask ordinands to accept the Nicene Creed but candidates for baptism only to accept the Apostles' Creed. Which are the items of the former, not included in the latter, to which you take exception?' At that moment a picture flashed into my mind. A few days earlier I had been in a village near Madurai where all the people belonged to a robber caste whose traditional occupation is stealing. The men of the village had decided to ask for baptism. The women had refused to follow them. A long struggle had ensued in which the women actually refused to prepare food for their husbands. But the men were firm and eventually the women had come round to their view. I had been invited to come and baptize the whole community. For an hour or more I sat cross-legged on the ground, questioning them about their faith. Those women were real amazons, tough, shrewd but – of course – illiterate. I tried to imagine the bishop in front of me sitting on the ground in that village and explaining to these women all the differences between the Nicene and Apostles' Creeds. I realized (and it should have been obvious) that this was not a discussion about the Church of South India at all. It was about English ecclesiastical and social and cultural differences. As I reflected later I realized that what was needed was something that would enable good people like that bishop to come with me into those villages and meet the people. The result was the writing of *A South India Diary*.

But of course we had many good friends in that room. George Bell of Chichester was in the chair and that was the beginning for me of a very precious friendship. Bill Lash of Bombay sat with us and gave us courage. The American bishops were very friendly. On the whole, we understood later, our cross-examination had helped to clear the air. During the ensuing days I was able to have good personal talks with the Archbishop of Canterbury and with most of the English bishops who were most deeply involved. I was also invited to join the special committee to deal with the tragic situation of Nandyal and shared with Stephen Neill the drafting of its report.

Until the end of the month I divided my time between Scotland, Rothbury and London. I was able to have long talks with the Archbishop and others who were eager to help the Church of South India, with Max Warren and the Church Missionary Society secretaries; with John McLeod Campbell of the Missionary Council and with the secretaries at Edinburgh House. The main thing was to ensure that there would be adequate support for the SPG workers whatever the outcome of the Lambeth discussions.

That outcome was a disappointment. The Conference was unable to come to a common mind. A majority took the view that the ordinations in the CSI should be acknowledged as true ordinations in the Church of God and that there could be a growing into full communion between the Anglican Churches and the CSI. A substantial minority was unwilling to make this acknowledgement. Moreover, the Conference made it clear that it was much more impressed by the Ceylon proposals which included the unification of the ministries by prayer and the imposition of episcopal hands (Lambeth Report, 283). Although the phrase 'supplemental ordination' was avoided, the rite proposed was clearly of that nature, including both the recognition of a previous ordination and an act which contained all the essentials of a fresh ordination.

These decisions were to have fateful consequences. The fact that relations between the CSI and the Church of England would be confused and ambiguous was a small matter. I do not think that any of the one million or so members of the CSI lost any sleep as the result of this. What mattered very much was that churches all over the world were served notice that the Anglican communion would not look with favour upon any plan of union which did not include the kind of 'unification of ministries' which the CSI had rejected. The only way of uniting Anglican with non-episcopal churches which had actually succeeded was rejected, and a way which had never been tried was commended as the only acceptable one. Alone among the pending schemes for unity, that of North India and Pakistan was able to struggle through to success twenty years later. The others – Nigeria, Ghana, Canada, Australia, New Zealand, East Africa – have been abandoned. It was one of those fateful turning-points in human affairs, for if the Lambeth Conference of 1948 had been able to give a cordial welcome to what had been done in South India, I am sure that the whole worldwide movement for unity among the Churches would have gone forward. The Anglican communion would have fulfilled its true ecumenical vocation to provide a centre around which reformed Christendom can be brought together in unity and in continuity with the historic ministry of the universal Church. That opportunity was lost, and is not likely to come again.

After a day or two at Rothbury I was off again for the Presbyterian Assembly in Geneva. Under the prevalent exchange controls it was quite impossible to get any Swiss money, so I decided to go without. At Geneva the rain was pouring down in torrents. I called a taxi and asked to be driven to the cathedral of Saint-Pierre, hoping to find a good Samaritan who would pay my taxi fare. The taxi stopped just outside the office of the Consistoire. I saw the plate 'Église Nationale de Genève', went in and ran up the stairs. Coming down was a truly magnificent figure, tall, white-haired, erect and soldierly. Breathlessly I explained my predicament. Without a moment's hesitation he enveloped me in a loving welcome, paid off the taxi driver in truly aristocratic style and carried me off to the place where the Assembly was meeting. It was Marc Boegner, President of the Reformed Church of France, member of the Académie française, President of the World Council of Churches: one of the truly great men of the ecumenical movement. He has given an amusing account of our first meeting, in his memoirs.[1] It was the beginning of a friendship which was to last until his death and which has enriched my life in ways that I can never forget. And it was my first introduction to Geneva, a city which I would later learn to love. I may add that he later made me pay for my taxi for, when I was quietly settling down into a back seat of the conference hall, I suddenly heard him announcing (in French) that a bishop had just arrived from India and would now say a few words. The Assembly itself was not particularly interesting but it provided opportunities for meeting old friends, for making new ones, and for explaining to the leading Reformed theologians of the world that we in South India had not betrayed the true faith. I organized a meeting for representatives of the younger churches who were a small minority very much on the periphery of the conference. I had for the first time the opportunity to get to know some of those who were to become close friends and colleagues: 'Wim' (Dr Visser 't Hooft), Hromadka of Czechoslovakia, Pierre Maury, Henri d'Espigne, Jim McCord and David Read. I had long discussions with Professor Jean de Saussure of the University of Geneva who was much concerned about the compatibility of the historic episcopate with good Reformed churchmanship. One day I spent with my sister Frances at Caux and had another meeting with Frank Buchman. And at the end we stood in front of the Reformation Memorial and sang 'Stand up, stand up for Jesus'. I noted in my diary: 'An extremely impressive delineation of the rugged strength of Calvinism, of its power to *stand*. It expresses its weakness too.'

On the evening of 17 August I joined the train at Basel for Holland. I was travelling third class with no sleeper, but the blessed John Mackay who was travelling first class invited me along to have dinner and introduced me to the great Karl Barth who was travelling with him. It was a brief meeting and I had not yet learned to appreciate either Barth or his theology as I was to do later. But I wrote to Helen: 'Barth is a most vigorous, jolly, human sort of person. I last saw him striding through the streets of Utrecht with a battered felt hat on his head, looking nothing like a Calvinist theologian . . .'

From Utrecht I made my way by bus to the Conference Centre at Woudschoten where about a hundred of the leading thinkers of the ecumenical movement, with attendant staff, were gathering for a two-day meeting to prepare the material for discussion in the four Assembly sections. The change in feeling and style from the Geneva meeting was electrifying. Everyone was alert and expectant. Everything was vigorous, purposeful and businesslike. People whose names were household words all over the world worked together with complete ease and familiarity. Everyone was an equal partner from the great ones like Barth, Niebuhr and Oldham to the veriest newcomer like myself. I was in the group on mission and evangelism with Kraemer and Stephen Neill as leaders and Ted Wickham, D. T. Niles and Pierre Maury as very vigorous and often clashing contributors.

While we were at Woudschoten the resolutions of the Lambeth Conference were published and I had to endure bitter disappointment with little comfort since all the Anglicans present told me that I ought to be thankful that they were not very much worse. I had my first long discussion with Michael Ramsey and noted in my diary that he 'correctly indicated the point of difference between us' but that we had not made much progress towards a resolution of it. It was in these days that I had my first opportunity of intimate talk with the beloved George Bell, Bishop of Chichester, who was of course both deeply sympathetic to us in South India and also able to speak with great authority about the Anglican position.

At the end of two days we all travelled by bus to Amsterdam and the next day, Sunday 2 August, we gathered in the great Nieuwe Kerk for the opening worship of the Assembly. It was a thrilling moment when the 450 official delegates of the Churches entered in procession with their very distinctive robes and I felt proud as I watched Bishop Jacob in the new and striking colour of a South India bishop. We all sang the Old Hundredth, prayers and lessons were read by the Archbishop of Canterbury and Marc Boegner, and then age and youth were represented in the preaching of John R. Mott and D. T. Niles. The former (according to my diary) rambled and the latter preached three excellent sermons. There were immense crowds and excitement everywhere, both because of the Assembly and because Amsterdam was preparing to celebrate the accession of Queen Juliana, and the whole city was *en fête*.

On Monday morning we had the session which formally constituted the World Council of Churches and in the afternoon the sharply contrasted addresses of Karl Barth and C. H. Dodd on the main theme, 'Man's Disorder and God's Design'. In my letter to Helen I wrote:

Karl Barth gave us a tremendous oration on the fundamental theme of the conference. It was real prophecy and compelled everyone, I think, to look beyond all our plans and self-importance to the living God. Some people were very annoyed by it, but I more and more feel that it was needed. In the evening at the reception Pierre Maury asked me what I thought of it. I said, 'It was magnificent, but where do we go from there?' Just at that moment Barth appeared, so Maury repeated my question to him. He said, 'Into the next room of course', and went! Which was the right answer; I mean that Barth demolishes all one's plans with his terrific prophetic words, and one is left wondering what to do next; and his answer always is, Just get on with the next plain duty.

On the following day we had the famous speeches of John Foster Dulles and Josef Hromadka which opened up with dramatic force the division between East and West. Hromadka's, I wrote to Helen, was a very courageous utterance 'but the vast majority of the audience (American) did not follow him'. In the following days as I talked with Indian friends we were more and more aware that the so-called East–West division which so dominated the majority of the Assembly was an intra-Western affair and that the real issues for Asia were right outside the consciousness of the delegates.

On the following day there was an opportunity to give the Asian Churches a voice. The programme called for eight meetings of confessional groups: Lutheran, Anglican, Reformed, Orthodox, Methodist, Congregational, Baptist and Disciples. I thought it was wrong for the Church of South India delegates to accept fragmentation and proposed a ninth group for the United Churches. It was a great success. In addition to CSI we had the united churches of China, Japan, the Philippines, North India and Canada and, to our delight, Visser 't Hooft chose to come to our meeting. I wrote to Helen:

In the upshot ours was a most thrilling meeting, whereas I gather all the others were terribly dull! Actually the meeting resolved itself into a sort of testimony meeting about the blessings that each Church had received from union. Visser 't Hooft was quite thrilled and said that we had a story to tell which had never been told, and urged us to prepare a book putting in permanent form the sort of testimony which had emerged at the meeting, I was pressed very strongly to undertake to edit this, and have asked time to consider it. We are to have a further meeting next week to carry the plan further. I think this is healthy, for the tendency of the older Churches is to regard organic unity as something so infinitely remote as not to be a matter of practical politics at all.

We did, in fact, try to get a book published, but did not succeed. In spite of Wim's encouragement it was to be many years before the WCC could itself take an official interest in plans for local unity. The power of the world confessional bodies and the bogy of the 'super Church' were still too formidable.

There was naturally considerable interest in the CSI and most of my free times were spent in discussion with those, chiefly Anglicans, from many parts of the world who wanted more information. In particular I had several long discussions with Michael Ramsey on the fundamental theological issues. Though we continued to disagree, I was increasingly attracted by both his spirit and his way of understanding the Gospel.

My official duties were in Section 2 on 'The Church's Witness' and in Committee 3 on the programme and administration of the WCC. The former was very frustrating. There was no real meeting of minds between those whose idea of mission was represented in Ted Wickham and those (like myself) who had a more traditional approach. On the work of Committee 3 I wrote to Helen:

> This is a very difficult job, partly because it is all so new and strange to most of us, and partly because the committee is dealing with astronomical budgetary figures which to the Americans seem to be nothing but to the rest of us seem to be out of all proportion to any contribution which our Churches could make. Consequently nearly all the talking is being done by the Americans and it is hard for the rest of us to play any constructive part.

I only came to understand later how fateful would be the consequences of this imbalance. I had a glimpse of it when I met Oldham coming out of one of the meetings in utter despair. His vision of what the WCC might be had been shattered and he saw no hope. I think that he would, if he had been in control, have designed something much more like the International Missionary

Council, a body with a very small central staff and a low public profile, putting all the emphasis upon local co-operation. Such a council would have reflected the economic realities of the member Churches. But the Americans were immensely rich, immensely generous, and full of splendid visions. They would be happy to foot the bill for an organization with real clout. And so it was for the first and formative decade of the council's life. I did not fully understand the issues then, for this was a strange and bewildering world. But I realize now that the basic principle was being forgotten – that the health of a body is a function of the health of its smallest units.

However, even if I had been able to play a part in these debates I was in fact drawn out of them by the work of drafting the Assembly message. I had been put on the committee appointed for the purpose and this increasingly took all the time there was. It seemed simple but it was to prove an incredibly difficult and complicated operation. After three meetings our chairman (George Bell) picked two rival teams: Neill, Niles, Schlink, and Kraemer as convener; Niebuhr, Niemöller, Maury, and me as convener. As Niemöller was the possessor of a typewriter I spent a lot of time in his room and came to love and admire him enormously. Both teams were judged to have failed the test and a new group was appointed (Kathleen Bliss, Maury, Neill, and myself). Kathleen (an old friend from Cambridge days) produced a draft which contained the famous words 'We intend to stay together', a gem that was to remain through all subsequent re-settings as the only memorable word spoken by the Assembly. We refined this but again the full committee rejected it. At 10 p.m. yet another team was picked – Berggrav, Bliss, Maury, Niebuhr, Visser 't Hooft, and me – and at 11 o'clock I was commissioned to write yet another draft. This was finished by 3.0 a.m., approved with amendments at breakfast by Maury and Wim, typed on Niemöller's machine for a meeting at 11 o'clock, accepted with some good amendments by 12.30, and retyped ready for translation and duplication by 2 o'clock. The next morning I read the message to the Assembly, after which it was distributed in the three languages. There was a full debate in the afternoon to which I replied, and with a few small amendments the message was adopted.

This was my first experience of an exercise in which I was later to get more practice. I have often wondered whether the result is worth the effort. It certainly provides good training in various virtues: patience, sheer physical endurance, and the readiness to see the products of much travail torn to shreds before one's eyes. Perhaps the results have some part to play in edifying the Church. And I do not think that we have yet found a better way of registering the points that we reach in our continuing struggle for unity.

I stayed in Amsterdam for another day in order to collect my thoughts and then returned by plane to Bombay and by train and bus to rejoin the family in Kodai.

Helen and I on honeymoon, 1936

My father, Edward Richmond Newbigin, c.1936

The family, 1945

The family, 1950

The family, 1960

After my consecration as bishop,
September 1947

At the WCC Second Assembly
at Evanston, 1954

Secretary of the IMC, 1960

With Wim (Visser t'Hooft), 1952

With J. H. Oldham, 1960

D. T. Niles, 1963

SCM Conference group, Vellore, 1957

After my installation as bishop in Madras, 1965

With social workers in Madras, 1968

The leprosy community, Keerasath, 1971

The Advisory Committee on the Main Theme of the Second Assembly, Bossey, 1953

Front row: Kathleen Bliss, Robert Calhoun, John Baillie, Willem Visser t'Hooft, L. N., George Florovsky, Karl Barth, C. H. Dodd, Pitney Van Dusen.

Back row: Walter Muelder, Owen Chadwick, Edgar Carlson, D. T. Niles, Roger Mehl, Edmund Schlink, Paul Minear, Heinrich Vogel, Christian Baeta, interpreter, Robert Bilheimer, Gustaf Wingren, Niels Ehrenstrom. V. E. Devadutt, Hendrik Kraemer.

The first All-India Faith and Order Conference, Nasrapur, 1972

A wayside conversation, c.1970

12

Madurai: Getting Down to the Job

The next four years were, in some ways, the toughest in my life. The honeymoon was over. We had got to know each other's defects as well as our virtues. The deep, bitter conflicts within the Madurai churches surfaced again. The former principal of the college, who had been persuaded to take early retirement, had leisure to employ his considerable abilities in organizing those who, for any reason, felt aggrieved – whether hard-line independents in the Anglican churches, or those whose troubles could plausibly be shown to be the result of caste discrimination. I was compelled to defend in the law courts the actions by which the various separate bodies had been incorporated in the diocese. High officials of the Education Department of Government were persuaded to rule that by the change of management the schools and training colleges had lost their recognition and would have to deposit enormous sums of money to acquire fresh recognition. The 'Backward Christians Forward League' was formed to campaign for the interests of one caste group and pamphlets were handed out where gatherings took place. Much more serious was the disintegration of morale in the college which reached such a point that the police came in with tear gas and only quelled the riot when they actually loaded their guns to fire at the students.

The general political situation was also explosive. Popular expectations of what independence would bring were disappointed. Congress was reviled and the Communist Party gained recruits rapidly, especially among the mill workers. As thousands of these were Christians, I was very much involved. Police repression was often brutal and the whole police apparatus rapidly became much larger and more formidable than it had been in the days of the British. Many of our church members in the mills were totally identified with the communists and I spent many long hours with them trying both to defend them against the police and also to help them to see that communism would not achieve what they hoped for.

In the villages – much the greatest part of the population – the overwhelming problem was hunger. For four successive years the rains failed. In one of my reports I wrote:

Whole congregations have simply abandoned their villages and left their homes to fall into ruins. At first they usually expect to be away only for a few months and to return with the rains. But as year has followed year and the famine has steadily worsened, their links with their old homes have practically ceased. In eastern and southern Ramnad it is now a common sight to see groups of ruined cottages which were once Christian homes. Their former inhabitants may be still wandering about as nomads in Tanjore District, camping by the roadside and moving on from place to place in search of work in the fields.

A great deal of my time was spent in organizing the import and distribution of American food under Truman's 'Point Four Programme'. The process was complicated and the red-tape endless. The wonderfully efficient organization of Inter-Church Aid by the World Council of Churches was still in the future. In spite of the difficulties, this help from the USA enabled us to feed thousands of children in our hostels and boarding homes and also to distribute directly in the villages. But it was a heartbreaking experience to tramp through the devastated area of eastern Ramnad District and find villages falling into ruin, their people gone.

One minor consequence of this was that more and more pastorates ran into debt. We had agreed to pay the ordained ministry from a central fund, but this depended upon the faithfulness of pastorates in contributing to that fund. The organizing of the finances of the new diocese was, in any case, a complicated task. The presence of mounting deficits was an added burden. It was an enormous relief when we were able to find in Mr G. G. Joshua an able young Indian treasurer who gradually brought the chaos of different funds and accounts into a smooth-running operation.

These were the years of the communist takeover in China and the traumatic termination of western missionary work there. From the point of view of an intelligent outside observer there was every reason to think that the same thing might happen in India. What lessons should western mission boards learn from China and apply to India? As far as I was concerned, this affected primarily the American Board in Boston. The SPG had washed its hands of South India. The CMS was our loyal friend and supporter but adhered to its principle of dealing not with bishops but only with its own missionary representatives in the field. During my whole twelve years in Madurai I therefore had no direct dealings with the CMS and they had no direct way of contributing to the policymaking of the diocese. The American Board had, however, been accustomed to keeping a fairly tight rein on its work in India. It still had thirty-six missionaries serving in the Madura Mission and was making large grants for the work. What were its responsibilities to be? The shrewd and far-sighted India secretary of the Board, Raymond Dudley, kept up a continuous correspondence with me, averaging several letters a month throughout my period there. I was privileged to have his confidence and we could write with complete frankness.

The Church had to be autonomous, but what would it be like? Would it 'slide into Anglicanism' as he feared? Would episcopacy corrupt the pure practice of congregationalism? On the last point I could assure him that, as far as I had learned to date, the job of a bishop was to help congregations to be in fact what congregationalism holds in theory that they are, but what (without someone like St Paul to prod them) they usually are not! But what is real autonomy? How can the Church be helped to become something that no communist flood can sweep away? This was the matter to which we constantly returned and on which we were agreed. We were convinced that the future lay not in the prestigious institutions but in small village congregations under local leadership. In February 1951 Dudley wrote to me:

In spite of 120 years of history, and in spite of our great institutions, even yet we know all too little as to how to redeem village life . . . Sometimes I wonder if the communists will combine with the outcastes (including the Christians) in a strenuous protest that missions have done little to raise the standard of living of poor village people.

And in December of the same year when I was obliged to plead for help for the newly started Lady Doak College for women, I wrote to him:

> Whether the Christian Church as a matter of fact ought to be running colleges like this is another question. There are large chunks of time when I think our members ought to be getting their education running revolutionary cells preparing the way for a pukka agrarian revolution. But that is not the way we have come so far. As Christian colleges go, I think this is a good one. But all this runs back again into the big question whether we are all too completely tied up with the western bourgeois set-up, and what the future of that set-up is in India.

The key to the future, as I saw it, was the development of a village-based voluntary ministry. Writing to Dudley in October 1951 about the problem of present debts and future ministry, I said:

> As you know, I believe that we have got to extend the volunteer principle much farther than we have done. I myself believe that if the Church is to be really rooted in the country and to Christianize the country through and through, our present pattern will have to be drastically modified. I think we ought to have an ordained Presbyter in every village, who would normally be a villager himself, earning his living with his hands, but sufficiently trained to be able to read and explain the Bible intelligibly, and to conduct the liturgy with understanding. I think there should be, further, a peripatetic ministry of teachers, on whom we could rely for instruction of the people in the faith in a systematic way, which might include both paid Presbyters and also the 'faith' workers who are already so popular a feature of church life. Further, there should be a fully trained and paid ministry of people – including a very much larger number of bishops than at present – with ultimate responsibility for the life and worship and teaching of the Church . . . I do not want to reduce the number of fully

trained and paid ministers, but I want greatly to increase the ministry and make it much more local and indigenous. I think something like what I have outlined is in line with the experience of the Church for its first thousand years in Europe, and even now in vast areas, and that our present pattern, the creation of the mercantile societies of the post-Renaissance West, is quite unsuited to the field we are working in.

The development of these ideas was to be one of my main preoccupations for the whole of the twelve years I was in Madurai. We had a small theological seminary for the training of catechists and Biblewomen. I asked them to stop this work and give their whole time to training volunteer leaders in the villages. At first these were asked to come to the seminary for short courses, but this was a mistake. Those who can leave the village for ten days are not those who carry weight in the village. Such courses were good for the professional men (government officers and teachers) whose standing in the village was secure in other ways. They formed a valuable part of the volunteer force. But for the real local leaders, the people whose roots were in the village, it was necessary for the seminary staff to go and camp in the villages and provide short courses during the times when there was no work in the fields. Through these two kinds of training we developed a cadre of over 300 volunteer leaders and it very soon became clear to me that the congregations under this kind of leadership were more lively and more active in evangelism than those under the care of the paid teachers. This experience led me to propose to the Diocesan Ministerial Committee that we should seek the permission of the Synod to ordain some of these village leaders to a full ministry of word and sacrament. For those who had struggled for decades to secure high academic standards of ministerial training, this was naturally shocking. Many years of debate were needed before it could be implemented. The outcome of the debate belongs to the next part of the story.

I was sure that the village congregations were the foundation for everything else. But they were not everything. If the Gospel was to make its full impact on all the vast, varied and profound experience of India, there were needed leaders who had really come to grips at a deep level with the issues which were posed for the Church not only by traditional Hinduism but also by the new intellectual and spiritual movements that were agitating the newly free nation. In April 1951 Kraemer paid an extended visit to the diocese at the end of which we had a long discussion which was to have far-reaching results. Kraemer expressed very strongly the conviction he had formed that the Church in India was not equipped and was not equipping itself for its real theological and missionary tasks – meeting the challenge of renascent Hinduism at a deep level, finding a prophetic and priestly role in the midst of the turmoil and conflict of nation-building, discovering its proper role in education and (above all) equipping its lay membership for its secular witness. Kraemer pointed out that the few Indian leaders capable of these tasks were completely absorbed in maintaining the big institutions. 'No one', he said, 'seems to have time to do any real thinking.' It was a powerful and just criticism which I felt had to be taken very seriously. We went on to think of a possible first step – the creation of a centre for study, research and training with a very small but highly competent team including both theological and socio-political training. Kraemer wrote a memorandum on this line urging the World Council of Churches and the International Missionary Council to support the idea.[1] I sent my own proposals to the National Christian Council and later in the year chaired a meeting under its auspices, with M. M. Thomas as one of the participants, which strongly endorsed the plan. There was to be a long and hard battle before the idea became a fact – the Christian Institute for the Study of Religion and Society, in Bangalore.

All of this was part of the struggle to move from mission to Church, from dependence to a genuine selfhood. The creation of high-quality leadership was essential, but so was the effort to help the village congregations to move from dependence on salaried teachers and catechists to a real spiritual autonomy, to a realization that where two or three were gathered in Jesus' name, there was not an outstation of the mission but the full reality of the catholic Church. The volunteer programme was vital. So also was the spiritual upbuilding of pastors and people. The greater part of my time was spent touring in the villages and holding small gatherings of pastors in each area for Bible study, teaching, discussion of their work and prayer. The village tours were extremely demanding. Every village wanted a visit and usually a full service with confirmations and communion. Sometimes there would be five of such visits in one day, with difficult journeys between the villages. Day after day I would be at full stretch from five a.m. till after midnight. It was exhausting but also exhilarating. And there was always the changing beauty of the countryside, the magic moments of sunrise and sunset, the faith of village people under incredible burdens, and the loving and generous hospitality of village homes. I would not have exchanged the job for anything in the world.

Among the things which raised difficult issues was the decision of Government to require all the elementary schools to switch to the Gandhian model of 'basic education'. This was in itself an excellent model. It called for a style of learning based on a village craft such as spinning, and was designed to equip children for better living in their village. It seemed to be a wholly welcome change from a model which unfitted children for village life and ultimately weakened the villages by draining the successful products into the slums of the cities. Implemented with flexibility and imagination it could be an unqualified blessing. Imposed with the wooden inflexibility of the state bureaucracy it could become something very different. I was eager that we should seize the opportunity to bring its best features into our village schools. But there was one big difficulty. The Hindu belief that all religions are equally valid paths to the one unknowable god was to be built into the programme. All training of teachers for basic schools was to be done in residential colleges where there was a tightly knit community centred in daily acts of worship understood in this syncretistic way. Any specifically Christian worship – even in the privacy of a teacher's home – was seen as schismatic and subversive. For young Christians fresh from a village elementary school this created an appalling problem of conscience. I agonized about the problem but, as often, God had other plans. In the most prestigious of the institutions in our part of India, where the rule was imposed with the greatest rigidity, the costly witness of a village boy who was willing to lose his teaching certificate rather than compromise his faith so shook the whole institution that I was soon baptizing students within the college campus. We ourselves took the initiative to establish the first Christian basic training college at post-graduate level and it did splendid work. But before long the whole attempt to impose basic education by Government order was abandoned and the schools went back to the old system.

I was heavily involved in wider responsibilities as convener of the Synod Theological Commission. This was chiefly engaged on two fronts. One was the development of discussions about unity with the Baptists and the Lutherans. The former withdrew after a short time, but with the latter we embarked upon a series of deep-going theological discussions which were to continue for twenty years and to produce a whole series of substantial doctrinal agreements and a draft plan of union. It ended, however, in nothing as the Lutheran Churches made it clear that they preferred to remain secure under the powerful wing of the Lutheran World Federation.

The other business was with the Church of England. The Lambeth Conference had asked the Church of South India to make changes at six points, and a Joint Committee of the Convocations of Canterbury and York had pressed us for answers on the same points. These concerned the statement of faith, the understanding of the sacraments, confirmation, the role of bishops in church government, future relations with non-episcopal Churches, and the continued recognition of ministers not episcopally ordained. All were directed to pressing the CSI into a strictly Anglican mould. We sent long and reasoned answers. The alternative statement of faith pressed on us by Lambeth would have left the door open for every kind of heresy. The idea that we should ultimately sever our relations with non-episcopal Churches and refuse to recognize their ministries was inconceivable. Yet these demands were pressed and no attempt was ever made to answer the theological arguments we advanced. The theological rationale of our method of union had been fully argued in my book *The Reunion of the Church*, which was in the hands of every member of the Lambeth Conference. Yet no attempt was ever made, as far as I could discover, to come to grips with the argument. There was simply a steady insistence that the CSI must conform to the Anglican model. The replies which we prepared covered thirty-four printed pages and were widely distributed. There was no formal response. Gradually the pressure ceased. The CSI was to be allowed to be itself.

And, as I have said, I do not think that many South India Christians lost much sleep over the anxieties of the Church of England.

By the end of this period two things had become clear. The first was that, whatever the internal shape of the Church might become, it was never going to sever its relationships with the non-episcopal Churches in order to satisfy the Anglican demands. The second was that it was not going to abandon the historic episcopate in deference to the demands of the Lutherans. It would continue to be a Church which treasures and maintains the historic episcopate; but it would refuse to be a Church which makes this the touchstone of church fellowship.

We did, however, have much cause to be grateful for the understanding and generosity of many Anglican leaders. Bishop George Bell of Chichester paid us a long visit and brought great encouragement. Bishop Hobson of Southern Ohio almost emptied his diocesan treasury to make good the losses suffered through the stopping of SPG funds. And the Archbishop of Brisbane, who had voted against recognition at Lambeth, paid us a visit on his way home and was able to report that we were not nearly so bad as he had thought. During the six months April to September 1950 I found time to write in a very staccato form an account of my daily experiences and this, published as *A South India Diary* and translated into many European languages, helped to reveal the fact that the CSI was a community of human beings and not just a bundle of ecclesiastical anomalies. Indeed I was vastly entertained to learn that the *Diary* was being used as devotional reading during mealtimes in monastic establishments where we had formerly been regarded with the greatest suspicion.

And there were some memorable experiences of the wider life of the Church. For six days spanning the New Year 1948-9 the Student Christian Movement brought together national leaders from a wide circle of Asian countries – the first meeting of its kind and one that would influence Christian leadership in the whole of South East Asia for a long time. The meeting was in Kandy, the lovely city in the hills of Ceylon (Sri Lanka). One memory of the conference remains vivid. Murray Rogers and I decided one day to play truant and climb a mountain which looked too delectable to be ignored. On the way back we lost our way and were wandering in the dark on a tree-clad hillside. Down below us there was a faint light. I climbed down the hill to see if there was someone to tell me the way. I found a woman crouching over a fire of sticks, stirring a pot of rice. When she saw me she jumped up and shouted (in Tamil) to the man inside the hut: 'Look! Our bishop has come to see us!' She was one of the many from Ramnad District who had fled from famine to seek a living in Ceylon.

As so often, the SCM led the way for the Church. A year later I went to Bangkok to attend the Conference of East Asian Churches organized jointly by the IMC and WCC. It was a thrilling meeting. Those vigorous, growing Churches hitherto tied to the apron strings of their parent bodies in the West, had never before met each other. In this respect the Churches were ahead of governments, for the Bandung Conference of South East Asian states was still in the future. The meeting took place under the shadow of the impending communist victory in China. Everyone felt the need for continuing fellowship and mutual consultation among the Asian Churches. The result was the appointment of Dr Rajah Manikam as joint IMC-WCC Secretary for the region, with a roving commission to visit all the churches. His fine work in the ensuing period laid the foundation for the later East Asia Christian Conference, now the Christian Conference of Asia.

There were other journeys to other parts of India for conferences and conventions. At the great Maraman Convention where 30,000 people gather each year on the dry bed of the river in Kerala, the beloved Metropolitan Mar Yuhanan honoured me by inviting me to give a series of addresses. On the first morning when a mere handful of 5000 or so had gathered, I rose – somewhat nervous – to give my first address. The Metropolitan pulled my sleeve and whispered: 'Keep your best stuff till later; the main crowds haven't come yet.' Another visit was to take a conference for a group of American missionaries in Western India who were going through a bad time. One of them had a tape-recorder but was short of tape. When he thought my remarks were falling below standard he would get up and switch off the machine. No doubt all this helps to avoid the danger of taking oneself too seriously!

But the most exciting of these extra-diocesan excursions was to take me briefly back to Europe. The WCC Central Committee in 1950 had decided that the Second Assembly should have as its theme 'Christ the Hope of the World' and that a group of twenty-five theologians should be assembled to prepare the Churches for the consideration of the theme. To my great astonishment I learned (from Oliver Tomkins who spent a memorable week with us in Madura) that my name was included in the twenty-five. My first reaction was total disbelief and reluctance to be party to the huge cost of a return air fare for such a crazy exercise. But Oliver's patient reasoning prevailed and I agreed to go.

As I flew into Geneva airport on 20 July 1951 and then took the lake steamer to the little lakeside village of Rolle, I could hardly believe that I was on the same planet as the one I had left. It would be hard to imagine a greater contrast than that between the slums of Bombay and the exquisitely manicured lawns of these lakeside villas. The same evening I joined Visser 't Hooft, John Baillie and Pitney van Dusen for a swim in the lake and after supper we got down to business.

The group was a formidable one. Among the Continentals Barth, Brunner, Schlink, Vogel and Wingren had deep differences among themselves. From the USA Reinhold Niebuhr, Bob Calhoun, Paul Minear, Francis Miller and van Dusen were separated from the Continentals by a vast gulf. Van Dusen was chairman and was, I believe, mainly responsible for the formation of the group. Barth was at his most polemical. 'How is it possible', he asked, 'to talk about hope when we meet in the neighbourhood of Chicago?' The Americans saw the title as merely an affirmation of the importance of Christ; the Continentals took the word 'hope' seriously and assumed that this was a discussion of eschatology. By the end of the third day we were near despair. Barth vented his wrath on Baillie. Niebuhr proposed that we drop the word 'hope' from the title. On the 23rd we were near the breaking-point. Niebuhr had almost made up his mind to leave. The group decided to appoint a small steering committee of which I was made chairman and next morning Schlink gave a brief meditation at morning prayer on the text 'These things must come to pass'. He drew the parallel between the Passion sayings and the warnings of the eschatological tribulation. It was very simple but it completely changed the atmosphere. Niebuhr unpacked his bag and we started again. I got Barth and the Americans to talk together and a long discussion between Niebuhr and Schlink in the plenary session brought us to a much deeper mutual understanding. My own prepared paper on the Apostolate of the Church was strongly attacked from all quarters and I was almost sunk until Barth came to my rescue with all guns firing – not, I think, because he agreed but because everyone else was against me!

We divided into three groups for drafting and I chaired the one which had to write the basic theological statement. It included Barth, Schlink and Florovsky, Bob Calhoun, George Thomas, Donald Mackinnon and Norman Goodall as secretary. It was tough work but I was delighted to be involved in it because it was a development of the concern that had dominated my thinking earlier: the concern to clarify the nature of our hope for human history as distinct both from the nineteenth-century idea of progress and the popular religious idea of personal immortality. Our first draft was strongly attacked by the Americans and a lot of rewriting had to be done in which Barth and Calhoun worked with Goodall and me. In the end the report was accepted, the three sections were brought together and I was asked to be the chairman of the whole group for the future meetings. I have often been puzzled by this decision but I suppose it was partly because I was theologically somewhere between the Americans and the Continentals and partly because I was the only member of the group who was a pastor while nearly all the others were professors. Anyhow, I agreed to serve and I noted in my diary: 'A good job, but a hefty one.'

The next four days were spent in conference at the Basel Mission House about their problems in South India and in a couple of days of mountain-climbing. Then I returned to Rolle for the Central Committee where I was to represent the CSI. As far as I was concerned, the meeting was memorable for three things. The first was the way in which Bishop Berggrav of Norway handled the deep and painful tensions in the meeting between the members from east and west of the Iron Curtain. The war in Korea had started. The Chinese had absented themselves from the meeting. The Americans were committed to a holy crusade against communism. The representatives of the East European Churches were a very small minority and Bishop

Bereczky of Hungary as their spokesman made a speech which sharply challenged the dominant western position. The atmosphere was extremely tense. Was the World Council to adopt the western line, or would it hold the deep conflict within the Christian fellowship? In a closed session Bishop Eivind Berggrav of Norway was the one who made it possible to hold together. In my letter to Helen at the time I wrote that it was 'a wonderful talk – as simple and direct as a father talking to his children. I suppose there is no one else in the world who could have done just what he did . . . It was an unforgettable experience and it completely transformed the situation.'

The second matter was the report of the committee of twenty-five which I had to present and defend. It was met with furious and almost unanimous anger. Dr Newton Flew described it as 'theologically contemptible' and there was an attempt to get it completely suppressed. Even a motion to send it to the Churches for study was rejected. Finally, after Wim had more or less read the riot act, the committee agreed to 'take note of the fact that the General Secretary will send it to the member Churches'. Meanwhile *Time Magazine* had asked for the entire text to be sent by cable! But eschatology was at that time an issue which the western liberal establishment was unwilling to face.

The third matter was the relation of unity and mission. I was asked to chair the section which dealt with this and I drafted the report on *The Calling of the Church to Mission and Unity*. Many of its ideas were to be developed further at Willingen in the following year and they helped to create the theological climate for the later integration of the IMC and the WCC. The discussion in the section also came sharply up against the resistance of the dominant Anglo-Saxon theology to any serious discussion of eschatology. In my first draft for the section I used – without quotation marks – the words of Jesus: 'This gospel of the kingdom will be preached throughout the whole world . . . and then the end will come.' An Anglican bishop successfully moved the deletion of the last six words![2] One sentence which I did succeed in getting into the draft was the text of what I tried to press upon the Willingen meeting a year later: 'Too large a proportion of the great volume of missionary giving and service which flows out from the older churches is at present required to prop up relatively static younger churches, rather than to make new advances for the Gospel.'³ That sentence represented my major concern as I looked at the whole ecumenical–missionary situation.

Meanwhile I was being drawn into ecumenical discussions at another point. The same central committee at Toronto which had set up the Committee of Twenty-five had also issued the famous 'Toronto Statement', which sought to meet the fears of those who thought that by accepting membership in the WCC they had compromised their own ecclesiologies. The statement sought to reassure them by affirming the neutrality of the Council in respect of their conflicting ecclesiologies. It was not committed to any of them but was a forum for all of them to meet. I was one of those invited to comment on this statement. In my response I argued that it was a dangerous business for the WCC to attempt to justify itself in the eyes of its members since the whole reason for its existence was the fact that 'Churches', in the sense of separated denominations, are living in sin! I argued that neutrality could be regarded as a legitimate starting-point, but that it could not be a permanent mark of the WCC because its own existence is a kind of answer to the ecclesiological question, and it is the wrong answer. A council of independent Churches is not the *una sancta* of the Creeds. Therefore the Council must face as a matter of urgency the question: What is the nature of the unity which is God's intention for the Church? If this is not faced, the Council will itself become 'some sort of a monster'.⁴ This conviction was to draw me more and more into the discussions of the Faith and Order division of the WCC and to an attempt to draft an answer to this basic question. These attempts were to lead in due course to the New Delhi Statement (1961), on the nature of the unity which is our goal and God's gift.

During these five years in Madurai the children had been growing happily. We had one shock when John, at the age of twenty-one months, was smitten with poliomyelitis. I got the news when I was visiting a remote village congregation and immediately drove up to Kodai and brought Helen and John to the Christian hospital at Vellore where he was given the best possible treatment and made a full recovery of the use of all his limbs. The girls divided their time between the American school in Kodai and holidays with us, and we had some glorious if brief times together in the hills and by the sea. In April 1952 we crossed over to Sri Lanka and had a splendid few days in Colombo as the guests of Gordon Burrows. We then sailed for England in the *Chusan*.

13

Madurai: Towards a Responsible Church in an Ecumenical Setting

For the nine months from May 1952 our home was in Edinburgh. It was a very happy summer with our children all together and with a glorious break at Rothbury which they were now old enough really to enjoy. In September Margaret and Alison went to Walthamstow Hall School, Sevenoaks, where they would be staying when we returned to India. I was – as before – much engaged with preaching, broadcasting and having long sessions of theological discussion with the Anglican critics of the South India union. Michael Bruce's Council for Defence of Church Principles had (I gathered from the notepaper) given place to the 'International League for Apostolic Faith and Order', but in spite of this semantic escalation I found the atmosphere more relaxed and friendly. At least there was a beginning of acceptance.

My main preoccupation during this period was the preparation and delivery of the Kerr Lectures which were later published as *The Household of God*. The outline for this had been taking shape in my mind for some time. During a chance meeting in a railway train five years previously, Alan Richardson had suggested to me that the ecclesiology implied in *The Reunion of the Church* could be detached from its immediate context in the South India debate and developed on its own. The invitation to give the Kerr Lectures provided an opportunity to do this. I had felt for some time that the Ecumenical Movement was not being undergirded by an adequate doctrine of the Church, and that all the books on this subject that I knew were essentially defensive of one tradition against the others. I started working from the Catholic-Protestant dichotomy as it had been so powerfully explored in the Amsterdam debates. But as I dug into the biblical material I became more and more convinced that this twofold approach did not reach the heart of the matter, and that these two traditions would only accept each other's truth if there was brought into the debate a third element – that which lays stress on the immediate experience of divine grace and power. For a long time I hesitated about how to name this third element. Finally I used the name Pentecostal. I had at that time almost no contact whatever with any of the Pentecostal bodies. I regarded them with the distaste of a well-educated university graduate. But the fact that I had made this element one of the three essential foundations for ecclesiology was to open the doors in later years to personal friendship with some Pentecostal leaders and to the enrichment of my own life through the charismatic movement much later, and it was to have considerable consequences for future thinking about the Church. The book was translated into French, German, Chinese and Japanese, and (to my deep delight) into a Russian text which was circulated in typescript. I was even told by one of the *periti* of the Second Vatican Council that it had influenced the writing of *Lumen Gentium*. When the lectures were actually delivered in Glasgow they appeared to fall completely flat and the professor who was my chairman told me that he could not make out what I was trying to say. But it has been a source of great joy in later years to meet people whose vision of the Church had been enlarged by the reading of the book.

During the summer of 1952 I was involved in three ecumenical meetings. The first was the International Missionary Council's conference at Willingen on 'The Missionary Obligation of the Church'. The purpose of the meeting was to attempt a restatement both of the basis of mission in the Gospel and of the present priorities for action – both necessary in view of radical changes in the world situation and of the movements in theology. The people of Willingen took us to their hearts and did all and more than all that could be asked to make us welcome. For me personally one of its richest rewards was the opportunity for deepening friendship with Walter Freytag. I have seldom met anyone with a surer gift for going right to the heart of a problem and putting familiar facts into new perspectives. I went to Willingen with the determination to challenge what I saw as the paralysis of missions, the practical exhaustion of the resources of the older churches in propping up relatively static churches in the old 'mission fields'. In the plenary session on 11 July I had the chance to put this challenge in a forcible way[1] and it was taken up in separate groups representing older and younger churches. On the whole the reaction of both was to question my oversweeping generalizations, but I think the challenge was not wholly without effect. And it was to influence the later idea of 'Joint Action for Mission'.

My main job at Willingen was with the theological group. This was dominated by the attempt, led chiefly by Hans Hoekendijk and Paul Lehmann, to swing missionary thinking away from the 'church-centred' model which had dominated it since Tambaram and to speak more of God's work in the secular world, in the political, cultural and scientific movements of the time. The report which the group prepared spoke of discerning by faith God's action of judgement and redemption in the revolutionary movements of our time.[2] But the Conference was not ready to accept these ideas. Their time was to come a few years later. At that moment, in spite of the passionate eloquence of Hoekendijk, they could not be incorporated into the findings of the meeting. Instead, as a member of the editorial committee, I was asked to draft a fresh statement on 'The Missionary Calling of the Church'. This based the missionary calling on the doctrine of the Trinity and used the words: 'There is no participation in Christ without participation in his mission to the world.' This statement was adopted with some enthusiasm, but Hoekendijk, Max Warren and Norman Goodall quite rightly insisted that it should not be treated as the report of the group but only as a statement 'arising out of the report', and that the latter, though not adopted by the Conference, should be sent to the Churches for study. I confess that I did not realize then that the ideas of Hoekendijk and others like him would become the overwhelmingly dominant ideas of the next decade.

The Willingen meeting gave me the chance for further work with Kraemer and some American and Indian leaders towards the creation of a Christian Study Centre for India. There were also many other very precious personal meetings and discussions far into the night round the tables in the hospitable inns of Willingen. At the end Norman Goodall, who had been mainly responsible for planning the meeting, declared that it had failed to achieve its purpose. Thirty years later one can look back and say that it was one of the most creative in the long series of missionary conferences.

After a family holiday at Rothbury I was back on the Continent, first at Lund where the world conference on Faith and Order was in session. I was not a member but attended the closing actions and was elected a member of the new Faith and Order Commission. The purpose of my visit was to share in the leadership of an informal gathering of representatives of united Churches and of Churches involved in unity negotiations. This was a follow-up of our meeting during the Amsterdam Assembly. The Faith and Order Commission was at that time unwilling to sponsor such a meeting and a few of us therefore arranged an informal meeting at which I gave the opening address. We were greatly helped and supported by the participation of the Bishop of Derby (Rawlinson), Fr Gabriel Hebert of Kelham, and other staunch Anglican friends. It was a really fruitful meeting.

From there I flew to Geneva for the second meeting of the Committee of Twenty-five at Bossey. This was, of course, the first time I had acted as chairman. It was not easy. As I wrote to Helen: 'They are all exceptionally able people with gleams of vision and favourite theories all of their own, and they are all accustomed to being listened to and not contradicted, but it is very hard to get them to stick to a certain line of thought.' However, we were able to build on the work of the previous year and made real progress. Barth was in good form and there were none of the earlier tantrums. Brunner was unable to come because of the tragic death of his son and because of his own illness. He wrote me a touching letter in which he said: 'I had a dream in which Karl Barth appeared to me, telling me in a most friendly way about your group and its work, at the same time pronouncing a most pessimistic view about its progress.' However, real progress was made, thanks especially to the roles played by Donald Mackinnon and D. T. Niles in bridging the gulf between the Americans and the Continentals. On the Sunday I had the joy of celebrating the CSI liturgy with Barth as the preacher. In my diary I wrote: 'The theme of the Commission is a challenge not to let the great hope of God's Kingdom be crowded out by little hopes.'

Early in February 1953 I returned alone to Madurai, leaving Helen in Edinburgh with the family. That summer I returned to Europe very briefly for the final meeting of 'The Twenty-five'. It was a difficult meeting and I may have been guilty of using too heavy a hand as chairman. But we parted as real friends – all grateful, I think, for the experience. My last memory is of Karl

Barth, to whom I had assigned the job of writing the final section. I found him sitting surrounded by papers in the middle of the Bossey lawn, looking much dishevelled. 'You look as if you are in trouble,' I said. 'I am,' he replied. 'This is a task for some great ecumenical theologian.'

After the meeting we had a family holiday at Rothbury and then, leaving Margaret and Alison as boarders at Walthamstow Hall, Helen and I returned with Janet and John to Madurai.

The six years in Madurai from 1953 to 1959 were, of course, filled to overflowing with all the ordinary duties of a bishop. My diary records day after day long tramps from village to village, sometimes wading through long reaches of flood, often sleeping rough on a station platform or on the mud floor of a village school. And there were also the unforgettable days spent in visiting the scattered communities of labourers who had left their village to work in the tea estates of the High Range or the High Wavies. There were times of disaster, famine, floods and cyclones, and the business of learning how to secure help in coping with them. Etched in my memory is the terrible cyclone of December 1955 when huge areas were under deep water and 168 of our village churches, schools and parsonages were destroyed in a single night. When it was clear that relief supplies were not reaching the villages I took a party down to the coast, commandeered a trainload of grain, got it loaded onto a boat and set out to sail round to Thondi in order to land the supplies where they were needed. Unfortunately the engines failed and we spent most of the night helplessly tossing in the Bay of Bengal. Eventually, however, we did get the grain to where it was needed and we were the first to reach them. The official authorities, who had blandly assured us that they needed no help, gave us responsibility for supplying 200 villages. Later we organized volunteers, mostly students, to help in the reconstruction of the ruined homes.

Such experiences emphasized the terrible vulnerability of the communities in which the Church was planted. How could we really strengthen those village communities? We were conscious of the fact that our hundreds of village schools, the pioneers in bringing education to the poorest of the poor, had often actually weakened the villages by creaming off their ablest young people for the city jobs which were judged the only proper ones for an educated person. The idea of 'development' was beginning to become popular. Missions had tried to develop rural husbandry and crafts. The 'Block Development' programmes of the Indian Government were getting into their stride. A group of dedicated laymen in the USA, called 'World Neighbours Inc.', was eager to pour large sums of money into village development projects provided that their name was prominently displayed and their hands were on the controls. We did indeed struggle to develop all kinds of projects for strengthening the village economy by building on local skills such as tanning and basket-making. But it was frustrating work. Foreign money poured into a desperately poor Church could only corrupt it. The essential thing was to evoke the commitment of the village people themselves, waiting patiently for their response, and then offering small amounts of aid commensurate with the scale of operations. We could not promise our generous American friends quick results.

Most of our congregations were made up of landless labourers from the Harijan communities. Without land of their own it was impossible for them to make use of the improved farming methods which people like 'World Neighbours' were eager to offer. Some of my missionary colleagues were impressed by the Bhoodan or 'land gift' movement led by Gandhi's most famous disciple, Vinobha Bhave. Many people were eager to hail it as the answer to the threat of communism. My Indian colleagues were sceptical and I shared their view. The long experience of missions had shown the futility of giving land to people who had no capital to invest in it, no resources against bad seasons, and no hereditary experience as landowners. The normal result was that the land was pledged in order to raise loans and it finished up as the property of city moneylenders. The village landlord might be rapacious but he had more understanding and compassion for the Harijans of his own village than a distant city capitalist would have. I spent a day following Vinobha on one of his long, patient walks on foot from village to village (followed by an army of officials in jeeps!). I listened to him preaching a superb sermon on a text from Romans 12. I was captivated by his beautiful spirit. But at the end of a long personal discussion with him my arguments were not effectively met and I remained unconvinced. I do not think that anyone now believes that the Bhoodan movement made a significant impact on India's rural economy or

141

on the condition of the Harijans. The procession of Government jeeps was a testimony to the fact that Vinobha was being used by Government as a counterweight to the communist threat. The fundamental need was not just the transfer of land but a change of consciousness. And this was happening in the communities of Christians who lived in the outcaste quarter of hundreds of villages. People who had lived for untold centuries as serfs were learning to think of themselves as children of God.

Sometimes the results were explosive and violent. In eastern Ramnad District the SPG had built up a fine congregation in the village of Veerambal. The dominant landowning caste in the area was the Thevars, notorious for their violent behaviour. People of the Harijan communities were required to prostrate themselves on the ground when meeting a Thevar. But the Christian congregation of Veerambal was much better educated than the Thevar landlords. They began to refuse the traditional gesture. There were violent reprisals which led to counter violence. One day in September 1957 when the Diocesan Executive was in session we received the news that 600 of the Thevars with guns had attacked the Veerambal congregation which was gathered in church, killing and wounding considerable numbers. A group of us rushed to the spot by car, passing burning villages by the way, and spent the next days comforting the bereaved, tending the wounded, visiting the Thevar villages and trying to bring about peace. But it could only be peace if it was based on a radical change in the relationship between the communities, not if it was a restoration of the traditional order. I found it very hard indeed to discern with those shattered and angry Christians of Veerambal how the message of the Gospel is to be so lived out that it brings justice and dignity without violence. There was no question that it was the Gospel which had so changed those Veerambal villagers that they refused to tolerate any longer the indignities that traditional rules had imposed on them.

These and other similar happenings were part of the larger struggle, the struggle to move from domination to freedom in national life, and in the life of the Christian society from the control of the foreign mission to the integrity and responsibility of the Indian Church. The Christians in Madura were accustomed to generous support from the USA. The Church was now – on paper – entirely autonomous and its leading positions (except that of bishop) were held by Indians. But the habit of asking for money from abroad was deeply rooted, and would not go away easily. It meant that the Church was not accepting full responsibility for its life. I pleaded continually that the practice of submitting an annual 'shopping list' to the Board should cease and that there should be instead a fixed annual block grant for the use of which the diocese must accept total responsibility. But I was not successful.

I saw the Gandhian Basic Education programme as a key to the strengthening of village life and spent a great deal of time both nationally as Vice-President of the National Christian Council and locally as bishop of the diocese, in urging the Church to take it seriously. We had the encouragement of Marjorie Sykes and other national figures in organizing a conference on 'The Role of the Church in Basic Education', in providing basic retraining for Christian teachers and (as already recorded) in starting our own graduate basic training college at Battlagundu.

But at this point we ran into the problem of compulsory 'common worship'. Two of the American Board missionaries, Lloyd Lorbeer and Dick Keithahn – saw no objection to accepting the Gandhian practice of common worship. My Indian colleagues were solidly with me in rejecting it. For Battlagundu we accepted the principle of a morning assembly in two parts: first, a silent period in which all were free to offer their devotions according to their several faiths, using their own sacred books; and second, a period of Christian worship, attendance at which was voluntary. I had understood that all had accepted this, but Lorbeer went into print with an attack on the subject and resigned from his position as correspondent of the training college. This became the occasion for hostile comment in the American religious press, where the position I had taken was regarded as reactionary. The Congregational Churches in the USA were at that time going through legal battles in connection with the proposed merger with the Evangelical and Reformed Churches. A powerful anti-union lobby had been formed. To those of this persuasion the Church of South India could easily become the target of their hostility to union in any form. If the suspicion of the CSI in the Church of England was abating, it seemed that among American Congregationalists suspicion was growing that the CSI was sliding into the typical errors of Anglicanism. It has to be admitted that some pastors at this time did tend towards an unthinking copying of Anglican liturgical practices but I think it is fair to say that one of the main reasons was that they had not been trained in a clear and firm liturgical tradition of a Reformed type. A vague New England liberalism, transplanted into Indian soil, did not produce a strong self-propagating growth.

In my view the practice of compulsory common worship touched the nerve centre of the Church's life. I was concerned that, while we must do whatever was in our power through education and 'development' activities to help the villages to become strong and healthy communities, our fundamental task, from which nothing ought to deflect us, was the preaching of the Gospel and the building up of genuinely free and responsible village congregations under their own leadership and with their own firm rooting in the Gospel itself. For this reason I spent much the greatest part of my time in the work of preaching and teaching, in residential periods of Bible study with pastors, village teachers, volunteer workers and lay people generally. I was convinced that, while we ought to do whatever we could to strengthen the fragile economic base of the village, the small projects which we could undertake were only significant as signs of something else. In relation to the vast mass of India's rural poverty they were so small as to be ridiculous. But as visible signs accompanying and illustrating the good news which we had to offer, they were significant. What mattered, I believed, was that these small and, humanly speaking, powerless village congregations should be so rooted in Christ that they would find their own resources of hope and courage. For this reason the job I was doing as chairman of the WCC Committee of Twenty-five and the job I was doing as pastor to these rural congregations were intimately linked in my mind. It was a matter of clarifying the great hope which alone could sustain the smaller hopes against repeated disappointment. Several times I passed within a few days from these village visits to the ecumenical discussions and back again and I tried to link them together, bringing the vivid experiences of the 'bottom of the heap' in India to Bossey, and bringing back from our discussions there something for the village congregations.

Closely linked with this was my commitment to the development of high-level ministerial training in Tamil. We had been splendidly served by the college in Bangalore, but as long as the whole of the training was in English it was inevitably dominated by the issues that were agitating Europe and North America. Meanwhile a colossal revival of Tamil culture was going on under the stimulus of C. N. Annadurai and his colleagues. New novels, poetry and drama, and new films were flooding the whole state with new ideas. But the Church was out of effective contact because its theological leadership was oriented towards the English-speaking world. During the whole of this period I was chairman of the governing council of the Tamilnadu Theological College at Tirumaraijur, where we were giving a high-level training in Tamil to ordinands from all the Tamil dioceses under the leadership of Thomas Settler and a fine group of Indian and European teachers.

Equally important for the growth of a truly responsible Indian Church were the plans for the study centre which Kraemer and I had dreamed of during his visit in 1951. I had many meetings about this, but the translation of the dream into actuality was made possible when the International Missionary Council took the matter up and assigned to Glora Wysner the job of midwife for this and several similar projects in other parts of the world. A group of us representing the National Christian Council met with her in Madras on 15 March 1955 and agreed to issue an invitation to Dr Paul Devanandan to become the first director of a Christian Institute for the Study of Religion and Society and to appoint a provisional council to plan with him the details of place, organization and programme. It fell to me to carry the main burden of negotiating the release of Devanandan from his commitment to the YMCA. In September 1955 this was received and the CISRS began officially to function in October 1957. Under the inspired leadership of Devanandan and M. M. Thomas the institute quickly began to give exactly the kind of leadership that was so much needed and it has continued to do so during the subsequent years.

The production of literature appropriate to the needs of village congregations was another major preoccupation. The 'Village Workers' Almanack' was issued annually to provide material for worship and preaching for each Sunday of the year. The 'Church Members' Manual' gave basic teaching material for new

Christians. And we gladly joined in the splendid scheme started earlier by Stephen Neill for Tinnevelley diocese for providing each year four newly written Tamil books for village teachers in biblical, theological and pastoral studies. As part of this programme I contributed a book on *Sin and Salvation* which was later published in English by the SCM Press and then in a number of Asian languages, in Arabic, and in Spanish and Portuguese for use in Latin America. I found as I wrote that book that my thinking had changed in a significant way. Twenty years earlier in writing on this theme I had referred to the Church only in a very marginal way at the end of the essay. In answer to the question 'How does the salvation wrought by Christ become ours?' I had begun with faith and then moved on to speak of the Holy Spirit and the Church. Now I found that I had to begin with the Church – the point at which the unbeliever first comes into contact with the redemptive work of Christ – and then go on to speak of word and sacraments, faith, regeneration and justification. I did not make that switch easily but I found that the experience of missionary work compelled me to make it. I saw that the kind of Protestantism in which I had been nourished belonged to a 'Christendom' context. In a missionary situation the Church had to have a different logical place.

In one part of the diocese an opportunity occurred to put into practice the convictions I had come to about the shape of a truly responsible Church. As the result of a great movement among the Paraiyar and Chuckliar castes in the area of Dharapuram, just over the northern boundary of the diocese, considerable numbers of these people in the area of Oddanchattram – our most northerly pastorate – were asking for baptism. How were we to respond? The traditional answer would have been to launch a big campaign in the American Churches, announce this as a great new evangelistic opportunity, raise a large fund, employ a staff of evangelists and catechists and post them in the villages to start schools, prepare and baptize the inquirers and build a network of churches. We could have done that but it would simply have reproduced the old pattern of dependence, and the movement would go on only so long as there were fresh supplies of foreign money.

With the complete support of the area chairman, Sam Devapragasam, and with the slowly won backing of the diocesan

146

council, we embarked on a quite different way. The essential
elements were:

1 Behind the request for baptism there is always the experience
of someone who has been touched and awakened by the Holy
Spirit to seek this new way. That touch may have come in
different ways – a word spoken by a friend, the testimony of
another life, an answer to prayer, a preaching heard, a dream, a
miraculous deliverance from danger. That touch has awakened
someone to strike out on the new path. The first thing is to find
the person, learn from him what has already happened, make
that the foundation for what follows, and accept him as the
leader whom God has already chosen and given to the new
congregation. No 'mission agent' appointed from outside can
replace him. This man must be acknowledged as leader and the
teacher sent from outside must be seen as helper and friend, not
as controller.

2 As soon as it is clear that the group has made up its mind 'to
turn from idols and serve the living God', baptize without delay.
The traditional practice of making baptism a certificate awarded
on satisfactory completion of a course of teaching subverts the
true order of grace and builds a debilitating Pelagianism into the
life of the Church from the start.

3 Provide a period of three to six months of intensive teaching.
For this purpose we appointed a team of four workers who were
available – like Paul's companions Timothy and Titus and
Tychicus – to spend time with the new congregation, not to take
over their leadership but to be their helpers and teachers in
learning what it means to belong to the household of God. While
the teaching is going on, we found that the new converts were
eager to pass on what they were receiving to their neighbours in
the adjacent village.

4 At the end of the period the new converts were confirmed
and received into full communion. Usually they had by then
started to build a mud-walled chapel for their worship. They
were now a living congregation of the one holy catholic Church.
Often their first action would be to invite the bishop to a
neighbouring village for the baptism of those to whom they had
been giving their witness.

5 A long period of training, normally four years, to enable the
local village leader to assume the full responsibility involved in

ordination. The training was given in short, intense periods of teaching during the seasons when no field work can be done, and by actual leadership in worship under the supervision and guidance of a trained pastor.

6 The work of this village leader to be supported and supplemented by the teaching ministry of the fully trained and salaried pastors who would then have a travelling ministry sustaining but not displacing the local ministry of village leaders.

From 1954 onwards we had the authority of Synod to prepare these village leaders for ordination. Three were in fact ordained before I left the diocese in 1959. My successor did not approve of these ideas and the programme was not continued. Nevertheless the experience of these six years convinced me that it was the right way. During that period more than twenty new village congregations were born, all through the spontaneous witness of the people themselves. And when the militant Hindu Arya Samaj mounted a very powerful anti-Christian propaganda in the area not one of these new congregations was shaken. They were, however small, truly indigenous and responsible expressions of Christian faith. I believed, and I still believe, that this is where the real power of the Gospel is to be seen and known. In a paper I wrote early in 1953 for discussion in the diocese, later published by the International Missionary Council, I wrote:

> When a new congregation understands from the beginning that the responsibility for its own life is a responsibility which it must itself discharge before God, it can stand on its own feet and propagate its own faith without the presence of a resident paid worker. On the other hand there is also abundant evidence to show that if, at the beginning, a new congregation is taught to lean upon a paid worker sent from outside, it will be almost impossible for it to outgrow that dependence.[3]

Madura diocese seemed to me to be as absorbing and challenging an assignment as anyone could wish for. But it was impossible to turn my back on the growing demand for involvement in wider ecumenical work. I did not find it difficult to deal with the flattering invitations of several good friends who obviously thought there were much more important (and lucrative!) jobs to be done elsewhere. But it was hard to know how much time to give to ecumenical happenings. I was appointed a delegate of CSI to the Second Assembly at Evanston and as chairman of 'The Twenty-five' I found on arrival that I was a VIP with a car and a chauffeur at my disposal and that some very able and astute representatives of the media were really anxious to understand what we were trying to say about the Christian hope. But the ecclesiastical leaders were not impressed by our effort, and the report had a generally hostile reception from the Assembly. I was in a difficult position because as chairman of 'The Twenty-five' I had to defend an unpopular document, while as chairman of the committee appointed to draft the 'message' of the Assembly I had to try faithfully to express what the delegates wanted to say. I was told afterwards that I had been too autocratic and probably the charge was just. I think it was a good message in the end, but I found the Assembly as a whole much more difficult than Amsterdam. One of the high spots for me was the moving address of Dag Hammarskjöld. Another was the celebration of the CSI Liturgy in which a very great number shared and of which I had many testimonies that it had been one of the great moments of the Assembly.

Immediately following the Assembly we had another consultation of representatives of united and uniting Churches at the McCormick Seminary for which D. T. Niles and I took turns as chairman. It was altogether a good occasion and brought a real meeting of minds. Michael Ramsey once again played a very important part in the discussions. After the Assembly I had a five-week programme of lecturing and preaching in various parts of the States, during the latter part of which Helen joined me. I had the chance to come to know the leadership of the American Board and also to meet some of the anti-merger Congregationalists who were financing separatist movements in South India. We were guests for a weekend of the much loved Angus and Kitty Dun of Washington of whom my most amusing memory concerns the moment when, during a drive round Washington, the Bishop asked: 'What do you think of this "supplemental ordination"?' I took a deep breath and was about to launch upon a well-argued theological statement when he said: 'As far as I can see, it means that when the Bishop lays on hands, he keeps his fingers crossed.'

Our final stay was at Union Theological Seminary in New York. Along with John Baillie I tried to present the message of

Evanston and was, of course, severely battered on the subject of eschatology. I decided that the Seminary was in danger of succumbing to a sort of a-historical gnosticism and therefore preached a sermon in chapel on 'The Son of God, who loved me and gave himself up for me'. Evidently I succeeded in arousing a more than ordinary amount of theological wrath, for that evening I was 'entertained' by a large body of the teaching staff and had to face an onslaught of angry criticism such as I had rarely experienced. It made me more and more sure that our Committee of Twenty-five had started something important.

I had been elected by the Assembly to the Central Committee but I felt I had been too much away from the diocese and did not attend the meeting in Switzerland in 1955. In 1956, however, I went both to the Central Committee in Hungary and to the preliminary meetings at Herrenalb in South Germany. The Herrenalb meetings involved me in a number of concerns which were to become very important for me later. In the Faith and Order Working Committee I pressed that the question about 'the nature of the unity we seek' should be central to the forthcoming Third Assembly. I had outlined my conviction on this point in the Thomas Lecture given in the University of Chicago two years previously. In that lecture I had answered the question 'What is the proper form of the Church's unity?' as follows: 'First, it must be such that all who are in Christ in any place are, in that place, visibly one fellowship. Second, it must be such that each local community is so ordered and so related to the whole that its fellowship with all Christ's people everywhere, and with all who have gone before and will come after, is made clear. That will mean at least this: a ministry universally recognized and visibly linked with the ministry of the Church throughout the centuries.'[4]

I was also one of the WCC representatives on the Joint Committee of the two World Councils, IMC and WCC, which met at Herrenalb. It was, as I remember, a stormy session. Much friction was being generated by the increasingly vigorous intervention of the WCC's Division of Inter-Church Aid in the areas hitherto the exclusive domain of the mission boards. While the latter had been struggling for decades to wean the 'younger churches' away from financial dependence on the West, the agents of Inter-Church Aid were, it seemed, going all over the place and offering apparently unlimited largesse to these same churches in order that they might become constructively involved in the development programmes for which the code name was 'Rapid Social Change'. An attempt was made to avoid conflict by defining the categories of aid which were proper for the WCC, and the 'Herrenalb categories' were to provide a framework for the operations of both parties for nearly a decade.

In spite of these tensions the Joint Committee was led to issue a formal statement to the effect that the time had come to consider the integration of the two councils into a single body, and both were asked to take the matter onto their agenda with a view to action at the Third Assembly. The most articulate and passionate opposition came from Max Warren of the Church Missionary Society who concluded an eloquent appeal to his fellow-delegates from the IMC with a challenge which echoed the ironic words of Micaiah the son of Imlah: 'Go up to Geneva and prosper!' At Herrenalb I represented the WCC in these discussions. Later I was to be the leader of the IMC team. But from whichever side I had to speak, I was convinced that integration was necessary, that from the point of view of the younger churches the existence of these two rival ecumenical bodies was an absurdity, and that while I admired and loved Max Warren I could not accept his deep distrust of the Church and his (as I thought) too simple belief that a missionary society based on the 'voluntary principle' was exempt from the temptations which beset all large institutions, whether churches or missionary societies.

From Herrenalb we moved to Hungary for the meeting of the Central Committee. It was a time (July–August 1956) of tension and hope which was to erupt a few months later in the streets of Budapest. My first visit was to Debreczen where, along with Hendrikus Berkhof, I preached to a packed congregation. In my diary I noted: 'The sense of eager longing was terrific . . . After the service the crowds seemed almost to cling to us. They wanted to talk and kept pressing little gifts into our hands. In the brief talks I was able to have, the phrase "real believers" came several times. There was an undertone of sorrow and wistfulness. We were the first outside church visitors without official Budapest interpreters.' Afterwards I had a moving letter from Professor Kallay who had been my interpreter.

At the Central Committee my main preoccupation was in the

group chaired by Angus Dunn which produced the statement on 'Christian Witness, Proselytism and Religious Liberty' – a matter of special sensitivity between Orthodox Churches and Protestant missions and therefore vital for the discussion of integration. The most memorable event of the plenary sessions was a powerful address from K. H. Ting of China – the first Chinese presence at a WCC meeting since 1949. His speech was a hard-hitting attack on the imperialist overtones of traditional missionary work and a claim (at least as I heard it) that only with its ending could the Church in China be truly free and responsible. The statement was so powerful that I seriously wondered whether it was right for me to stay in Madurai. I shared my question with Ting and for an hour he pleaded with me not to leave India, giving, as an example to convince me, the crucial importance of the work of R. O. Hall in laying (as Ting affirmed) the foundations for the real selfhood of the Chinese Church.

The other memorable conversation occurred during a brief halt of our bus in a small country town where we stopped for a drink. A crowd of local folk gathered round us and one of them asked Niemöller: 'Are you a pastor?' 'Yes.' 'From which country?' 'Germany.' 'Then tell me, where is Niemöller?'

These summer meetings in 1956 took me away from the diocese for nearly eight weeks. Early in June we had installed John as a boarder at Kodaikanal School, and Helen had sailed home with Janet so that she could make a start at school in England. After the WCC meetings in Hungary I had nearly five weeks in Britain, including a brief but lovely spell of holiday at Rothbury with Helen and the three girls. When I returned to India, Helen stayed on to see Janet settled at Walthamstow Hall and then returned to India by sea.

In the following year I was again away for nearly twelve weeks in Europe and North America. The first engagement was a conference at Bossey of seventy pastors and missionaries about the mission of the Church in the contemporary world. I had been asked to give a lecture for which I was quite unprepared. I therefore spent the entire night hours on the plane from Bombay to Rome reading right through the New Testament and noting every reference to 'the world'. The result of this was to set my mind moving in a new direction in which it was to travel for the next ten years. My thoughts for the past decade had been centred in the Church. This fresh exposure to the word of God set me thinking about the work of God in the world outside the Church. The result was a lecture in which I advanced the thesis that 'what we are witnessing is the process by which more and more of the human race is being gathered up into that history whose centre is the cross, and whose end is the final judgement and mercy of God'. I was talking not just about missions but about the total shift from a cyclical to a linear way of understanding history, brought about by the impact of 'development'.[5] This thesis was taken by one of the participants, Arendt van Leeuwen, as the starting-point for a very ambitious and influential book on *Christianity and World History*.[6] As far as I was concerned, this was the beginning of a shift in perspective which enabled me to understand the concern of people like Hoekendijk and Paul Lehmann which I had failed to understand at Willingen. It meant that I began the 'secular decade' of the 1960s with some enthusiasm for the 'secular interpretation of the Gospel', and was the more ready to see its weaknesses before that decade ended.

In the United States my first assignment was to preach at the inauguration of the union of the Congregational with the Evangelical and Reformed Churches to form the United Church of Christ. A heavy lecturing programme was interrupted by a spell of illness in which I was most lovingly cared for by Bishop Hobson of Southern Ohio. From 20 July to 7 August I was at Yale Divinity School for the annual cluster of WCC meetings. The Faith and Order Commission elected me as vice-chairman and I was elected to a committee to consider the future of Faith and Order within the WCC. This was to give me an opportunity to press further the issue of the nature of the unity we seek, and to urge that it have a central place in the Third Assembly.

In the Central Committee my main job was the drafting and presenting of a statement on IMC–WCC integration, especially in view of the strong opposition of the Orthodox, for whom 'mission' meant destructive proselytizing by irresponsible Protestant sects. The integration discussion was full of tensions. Apart from the deep suspicions of the Orthodox there was the clash between the younger people who were revolting against the 'colonial' style of missions and the older ones for whom the old patterns were sacred. During the meeting at Yale I tried to defuse some of these tensions both by means of an informal meeting of third-world churchmen and younger missionaries and also by means of personal discussions with Orthodox leaders. The statement we eventually produced did prepare the way for the integration four years later.

As at many other ecumenical meetings I was glad to relieve the times of weariness with the composition of appropriate limericks. Perhaps this is the only point at which I might refer to this because the limerick in question achieved a wide circulation. It was a hot and drowsy afternoon. George Florovsky was making a very long and largely incomprehensible speech. Franklin Fry in the chair was maintaining a firm and soldierly appearance, as of one in full control. Ernest Payne, the vice-chairman, at his side, was visibly wilting. The following lines seemed to flow unbidden onto the pad on my knee:

> Florovsky is speaking again.
> His meaning is not at all plain.
> But while Franklin C. Fry
> Will never say die
> It clearly gives Ernest A. Payne.

Unfortunately D. T. Niles at my side saw, read, seized and passed the paper along the row. I don't think the chairman ever understood why the committee's decorum so suddenly disintegrated.

On the way back to India I spent four days in Iran as guest both of the Presbyterians in Tehran and of the Anglican bishop (Thompson) of Isfahan. The Anglicans in particular were eager to discuss the possibility of union even, apparently, if it meant giving up episcopacy. I felt sad that the Presbyterians seemed to be losing their trained leadership in a continuing 'brain drain' to the USA. I found the small Anglican community very impressive and this was the occasion when I first came to know and admire a young priest named Hassan Deqani Tafti. From Iran I returned home via Zahidan, Karachi and Bombay and within a few days I was again fully immersed in the usual business of the diocese. Helen had meanwhile been with John in Kodai. After I returned, John went back into boarding and Helen joined me in Madurai. The house felt very strange with no children, though John was with us for the cold-weather holiday, and there were other boys in the compound for him to play with. After New Year we took him back to Kodai, and then Helen and I were on our own again until the summer.

14
Madurai: A New Assignment

In the last few days of 1957 a letter came which was to bring a new and totally unexpected change in our lives. It was a confidential inquiry from Dr Alford Carleton of the American Board to find out whether I would be willing to be considered for the post of General Secretary of the International Missionary Council. The Assembly of the IMC was due to convene at Accra, Ghana, over the turn of the year. The two main matters on the agenda would be the launching of the four-million-dollar Theological Education Fund and the question of integration with the World Council of Churches. It was expected that Charles Ranson would leave the General Secretaryship in order to become Director of the TEF, of which he was the originator and architect. This would mean that someone was needed to take his place and (if integration were agreed) to carry the IMC through the final negotiations and into the integrated Council and to become the director of the proposed Division of World Mission and Evangelism in the WCC. Would I be willing to come if invited?

One paragraph of the letter I sent in reply will show how one part of my mind responded to the suggestion:

The possibility which your letter raises is one which touches my deepest convictions about the future of the Christian task in the world during the next few decades. I have come to feel increasingly that there is a dangerous dichotomy at the present time between what we (in the missionary enterprise) are saying and what we are doing. This in two respects: (1) We are saying that our working picture is not the nineteenth-century one but one of a global fellowship facing a global task, with the missionary frontier running through every village. But we are not acting according to that picture. We are (if you will forgive a horribly crude metaphor) trying to maintain a bunch of adolescent children tied up with a set of uncut umbilical cords to their mothers. (2) We are saying that we have recovered a radically missionary theology of the Church. But the actual structure of our Churches (younger as well as older) does not reflect that theology. On the contrary it continues placidly to reflect the static 'Christendom' theology of the eighteenth century. At Yale I said that I supported IMC-WCC integration simply as a preliminary step to the much more radical changes which I believed to be necessary in the whole structure and functioning of the missionary enterprise. This last weekend I spent with a WSCF conference trying to plead with them that the WSCF should take up the task which the Churches are still too tradition-bound to undertake, and do the pioneer thinking needed for such radical changes. You will therefore understand that your letter-which is lying in the mail waiting for me on my return – had something of the character of a providential word to me personally. But whether the leadership of the Churches would welcome to such a responsible position a person advocating these ideas, I do not know.

Added to these considerations was the fact that we had decided that the family needed a home in England and that from our furlough in 1958 Helen should remain with them. But my emotional ties with the diocese were terribly strong. I could not bear to think of cutting them. And I believed that two or three more years were needed before the diocese should be asked to elect an Indian bishop. I said I hoped I would not be asked to leave before 1960.

On 4 January I received a cable from Accra asking me to accept nomination for the post. I replied by cable that I was not available before 1960. The next word I had was a letter from one of the Indian delegates informing me that I had been elected chairman. From the official letter I learned that, in the hope that I would later accept the full-time appointment, search was being made for someone to hold the Secretary's post. During the ensuing weeks I had to wrestle with conflicting calls. Those who knew that I had been proposed for the Secretary's post urged me to accept. Letters from Paul Devanandan, Norman Goodall, Visser 't Hooft and others were hard to resist. I did not want to go. I loved the Tamil people and country and had learned to be at home in their language and ways of life. I loved the Church of South India and believed that it was tremendously important for the whole movement for unity. I loved the work of a bishop. I could not bear the thought of cutting these bonds and becoming an ecumenical office-wallah. It was Michael Hollis who persuaded me that I ought to go. It was, he suggested, a clear call from God which I had not sought and did not want, and I should not easily refuse it. Moreover, he thought that the CSI would be willing to second me for this service, giving me leave of absence for five years so that I could see the integration through and be free to return to South India. On these terms I felt I could and must agree. And it was clear that if I were to go, there ought not to be too much delay, for a bishop on the way out is in a weak position. And so in March 1958 I wrote that, provided the CSI was willing to second me for five years, I would be available from 1 July 1959. In September 1958 the Synod Executive gave the necessary permission for me to serve for a period of five years from July 1959 'as a bishop of the Church of South India without diocesan charge, released for service with the International Missionary Council'.

Meanwhile, willy-nilly, I was chairman of the IMC. I had never seen a copy of its constitution and had no idea what the duties of the chairman were. I knew that, since its inception, it had had only two chairmen: John R. Mott for the first thirty years and John Mackay for the last ten. How could I possibly occupy the place of these giants? And many confidential letters were coming in to tell me that the IMC staff was in considerable disarray. They were not of one mind on the matter of integration. The Ghana Assembly had made the decision in principle, but there had been little unity and clarity of thinking. Above all there was needed a theological lead. The discussion of integration had been too much on the level of administrative adjustment. There had not emerged a clear and compelling vision of the future shape of missions.

And I was in Madurai with all the daunting and demanding tasks of a diocese of the CSI, and of the National Christian Council of which I was still an officer. The pressure of these responsibilities continued unabated. But I was more and more involved in correspondence with the IMC staff, most of whom were personally unknown to me.

We were due for normal furlough in the summer of 1958 and

had agreed to break our journey at Beirut so that I could give two series of lectures for the Near East Christian Council and the Near East School of Theology. In view of the strong opposition to integration which was being voiced by Orthodox member churches of the WCC it was proposed by Metropolitan James and Visser 't Hooft that I should pay a formal visit to the Ecumenical Patriarch in Istanbul with the hope of smoothing the path. We had also a long-cherished ambition to visit Rome, and Bishop George Bell had urged me to do so and had arranged introductions to several Catholic theologians there.

The twelve-day stay in Lebanon enabled me to have contact with representatives of the churches in the area and also, along with Helen and John, to visit Biblos and Baalbeck with its gigantic ruins. We saw the sockets from which the huge marble pillars had been taken to support the dome of St Sophia under which we were to stand in awe a few days later. At Istanbul we were received by a representative of the Patriarch, drove past the mighty walls which had defended Christendom against Islam for so many centuries, and the ancient cannon (made in 'Christian' Venice) which had breached those defences. To be the guests of the Patriarch Athenagoras was a truly great experience. He received my visit with the greatest kindness, courtesy and understanding, and I left with the feeling of having been in the company of a great and noble Christian. In Rome we were met by Margaret and a friend and we had several days of sight-seeing including a long visit to the new excavations under St Peter's, guided by Father Kirchbaum the archaeologist in charge of the work. I was also able to have some very good discussions with theologians interested in the Church of South India and the Faith and Order Movement. The longest and most useful was with Father Boyer, SJ, the President of Unitas, on the whole question of infallibility and impeccability. With Cardinal Tisserant I made little progress, as theology seemed to be crowded out by the fear of communism taking India over.

After four wonderful days in Florence we stopped briefly in Geneva for talk with Wim and other members of WCC staff and went on to London and to Edinburgh for the General Assembly to which I had to bring the greetings of the CSI and in which I had to listen sadly to the debate on the famous 'Bishop's Report'.

For the next six months our home was again in Edinburgh but I was almost continually on the move both in the UK and abroad. In June I was in the USA and Canada for the first meeting of the Committee of the Theological Education Fund, with officers and staff of the IMC, and with leaders of the US mission boards. I had had misgivings about the TEF because its emphasis seemed to be on a concept of 'excellence' which was wholly western. I had sought out Mr Yorke Allen, the man deputed by Mr John D. Rockefeller to make a preliminary survey of needs and possibilities, and had urged on him the importance of the non-European languages, but found him totally allergic to my ideas. However, the first meeting of the new TEF committee was reassuring and I was impressed by Bengt Sundkler's argument that it may be necessary to achieve the highest standards in English-medium theological work before returning to recover the proper primacy of the mother tongue.

In July I had a long series of visits in Germany, including Berlin, Bielefeld, Dortmund, Wuppertal, Kaiserswerth, and Hamburg. These were partly to share with German church leaders the Indian experience of unity, and partly to talk with the missionary society leaders about integration. Obviously the two concerns were interlocked and my thesis that the Church must itself be understood as a missionary society seemed to come to many in my audiences as a new idea. It was an especial joy to have long discussions with Pastor Bodelschwingh of Bethel, Präses Scharf of Berlin, Professor Gollwitzen, Klaus von Bismarck and Präses Wilm. Von Bismarck and I were tempted to think about eschatology while we sat in the back seat of Wilm's car and watched the countryside passing at 150 kilometres an hour, but at one of our stops, von Bismarck made a remark that has always remained with me: 'That' (pointing to Wilm) 'is the sort of pastor a real layman needs.' I understood what he meant. He did not need someone to arrange 'Church activities' for him. He needed someone to bring to him the healing grace of God in the midst of the fearful dilemmas and responsibilities of public life.

The German trip was interrupted by three days in Geneva for meetings of the Committee on the Future of Faith and Order and the Working Committee which followed. These meetings gave me the chance which I had long sought to thrust the question of the nature of the unity we seek into the centre of the WCC's agenda. The first paragraph of the report of the Committee embodied my convictions:

It is our strong conviction that to proclaim the essential oneness of the Church of Christ involves facing the question: What kind of unity does God demand of His Church? We agree that no one definition of the nature of unity can be a condition of membership in the WCC, but Faith and Order exists in order to stand for the unity of the Church as the will of God and for a ceaseless effort to know what obedience to that will means concretely. Only so can it be 'manifest'. The WCC can have no 'neutrality' on whether that question is answered or not. Clearly the World Council is not in a position to say what the answer is in all its fullness; if it were, our quest for the 'manifest unity' would already be at an end. As the Toronto statement of 1950 put it (pp. 8–9; para. VI.1), 'the Ecumenical Movement inevitably creates a situation in which the relationship of the Churches can not remain unchanged . . . the Council exists to break the deadlock between the Churches'. All the Churches in the Council confront each other under the demand of God Himself that they should learn from Him the nature of the unity which we seek. It has been characteristic of Faith and Order to recognize that patience and thoroughness are needed for this task. But it is also necessary to recognize that in such matters we are not entirely free to proceed at our own pace, that events are forcing upon us various kinds of Christian co-operation, and that if we do not find the right form of churchly unity we shall find ourselves remaining content with a form of organizational unity which is not a true churchly unity because it leaves unfulfilled many of the central requirements of the Church's life. There is need therefore for a proper sense of urgency lest we lose the time that God gives us. Faith and Order must constantly press upon the Council and the Churches the fact that the question of unity is one upon which an answer has to be given, and that to give no answer means to be shut up to the wrong answer. Specifically Faith and Order must raise this question:

(a) in Assemblies so far as its programme for the whole WCC allows;

(b) in Central Committee from time to time as best serves, as well as in the Theological Commissions which all at least bear upon the answer.

These ideas were not universally welcomed in the subsequent sessions of the Working Committee. The Orthodox insisted that they were not committed by membership in the WCC to any particular view the Council might develop about unity. Some of the Lutherans objected to the stress on 'churchly unity' which would mean structural uniformity at the cost of doctrinal laxity. Some of the old stalwarts of Faith and Order feared that the traditional leisurely pace of its work would be threatened. The idea that decisions might have to be made was alarming to the academic soul! There was reluctance to allow Faith and Order to be represented even by observers at meetings to discuss specific plans of union. These fears were to be expressed again when the report came to the Central Committee in Denmark later in the summer.

From Germany I returned to London for a brief visit to the Lambeth Conference. I had been urging the Archbishop in letters from Madurai that the CSI should be represented at the Conference by means of 'observers' or 'fraternal delegates', and that it was very hard for the ex-Anglican element in South India to be completely excluded from the Conference. He had not been able to accept this suggestion, but in April he had written very cordially inviting me to come as his guest 'so that there might be a celebration of the Holy Communion with the CSI liturgy which, of course, all the bishops would be free to attend if they wished to, and certainly some would wish to communicate'. I was delighted to accept this invitation and the service took place on the morning of 18 July. As fellow-ministers I had Leslie Brown, then Bishop of Uganda, E. C. John studying in Cambridge, and V. Gnanamuthu working in a Methodist circuit. About 160 of the bishops received communion, the first four being the two English Archbishops (Fisher and Ramsey), Sherrill, Presiding Bishop of the US Church and Yashiro of Japan. At the end Mrs Fisher leaned over, squeezed Helen's hand and said 'Lovely'. It was a healing moment.

162

Ten miles up the Coquet valley from Rothbury the village of Harbottle lies at the foot of the Cheviot hills, and its one church (now, alas, abandoned) was Presbyterian. Through the kindness of the minister we were able to occupy the manse for four weeks in the summer, and for that brief spell I was the minister of a congregation which included the shepherds' families whose homes had so often made us welcome on our Cheviot walks. All six of us were together and we had a wonderful holiday. It was interrupted for me by the necessity to attend the meetings of the IMC/WCC Joint Committee at Nyborgstrand in Denmark. This was hard going. I wrote in my diary: 'I am impressed by the spiritual difficulties of this work.' The two sides knew that integration was necessary but they did not fully trust each other. Only one shaft of humour lightens the scene in my memory. Picture a long room with a row of mission board executives down one side and a row of church officials down the other. The question is the old one – the clash of policies about financial aid for the 'younger churches'. Guns are firing from both sides. Suddenly everyone remembers that there is, in fact, one representative of these 'younger churches' present: Dr Thakur Das from Pakistan has been sitting at the bottom end of the table, quietly smoking. All heads turn in his direction. 'What is the opinion of the younger churches?' Thakur Das slowly removes his pipe and the oracle speaks. 'If this animal has two teats, I don't mind getting hold of both.'

Immediately after the Harbottle holiday I had to return to Nyborgstrand for the meetings of the WCC Central Committee. I was responsible for the Bible studies and was much involved in advocating and defending the proposals for a new and more active role for Faith and Order. I urged again that while the patient, long-term theological study programme must be continued, it must not be based on the assumption that no conclusions will ever be reached. This view was naturally alarming to some members, but the report had a favourable hearing in spite of the fact that it did call for a change in direction. The Nyborgstrand meeting remains in my memory chiefly because of the sermon of George Bell. It was to be his last public contribution to the Ecumenical Movement which he had served with such devotion, and it was the speech of a man still pressing forward towards the goal.

From Nyborgstrand I went on to a series of meetings in Copenhagen and Helsinki with the four northern missions councils. It was part of the necessary exploration of the constituency of which I was now chairman. I was not encouraged by the opening remark of my host at one of the numerous dinners which were laid on: 'Well, Bishop Newbigin, I don't believe in giving responsibility to natives, do you?' I was beginning to understand the dimensions of my new job.

It was clear that integration could not be a merely structural matter but that it involved profound psychological, cultural and, above all, theological issues. The remark just quoted revealed the extent to which missions were still tied up with the psychology of colonialism. It was not surprising that the very idea of missions was being rejected by younger people in both older and younger churches, that the word 'missionary' was being dropped in favour of 'fraternal worker', and that inter-church aid under the umbrella of the World Council was seen as a very acceptable replacement for the discredited enterprise of missions. The problem was not primarily administrative; it was theological. How could the fundamental Gospel calling to mission be re-stated in terms which were free from the stench of colonialism? I had tried to sketch an answer to the question in my first meeting with the officers and staff of the IMC in Canada. I had been encouraged to develop it. I accordingly wrote a 12,000-word paper which was taken as a basis for discussion at a three-day consultation in Oxford of younger church and mission board leaders. In the light of the discussion there the paper was revised and published as *One Body, One Gospel, One World*. Widely translated and circulated in several editions it served as a rallying point for discussion about the proposed integration. It sought to affirm the validity of missions as distinct activities within the total mission of the Church and to define their specific character in terms of *intention*. While all the activities of the Church have a missionary *dimension*, there are needed specific activities which have the *intention* of crossing the frontier between faith and unbelief – and that frontier is no longer the old geographical one, but runs through every land.

After the Oxford meeting I paid a visit to Geneva to share with the World Council staff the thinking of the IMC. Although there was a good discussion, I was made painfully aware of the deep scepticism with which some of the younger members of the staff viewed this attempt to rehabilitate a discredited concept. It was a signal to indicate some of the struggles to come.

During the remainder of 1958 I was busy with speaking engagements in various parts of the country, and with the delivery of the Noble Lectures at Harvard University which were later published as *A Faith for this One World?*. This was an attempt to state the case for the missionary calling in the context of proposals for the unity of all the religions. I was the guest of Nathan and Anne Pusey whose friendship has been a great enrichment to my life. I was introduced by him to many of his colleagues, with whom I had rewarding discussions, the most memorable being with Paul Tillich whom I found a very gracious person. On 7 January I returned to India, leaving Helen and all the children behind.

My last six months in Madurai were packed with all the normal duties, joys and sorrows. Although I was without the family, I had good company. Following the retirement of Raymond Dudley, the American Board had appointed Telfer Mook in his place. Telfer had both legal and theological training and a mastery of Japanese, but had no previous experience of India. It was therefore agreed that he should share my home and my programme for these six months, and it was a great joy to have Telfer, Jane and their small daughter Margie during the final days in Madurai.

In May I took part in the founding Assembly of the East Asia Christian Conference at Kuala Lumpur. It was a fine meeting, full of fresh thinking. D. T. Niles was the main architect and driving force. He had, in my view, the right idea about how such an organization should work. There was to be no central office. The staff would be located in different places, rooted in local situations but keeping in touch through frequent meetings. As long as he remained at the head of the EACC this was the pattern, and it made for variety, freshness and a real relevance to actual situations.

At the first Assembly Niles instituted the John R. Mott memorial lectures, and the first set was given by Niles, Goodall, Visser 't Hooft and me. In my two lectures I posed the dilemma of the foreign missionary. On the one hand, looking at the Asian Churches, he is tempted to call for the total withdrawal of foreign workers and funds as the only way to enable the Church to become truly itself. 'I am tempted', I said, 'to pray that somehow some catastrophe might happen by which foreign aid was cut off and the Church was compelled to depend on God alone.' But on the other hand, looking at the vast unfinished task of evangelism, how could I responsibly tell the sending churches: 'Your gifts and your missionaries are no longer needed'? The dilemma arises, I argued, from the fact that we have adopted wrong missionary methods, methods modelled on the style of colonialism and not on the sovereignty of the Spirit as the true agent of mission. I argued for a style of mission on the lines sketched by Roland Allen and called for a radical reordering of the pattern of Church and ministry as the only way out of the dilemma.

It was these ideas which I hoped to develop later in the WCC study on 'The Missionary Structure of the Congregation'. In the event, this study was swept into the powerful current of secularization which flowed through the following decade, and went in a direction different from what I had hoped.

Early in June I paid my last visit to the Oddanchattram pastorate for the ordination of the first three 'local' pastors and for a large number of confirmations and baptisms. In one village those baptized included some of the high-caste landowners. One of these proved to be very well versed in the Hindu scriptures. I asked him: 'What made you decide to be a Christian?' Before he could answer, one of the (pariah) Christians quietly said: 'I told him', and the landlord at once acknowledged that it was so. In my diary I wrote: 'So the Spirit uses the things that are despised to bring to nought the things that are.' A small incident, but it seemed to affirm the rightness of the way we had tried to follow.

At the end of June I left Madurai for good. It was very hard, for I did not want to go. In my diary I wrote:

There was a great crowd at the station. At the end they just stood in a great mass and gazed and gazed at me till I felt I would weep. We sang (a Tamil lyric) and at last the train moved off and the group became only a blob in the distance . . . There was a group at Kodai Road station with fruit and flowers and honey and they asked me to bless them before the train left. At Dindigul there was another big group with many presents.

Then that was left behind too, and as the train went on through the night I tried to face the fact that I was no longer their bishop. I realized that I loved them and that they loved me and I prayed that God would keep them and would help me still to be a bishop even in this new task which is so strange and perplexing.

15

London: The International Missionary Council

It was indeed a deeply perplexing situation into which I had been called. As General Secretary of the IMC I would be expected to give some kind of lead to missionary planning and policy. But in which direction? Seven years ago, at Willingen, one of the greatest of missionary leaders, Max Warren, had said: 'We have to be ready to see the day of missions, as we have known them, as having already come to an end.'[1] And at the Ghana Assembly Walter Freytag had spoken in a poignant phrase of 'the lost directness of missions'.[2] There was no longer the simple call to go and bring the Gospel to the heathen. It was a matter of supporting 'younger churches'. The vast majority of the missionaries sent by the churches and societies involved in the IMC were not sent to preach the Gospel to unbelievers but to serve the churches as teachers, doctors, administrators, technical 'experts' and theological educators. And most of them, especially the powerful North American boards, were content to have it so. The missiology of W. E. Hocking and the 'Laymen's Inquiry' was by no means extinct. There was immense faith in the validity of modern western technology as a tool for 'development', but much less conviction about the validity of the Gospel as 'the power of God for salvation'. Mission was being absorbed into inter-church aid.

And in a sense this was right. It was necessary that the Churches in Asia (for example) should be released from the one-track relation with a western mission board and be free to develop mature relations with other Churches quite outside the traditional ones which were so loaded with the spiritual legacy of paternalism. Without this, as Freytag among many others urged, they would not become genuinely free.

The coming into existence of the World Council of Churches and the new move to extend the operations of inter-church aid beyond Europe, were a providentially given opportunity to create a new pattern of relations. But because the missionary agencies were in fact much more in the business of inter-church aid than in the business of missions as traditionally understood, the entry of the WCC was perceived by them as a threat. The logical step for missions would surely be to accept wholeheartedly the existence of an agency of inter-church aid as an opportunity to recover a proper concentration on the specifically missionary task. But, first, missions cannot bypass the Churches which they have brought to birth; missionary outreach must therefore be in the form of inter-church aid for *mission*. Therefore, secondly, it becomes necessary to define a missionary *focus* within the total operation of inter-church aid. How can that focus be defined in practice? Is help for a hospital in a backward rural area mission or not? Is action to challenge social wrongs mission or not? How can a world organization embody in its structures a valid way of relating inter-church aid and mission? How can the huge new resources made available to inter-church aid agencies in the booming economies of the West be used in ways that do not destroy the real freedom of the younger churches struggling with dire poverty? Does inter-church aid with its short-term *ad hoc* 'projects' offer an adequate alternative to the life-long involvement of the traditional missionary who learns the language and becomes part of the culture of the people to whom he is sent?

Added to these basic problems was the profound difference in ethos and organization between the IMC and the WCC. The latter was rapidly building up a very large staff in Geneva, which necessarily became a centre of initiatives for action and study of all kinds. The IMC had a very small staff divided between three offices in New York, London and East Asia, made no attempt to create a public image of itself, and saw its role as that of a servant to the national councils which constituted its membership. Apart from the emergency wartime programme for orphaned missions and the new and untried model of the Theological Education Fund, the IMC had not engaged in large operations. Its very small but exceptionally gifted staff had provided a resource to help national councils to recognize and cope with the emerging problems of a rapidly changing world.

I found it very hard to know what I ought to be trying to do. I had no experience of the operation of the high-powered church and mission bureaucracies into which I was suddenly introduced. My ignorance was vast and profound. I remember that on one of my first days in Edinburgh House I had to cope with an urgent question concerning Christian literature for French-speaking West Africa. Up to that moment I had hardly been aware of the fact that such an area existed! Fortunately I inherited from Erik Nielsen the services of Marjorie Sandle as my secretary, one of that remarkable group of able and devoted women which the IMC had attracted into its service. Her amused tolerance of my abysmal ignorance, her cheerful readiness to engage in whatever games the ecumenical circus was playing at any moment, and her total competence kept me both from thinking too well of myself and from appearing too incompetent to others.

The summer of 1959 was so filled with meetings that I had little time to wonder about which of a hundred different lines was the important one to pursue. There were meetings of the IMC Administrative Committee and of the TEF in Paris, a big conference at Thessalonica on 'The Christian Responsibility for Areas of Rapid Social Change' and the usual cluster of WCC committees at Spittal in Austria, in Athens and on the lovely island of Rhodes where the Central Committee were the guests of the Church of Greece. The Thessalonica meeting reflected the dynamic leadership of M. M. Thomas and Paul Abrecht. It developed strategies for helping the younger churches, especially in Africa, to become constructively involved in national development as the new governments took over from the colonial powers. It proposed, and the Central Committee later authorized the seeking of 'an international fund to promote additional experiments in technical assistance under Christian auspices', and the IMC was invited to collaborate. Obviously it was dealing with issues in which missions had been involved for decades. But its atmosphere was, understandably, antipathetic to traditional missions. To compound the problem, the one missionary who had been invited to address the conference was a disaster. His speech was an unconscious caricature of the nineteenth-century missionary as perceived by the younger generation. It merely served to confirm the image of missions as the religious aspect of colonialism. The IMC was challenged to help swing the resources of missions behind these courageous new initiatives. But where, in all this, was the role of evangelism?

At Spittal in Austria I took part for the last time in the Faith and Order Working Committee and had to resign from my place as vice-chairman, being now a staff secretary. As a result of the discussions in the previous summer I had been asked to prepare a paper stating what I meant by 'churchly unity' and the debate on this paper resulted in the following minute addressed to the Central Committee:

> The Faith and Order Movement was born in the hope that it would be, under God, a help to the 'churches' in realizing His will for the unity of the Church. The formation of the World Council of Churches and the incorporation of Faith and Order in it, have changed the circumstances under which Faith and Order works, but have not changed its purpose. We have become convinced that the time has come for a reaffirmation of this purpose, and for a re-examination of the means by which Faith and Order should, within the World Council of Churches, seek its realization.
>
> We believe that the unity which is both God's will and His gift to His Church is one which brings all in each place[3] who confess Christ Jesus as Lord into a fully committed fellowship with one another through one baptism into Him, preaching the one Gospel and breaking the one bread, and having a corporate life reaching out in witness and service to all; and which at the same time unites them with the whole Christian fellowship in all places and all ages in such wise that ministry and members are acknowledged by all, and that all can act and speak together as occasion requires for the tasks to which God calls the Church.
>
> It is for such true *churchly* unity that we believe we and all the World Council must pray and work. Such a vision has indeed been the inspiration of the Faith and Order Movement in the past, and we reaffirm that this is still our goal. We recognize that the brief definition of our objective which we have given above leaves many questions unanswered. We can see that its achievement involves nothing less than a death and rebirth for many forms of church life as we have known them. We believe that nothing less costly can finally suffice.

At its meeting in Rhodes the Central Committee agreed that 'the issues of "churchly unity" would be discussed in the section on unity in the Third Assembly'. Because of my new responsibilities I was no longer involved in the processes by which the New Delhi Assembly did eventually adopt substantially the wording of this minute. At that time I hoped and believed that the WCC had really committed itself to something beyond the ecclesiological neutrality of the Toronto declaration. Events in the following decade were, however, to prove that I was too optimistic. The impact of the Second Vatican Council would relegate the issue of local unity to the margin and bring back into the centre of the stage the development of theological discussion among globally organized denominations which show little sign of readiness to disappear.

At the Rhodes meeting my main concern was with the debate about integration and especially about seeking to reassure the Orthodox. It was clear that while there was still opposition, integration would probably be accepted in a form which would enable the member councils of the IMC to continue to have a significant role in the integrated WCC.

The meeting was notable for a most wise and sensitive paper from the Division of Inter-Church Aid setting out its vision of its distinctive task *vis-à-vis* that of the missions. I was particularly grateful for the following sentences in the paper:

Inter-Church Aid as hitherto conceived does not produce, and is not likely to produce, that kind of servant of Christ and the Church who, standing at the meeting place of the missionary outreach and the growing Church which results from it, bears in himself the responsibility for all the real and imaginary sins of the missionary enterprise in the past, endures all the criticisms that he is really a vestige of a dying imperialism, responds to maximum demands and yet is content with minimum authority, because he has responded to a specific call of God, to a specific form of life service. While the procedures of Inter-Church Aid make possible a great deal of flexibility in the concentration of resources upon areas of need in pioneering projects in the hinterland between church and mission, and in the bringing of special aid for special purposes, they can never be a substitute for, though they may be complementary to, the continuing and sustained relationships of churches to one another which are established in the missionary enterprise.

I found this a very moving signal of understanding from the 'other side'.

I came home for a glorious family holiday on the Isle of Arran and then, in the middle of September, started my new career as an ecumenical bureaucrat sitting behind a desk in Edinburgh House and joining the cataract of commuters in the daily rush-hour. For three months we found a temporary home in Kew and then, on a day of freezing fog, moved into a house in Bromley, Kent, which was to be our home for the next two years.

My room was the one Bill Paton had occupied, and his portrait hung on the wall to remind me of the formidable job I had inherited. But I did not spend much time there. During eighteen of the next twenty-four months I was travelling. I suppose that (perhaps unconsciously) I saw my new job in the terms to which I had become accustomed by the previous experience of a missionary and a bishop. The units for which I had to be concerned were now not village pastorates but national councils. Yet the principles were the same. They must be visited so that I could understand their problems, know their leaders personally and become aware of the points at which help from outside would be welcome. And, as in Madurai, the core of the programme of such visits must be Bible study. If missions were to recover a sense of direction, if in the circumstances of integration we were to discern the distinctive missionary focus within the total life of the worldwide Church, then the only way was to open ourselves afresh to the biblical perspectives. I felt that there was a danger that I might see everything through Indian and Asian spectacles and therefore decided to concentrate on the other continents. I set about planning long tours in Africa and Latin America and visits to mission councils in Europe and North America. I had already, before accepting the new appointment, promised to lead Bible studies at the national conference of Australian Churches, and the visit was extended to cover New Zealand and the Pacific. There were also many invitations to talk to students and, in gratitude for all that I owed to the SCM, I felt that these had to have a high priority.

Over the turn of the year 1959–60 I was part of the great Ecumenical Student Conference on the Christian World Mission at Athens, Ohio, attended by 3600 students of whom 1000 were from overseas. In the years following I have met people all over the world for whom that conference was a turning-point. The mornings were divided between Bible studies which were my responsibility and addresses by Martin Luther King. Because of the great numbers we were divided between two halls and, to my lasting regret, I was never able to hear that great man. We could only greet each other briefly as we passed every day on the way to the audience the other had left. I believe that it was from those meetings that the first impetus was created for student leadership in the civil rights struggle in the South.

From the conference I went on to a series of meetings with mission and church leaders in Canada and then right across the Pacific to Australia. The letter of greeting from my old Cambridge friend, Archbishop Frank Woods of Melbourne, should have warned me of what was in store: 'Don't let them kill you in Sydney; we would rather do it in Melbourne.' In the course of a month's visit I had to give forty major public addresses plus eighteen radio and television programmes, many of which were re-broadcast several times. The great event was the first national conference of Australian Churches which was a truly heart-warming occasion during which I had the joy of sharing leadership with M. M. Thomas, Masao Takenaka, Hans-Reudi Weber and Renuka Mukerji. It did seem that this was an occasion when old denominational and theological barriers were lowered and trust was created at a deep level. Next followed a two weeks' tour of New Zealand and then a week in Fiji to bring together the representatives of the scattered and divided Pacific Island Churches and to lay the foundations for the first conference of these Churches to be held in the following year. While in Fiji I was able to contact the Indian community and to explore ways of enlisting the help of the Churches in India for the work of the Fijian Indian congregations.

The journey back through the United States was punctuated by a number of conferences with mission and church leaders and I then had a spell mostly at home and on short visits to various European countries. A crucial event was the conference called at Strasbourg in July 1960 by the World's Student Christian Federation on 'The Life and Mission of the Church'. It was the brain-child of D. T. Niles and Philippe Maury who believed, as I did, that there was an emerging theological consensus about the missionary nature of the Church and that the coming generation

174

of student leaders could be captured and fired by the vision so that a new generation of ecumenical leaders could be prepared to take the place of those who were growing old. There was an immensely impressive array of speakers including even Karl Barth, but the event proved very different from the expectations. To quote the report in the WSCF's journal: 'It must have been striking to everyone how much indifference there was to the theological issues and ecumenical achievements of an earlier generation.' The convictions to which I and those of my generation – D. T. Niles, Visser 't Hooft and Philippe Maury – had come with much wrestling were dismissed, to quote the same report, as 'pious talk and Geneva ideology'. The new vision was of the world, not the Church, as the place where God is to be found. Consequently 'the mission and renewal of the Church in our day depends on acceptance and affirmation of the secular world in place of traditional Christian tendencies to reject it'.[4] The most articulate exponent of the dominant mood was Hans Hoekendijk whose address called us 'to begin radically to de-sacralize the Church' and to recognize that 'Christianity is a secular movement – this is basic for an understanding of it'.[5]

On a theological level I had to recognize the big element of truth in what was being said, but I was acutely aware at the same time of what was being ignored or denied. At the end of Hoekendijk's immensely powerful address I remarked to my neighbour that I would like to hear him preach a sermon on the transfiguration. On a personal level I found the event very painful. It was painful to experience the contempt in which missions were held and to see, for example, a courageous and sensitive person like Hank Crane, fresh from the agony of the Congo, treated as unworthy of attention because he was just a traditional missionary. If one of the WSCF leaders could write of the conference as 'a nightmare and a terrible storm of impressions which, on first reflection, we feel fortunate to have survived',[6] it was certainly for me a very sobering indication of the difficulty of the way ahead. I did not yet know how far the decade that had just begun would take us from the lines on which my own theological development had brought me. I had been pleading for a 'churchly' unity because I believed that God's purpose of reconciliation could not be achieved by a concatenation of programmes and projects unless these were leading towards the life of a reconciled family within the household of God. I was soon to learn that 'churchly' was an adjective of abuse, and that the only way to be really part of God's work as understood in the 1960s was to leave the Church behind. The 'secular decade' had arrived. The SCM would not again in my lifetime be, as it had been, the most powerful source of new life for the ecumenical movement. In the 1970s there would be a dramatic rediscovery of the realm of the spirit, but it would not be integrally related to a new vision of the Church as one body.

August was spent in St Andrews for meetings of the IMC and the WCC Central Committee. Our friends Wilfred and Mary Hulbert had given us the use of their home in St Andrews for the period of the meetings, and so we were able to be all together as a family, which we thoroughly enjoyed. It was not all work, and on one memorable day we all travelled to Dunblane for the opening of the Scottish Churches' House – one of the many fruits of Robert Mackie's quiet work in the ecumenical cause. In my diary, however, I noted that the meetings of the Central Committee were 'a bit of a trial and gave many occasions for doubts about the direction we were taking'. However, the Spittal statement about the nature of the unity we seek was well received and, with a strong commendation from the Archbishop of Canterbury, was sent forward to the Third Assembly. On integration most of the Orthodox anxieties were allayed. Professor Ioannidis of the Church of Greece was able to say 'We will report to the Ecumenical Patriarch that all doubts are cleared up', and Bishop John of San Francisco was able to announce to the Committee that he was now 'in a state of brotherly favourable abstention'. From the side of the IMC I stressed the need for a proper continuity so that the distinctive contribution of the IMC might be fully carried over into the new council.

The summer of 1960 was also the fiftieth anniversary of the Edinburgh World Missionary Conference. This was marked by a service in St Giles Cathedral at which the Queen Mother was present, and also by a TV programme which I shared with J. H. Oldham whose genius it was to have made that conference a real turning-point in the history of the Church.

After a brief holiday at Rothbury I set out for a journey through Africa which was to include visits to fifteen countries and a series of major conferences with church leaders at half-a-dozen centres. For the whole of the time I had as my colleague Dr Donald M'Timkulu of South Africa, the newly appointed Secretary of the All-Africa Conference of Churches which was in process of formation. It was an ideal arrangement. I needed a pair of African eyes to help me to understand what I was seeing. He had no previous contact with the rest of the continent and needed an opportunity to present the newly formed AACC to the Churches. We were both eager to share with church leaders, African and ex-patriate, in fundamental, Bible-centred reflection about the future of the Christian mission in Africa. Most of the countries we visited were still under foreign rule but struggling towards independence. Cameroun and the Congo were in the throes of civil war. Everywhere the old colonial patterns were disappearing or were under immediate attack. I had prepared for the visit by questions sent in advance to each centre. In some places we had meetings of one or two days to discuss the needs of each situation. In others we had prolonged conferences of several days in which representatives came from several countries. I took the Letter to the Ephesians as the basis for all our meetings and in the light of a careful study of the text we looked at the contemporary situation. In each place I tried to discover what, if any, were the needs which the IMC and the WCC might help to meet. I sent back a stream of reports for my colleagues, running into nearly 12,000 words, in the hope that the first impressions of a stranger might have value even for those who already knew Africa well.

In West Africa I was at once struck by the fact that there was nothing of what one might call the moral and cultural equivalent of Gandhi. In India I had been accustomed to the idea that even well-to-do people were deeply affected by the Gandhian ideal of simplicity and the *swadehi* style and would scorn to fill their houses with the trappings of western affluence. Here I found that people with money imitated the European style. I wrote: 'I understand why Bishop Sumitra, when he came back from Nigeria, said that the thing that impressed him most was the number of *things* everywhere, and the lack of a sense of space.'

I was greatly struck by the contrast between a highly educated laity and a largely uneducated clergy. None of the graduates of the splendid universities was thinking of the ministry. 'The Church', I wrote, 'is educating its laity out of the Church.' The

TEF had not come a moment too soon, but I urged the need to encourage some of the outstanding laymen to take early retirement and offer for the ministry, for I saw little hope otherwise of changing the poor image of the ordinary pastoral ministry.

Over and over again I was made to realize that there was a sharp difference of opinion between the African leaders and their counterparts in the 'sending churches' about what kind of missionaries they wanted. I summarized a magnificent intervention of Pastor Jean Kotto of Cameroun as follows: 'We do need people to help us as experts in subjects where we are weak, but we do not want them only as technicians, we want them as bearers of the Gospel. We need them as symbols of the universality of the Church. This will be a permanent need. I do not know whether missionary societies will always exist, but there must always be missionaries. The missionary must be the salt which dissolves in the meat, disappears and dies in it. The missionary is not, and can never be, a temporary visitor, he is not one who comes and shakes hands with the Church and goes away, he is one who gives himself completely to the Church so that like salt he is lost in it.' A few days later, reflecting on the agony through which the Congo missionaries were passing, I noted:

> In all our efforts to provide technical assistance of all kinds to a newly independent country like the Congo, we are surely going to have to be terribly careful lest we get into a new sort of colonialism. If we are thinking all the time of the things and skills that 'we' have and 'they' haven't, and if we conceive inter-church aid exclusively in these terms, we shall very quickly run into this danger. Which means, surely, that in the end of the day there is nothing so important as the coming to the Congo of missionaries who know that the one thing they bring is the Gospel which they share with the Congolese Christians, and who are ready to disappear into the Church in the Congo and become part of it, dying that it may live.

And again, still reflecting on the Congo situation, I wrote:

> Before one begins to think about what one can do to help the Church in the Congo it is necessary to say as sharply as

possible that the most fundamental need is *not* education, or technical training, or relief – important as these are. It is that missions should be enabled to face the act of repentance that is needed for the paternalism of the past, and that the Congolese Churches should be enabled to understand what it means to be the Body of Christ. I cannot emphasize too strongly the fact that the real need is in the realm of spiritual illumination.

The missionaries felt battered and bruised, yet there was also the sense of new life and new powers being released. After a late-night party in Leopoldville (as it was then called) I wrote:

At almost 11 p.m. we drove out to the Stanley statue to see the lights of Leopoldville. It was a memorable moment for me, with all kinds of conflicting thoughts in my mind. Below me was the vast sweep of the river, narrowing towards the rapids whose thunder formed the undertone of every other sound. To the right the glittering lights of Leopoldville, the great expanse of the Stanley Pool dimly glimpsed in the moonlight. Across the river the lesser lights of Brazzaville. Above us towered the immense figure of Stanley looking out into the unexplored regions beyond. Around us a bunch of cheerful young Africans laughing and talking and occasionally giving a friendly slap to one of the lesser statues that form part of the monument. I suppose that much more history will have to unroll before we shall be able to see in one perspective the courage and vision of the white man's opening-up of Africa, and the bubbling gaiety of the young Africa which the white man – to his perplexity – awaked.

In Ruanda I had my first contact with the revival movement and was deeply impressed. The level of education was much lower than in West Africa, but 'what was immediately striking was the spiritual maturity of the Africans and the completely frank and open relationships between them and the missionaries. It was . . . the most refreshing experience we had had.' By contrast, a few days and a long road journey later, at our meeting in Kitwe, 'No one could fail to feel the sense of constraint in the air . . . Each person made a long and polite speech, but there was little real opening of the heart the one to the other, at least till we reached the end of the second day.'

In South Africa I experienced at the same time the liberating glory of the vast sense of space, and the suffocating absurdity of the rules which required Donald and me to go through separate doors and sit on separate seats. We had some vigorous and hopeful theological discussions with the Dutch Reformed Church leaders including van der Merwe and Beyere Naudé, and (with the backing of the TEF behind us) I was able to help lay the plans for a Federated Theological Seminary at Fort Hare.

The last part of the journey included periods in Southern Rhodesia, Nyasaland and Tanganyika (as they were then), Kenya and Uganda and a very good discussion on church union for East Africa. One of the last days of the tour was memorable for me, as my old friend Leslie Brown invited me to lead a retreat for the bishops in preparation for the election of the first archbishop for the new province. It was not a surprise that Leslie himself was chosen, and the days I spent as his guest helped me to understand something both of the glory of the Uganda Church and of the terrible political tensions in the midst of which it had to serve.

At the end of the long tour, Donald and I spent three hours going through our notes together and finding 'how clear and unanimous are the main convictions which have emerged from these consultations'. At the end of my last report I wrote:

I confess that I embarked upon this tour with considerable trepidation, but as I look back upon it now I can only look back with deep thanksgiving. At every point we have been made to understand that the people we met were profoundly grateful for this opportunity of studying the word of God together, of facing their problems as Africans and missionaries side by side in really frank encounter, and of facing the actual issues which the present situation in Africa poses, and doing so in the light of the word of God. We have had a very great many moving expressions of gratitude for the experiences which these consultations have provided, and I can only conclude by expressing my own gratitude to all of those who have remembered us in their prayers.

Coming when it did, this journey did much to steady my own convictions. After all, the passing theological fashions of Europe were not the only things that had to be taken into account.

After ten days at home I was off again to the United States for a four-week trip which included a visit to the Los Alamos atomic research establishment for discussion of the implications of the new technology, the meeting of the National Council of Churches at which I spoke, and the launching of the 'Blake-Pike Plan' for church union with a sermon and celebration of the CSI liturgy in the Grace Cathedral, San Francisco. A great deal of time was spent in sharing with the mission board leaders in the United States the impressions of our Africa tour. In my diary I noted: 'I found much sense of spiritual defeat and uncertainty about whether we have any gospel to offer.'

For the first three months of 1961 I was in England except for visits to Geneva and to Norway where there was substantial opposition to integration. As a follow-up of the Africa tour I spent a lot of time organizing a campaign to recruit teachers for Africa, as I was sure that the next few years could be crucial in this regard. I was also engaged in a vigorous and sometimes highly polemical discussion with Archbishop Fisher on account of the critical remarks about the Lambeth decision which I had made in the introduction to a newly published second edition of *The Reunion of the Church*. In my diary for 24 March I refer to 'an all-out assault' on the subject which ended in my being almost thrown out of the Palace. However, I think he really rather enjoyed these arguments and when in a charming note he acknowledged my letter at the time of his retirement he wrote that he was going to miss our theological battles.

In April I was off again on my travels which included the founding conference of the Pacific Council of Churches, the setting up of the united theological college for the Pacific Churches, and numerous meetings in the USA on the outward and homeward journeys. From 24 April to 6 May I shared in the lavish and gracious hospitality of the Samoan Church. The conference was housed in the beautiful buildings of the Malua Theological College on a lovely grassy site beside the sea. In my first letter home I wrote: 'This is a real medieval situation – the *corpus Christianum* untouched by the acids of modernity! The representatives of the chiefly families are the pastors. The chief people in Church and State are the same people, and it is inconceivable that anyone should claim to be something other than a Christian! On the other hand we have delegates from New Guinea where the Church is standing on the frontier of

completely untouched areas of cannibalism. I have never been at
a meeting of such terrific contrasts.' These widely scattered
Churches, born out of vastly different Church traditions, French
and English, had never met before. Each had lived in isolation
apart from the link with the parent mission. There was a vast
amount to learn. And they desperately needed to strengthen
each other, for the tourist invasion was beginning, and instead of
receiving from the western world missionaries of the Gospel
they were being asked to receive promoters of a new industry
which threatened to turn these lovely islands into brothels for
rich tourists. It was clear that the Pacific Churches were in a
situation quite different from those in Asia and Africa and a
distinct regional organization was needed. The marvellous Bible
studies of Hans-Reudi Weber drew us all together into a deep
understanding of the Gospel, and by the end of the meeting there
was a unanimous readiness to move forward to a Pacific Council
of Churches with a full-time secretary in the person of Vavae
Toma. But the Conference was much more than this. In the
words of the official history of the ecumenical movement it was
'a reformation event' in which Paul's Letter to the Galatians
'spoke in a disturbing and renewing way to the basic topic which
the advisory group (in the previous year) had so clearly
outlined'.[7] For myself the chief memories, apart from the Bible
studies, are of the Samoan dancing, and of the church in Apia. Of
the former I wrote in a letter home:

> There is something quite special about the rhythm of the
> Samoan music and dancing; it all seemed so effortless and
> spontaneous, yet full of energy and fire. Picture a great
> expanse of bright green grass, with an incredibly blue lagoon
> beyond, a few big shady trees scattered about, and a company
> of about a hundred Samoan girls doing a seemingly endless
> dance that stretched over the whole field for about a hundred
> yards, all with absolutely perfect time and faultless grace of
> movement. They had full-length grass skirts and their hair
> long, and the dancing had a slow, meditative sort of rhythm,
> and it seemed to go on endlessly, yet one felt one could sit all
> day and watch it. It really was beautiful. I just wished you could
> have been there. Surely audiences in London or New York
> would have paid the earth to see a thing like that, and yet the

whole point is that they could not have seen it, for it was essentially a spontaneous thing which seemed to come out of their own life and would be inconceivable as a paid professional job. There was lots of joking and chaffing from the Samoans in the audience; for instance, apparently Saturday is the day they all go fishing and some of the men in the audience thought bits of the dancing looked like fishing and shouted out to know if they were catching fish. It was all thoroughly integrated in the ordinary life of the community, and essentially not a show put on. I think that was part of its beauty.

It was a nice comment on the oft-repeated assertion that missions have destroyed native culture.

On the Sunday I preached in the old LMS church which stands on the waterfront of Apia harbour. The body of John Williams is buried under its steps. All the missionaries sent out from the Samoan Church – many of them to die as martyrs – are commissioned for service in the Church, sent out over John Williams's body and so out across the water. When (or if) they return, they come the same way. If in Samoa I found a new *corpus Christianum* I found also a Church with a living missionary faith.

Following the Malua Conference I returned to Suva for a TEF consultation on ministerial training for the Pacific Churches, which laid plans for the Theological College of the Pacific. I also learned of the existence of an isolated village in the hills where the whole population was Tamil and where no Christian witness has been given. I insisted on visiting the village. In my letter home I wrote:

It was a lovely run through beautiful hill country all glowing with the radiance of the setting sun, and then after dusk we drove through the most hair-raising places right off the road and finally walked till we reached the village – a very isolated place. It was just like being back on an ordinary pastoral visit in the diocese, picking one's way along muddy footpaths in the light of a Petromax lamp, and then coming to the village and finding a *pandal* and everything set out for a meeting, and garlands and cups of tea! I think they were quite thrilled to have the visit, though some of the children did not really know much Tamil. I spoke and sang and we talked for a long time and finally it was after nine when we got back to the doctor's house.

So, with the mud of a Fijian village still on my shoes I boarded the jet at Nandi for San Francisco and a fortnight of meetings in the USA with IMC and US mission board staff at the Stony Point missionary training centre. Most of the next month was spent in Geneva and then for five weeks I was travelling in Latin America. I had prepared for this over the preceding weeks by trying (helped by linguaphone records) to learn enough Spanish to be able to understand conversation and to deliver in a reasonable manner addresses prepared in English and translated for me by friends. This proved a very useful investment of time.

Latin America was an altogether new experience for me, and much more difficult to cope with than Africa or the Pacific. To begin with, as I soon began to realize, evangelical Christianity in this vast continent had been founded on a negation. Not the beauty of the Gospel but the horror of Rome seemed to be the deepest motive. In one of my early reports I wrote:

One of the distressing features of the situation is the obsessive fear of Rome. Of all places this seems to be one where it is unnecessary in view of the fact that the Roman authorities themselves acknowledge that there are now more Protestants than practising Catholics in the country. One is conscious all the time of the profound spiritual consequences which have flowed from the fact that evangelical missions in this country felt it their duty to begin by saying 'No'. When one begins by exalting a negative it is very difficult to get out of that posture. I think that this is where the message of the ecumenical movement with its insistence upon the positive affirmation of Jesus Christ as God and Saviour has a profoundly important feeding and strengthening role to play. I found that there was a real response to this approach.

But the response was always under threat. Wherever I went, there was in the same town at the same time a representative of North American 'evangelical' Christianity to warn against the danger of being mis-mated with ungodliness. Ecumenism and communism were linked with murder and adultery among the mortal sins.

The other overwhelming impression was of the juxtaposition of extreme wealth and extreme poverty. In my first report from Sao Paulo I wrote:

> The contrasts, especially in Rio, between glitter and squalor are quite staggering. I spent the whole of my first evening on a work-camp site in one of the slums of Rio with a group of young people. I must say I found it a most moving experience. These young people were doing a grand job and had obviously got a remarkable degree of co-operation from the local people. They were not content merely with doing good but were making a serious attempt to get behind the symptoms to the basic economic and political facts. I was told that the churches are not happy to have their young people engaging in the kind of political and economic analysis which I saw going on in this group, and that they feverishly tried to organize meetings which will keep the young people inside the church organization. When I repeated this to church leaders I was told that this is not fair, but I suspect that there is a large degree of truth in it.

As on the African journey I tried to make the centre of the programme the gathering of pastors and others from the widest possible range of traditions to do Bible study together and to reflect upon the local situation in the light of this study. Some of the meetings in Brazil and Buenos Aires were disappointing. Much the most fruitful was a week-long series of sessions in Santiago which included a good number of Pentecostal leaders. The phenomenal growth of Pentecostalism in Chile is well documented, and just because they were conscious of their strength and were free from domination by North American missions they were ready for frank criticism and open discussion. I preached in one of the largest of their churches. In my report I wrote:

> It was really quite an experience, beginning with the plush American car in which the pastor's son brought me to the church. It was a very large hall filled with people. The band produced a degree of percussion which I have not experienced in any other circumstances and the vigour of the singing was such as to make it almost impossible to remain still and not to

join in the jumping and dancing which was going on around. There was a circle of Elders who formed up to fend off the various holy rollers and dancers and to prevent them colliding too violently with each other or doing themselves damage. My sermon proceeded rather slowly since after about every third sentence the entire congregation leaped to its feet and shouted 'Praise the Lord, praise the Lord, praise the Lord', waving their arms in the air. Under the circumstances it was impossible to produce a very careful exegesis, but I have no doubt that something got across. Certainly nothing could have exceeded the enthusiasm or the warmth of the welcome.

It was encouraging that, after such a service, the Pentecostal pastors were willing to receive without resentment my question whether, along with the Holy Spirit, other spirits were also at work in that gathering. When, at the end of the week, a real depth of trust had been achieved, I put to them the question: 'Tell me, what are your real problems?' I received the unanimous reply: 'Caudillismo', which I mentally translated as 'bossism'. While I could not fail to recognize the dynamic character of these movements, I found them also willing to recognize the need to learn from older theological traditions.

The central event of the whole tour was the Second Latin American Evangelical Conference in Lima. At this I had to give a major address and lead Bible studies. The hope of many was that it might make possible the launching of a regional council of churches similar to those in Asia, Africa and the Pacific. There were many younger churchmen who, through the work of the WCC's 'Rapid Social Change' programme had been inspired by a new vision for the Church as a witness for justice in society. But the power of the North American Evangelical missions was too great. A proposal to convene representatives of the national councils to discuss future collaboration was carried, but under pressure from the Peruvian Council this was diluted to become an affair of very loose 'fraternal relations', the leadership to pass each year in rotation to another council. The secretary of the Peruvian Council volunteered to act for the first year. It was a plan almost guaranteed to fail and it did. At the end of my report to colleagues I wrote:

After the shouting was all over, I got Herbert Money aside and had a frank talk with him. He is the secretary of the Peruvian Council and appears to dominate it completely. I told him that, in my opinion, the example of the Congo Protestant Council showed that the policy of unity at all costs might be disastrous, that it might mean that the Christian voice was totally ineffective when the moment of need arose, and that it might not be that we had sufficient time before us in Latin America to wait for all the conservative evangelical groups, who appear to have so little sense of the realities of the world we live in. I said to him frankly, 'You and I know that, if it had not been for the Peruvian Council, this Conference would have passed a proposal for a much stronger Latin American Confederation. Now you are going into this to be its Secretary. I want to ask you frankly, are you going into it to make it work, or to sabotage it?' I must say he took it very well. He said; 'I give you my word that I am going to make it work.' I believe he will try.

I have no reason to believe that he did not, but the whole plan was a recipe for failure. The Latin American churches had to wait a long time for an effective regional organization.

The Lima Conference was so over-populated with Anglo-Saxon missionaries that I did not feel guilty about leaving it for a couple of days when the chance appeared for a trip over the Andes to the jungles of the Upper Amazon basin. I had better let my report at the time tell the story:

On Sunday I had an opportunity of preaching at the Union church and also of meeting a group of conservative evangelical missionaries at the headquarters of the Wycliffe Bible Translators where Sir Kenneth Grubb gave extracts from his autobiography. It was a quite fascinating story full of tales of rapine, murder and sudden death told in a casual tone of voice, but suggesting that any Sunday afternoon which did not have at least one corpse in it was a bit of a bore. That evening I learned that there was a possibility of accompanying him on a visit to the jungle tribes work of the Wycliffe Translators. A seat had been arranged for Clyde Taylor, but he had called off and I jumped at the opportunity of going. Next morning, therefore, we were up shortly after five o'clock and took the plane over the Andes to a jungle base at Pucallpa. The plane flew at 18,000 feet and as the cabin was unpressurized we used oxygen. There were the most magnificent views of snow-capped peaks, Indian villages and terraced agriculture dating from the Inca days. Then there came an abrupt change as we had crossed the *cordillera* and began to descend into the steamy heat of the Amazon jungles. At Pucallpa we were welcomed by one of the missionaries and taken in the mission plane to the base at Yarinacocha. After lunch we transferred to another plane with floats and set off on a long trip southwards. We were to visit a group of Piro Indians whose language has been reduced to writing by this group. We had with us on the plane Miss Matteson who had done the job and translated the New Testament into their language. It was a long flight at not much above tree-top level with no sign of human habitation except an occasional clearing by the riverside. We made two stops to visit isolated mission groups and finally fetched up at the place where we were to stay the night, the village of Meeyaria. This is a new settlement of about a dozen houses recently made by the Piro Indians. We were courteously accommodated for the night in one of their huts and we attended worship with them in the evening and the morning. We also spent a long time talking with the young man who is the leader of the congregation and who told us of his experience in the faith. Next morning we flew further up the Urubamba river to the point where the Camisea joins it; where there is a settlement of the Mechiquenga tribe. This was formerly a very warlike tribe which successfully resisted the Incas and was never subdued by them. One of the Wycliffe families is living there; I should think it is about the most lonely mission station in the world. They live in a hut which is exactly the same as the other Indian huts in the village, and they have no kind of communication with the outside world except what is provided by the mission plane and radio. There are no mails and no other forms of contact whatever. They are doing a wonderful job helping this tribe to develop crops and poultry while they continue their fundamental work on the language and the translation of the New Testament. Mr Small was at work on St John at the moment that we arrived. The Mechiquenga, of course, still rely primarily upon their bow and arrow for game and fish and they gave us some demonstrations of their shooting. We had all kinds of fascinating tales about the experience of this missionary couple. Mr Small has twice been through the very dangerous Bongo Demainique rapids in which many people have lost their lives. He told us that he has information from the Indian tribes about the whereabouts of the forgotten Inca city Pachitis, which is being searched for by various archaeologists. His policy seems to be to keep the secret. I had a quick bathe in the river which was beautifully cool in the tropical heat since it is only about fifty miles from the mountains. One gets an impression of the colossal size of this river basin when one remembers that the river, at the point where we camped, is 4000 miles from the mouth and is yet as wide as the Thames at London Bridge. In the afternoon we flew back to Pucallpa and in the evening Kenneth Grubb and I addressed the whole group of missionaries at the base and in the area around about. The presence of Kenneth Grubb in their midst, with his tales of what he had done in those areas long before they were born, had rather the effect that one would expect if Christopher Columbus were suddenly to turn up on the New York Stock Exchange. It was a tremendous success.

From Lima I went on to Bogota and San José for a very fruitful visit. I found in the Latin American mission and its seminary there, a combination of evangelical commitment with ecumenical openness which I had not met elsewhere. A brief visit to Mexico fired me with the desire to return, and – if possible – to have the next major ecumenical meeting in that city. In my report I wrote:

It is absurd to have spent only a day and a half in Mexico, and yet even in this time one feels the terrific impact of this extraordinary country, the glamour of the Cathedral and the city square, lit more beautifully than any other lighting of the kind that I have seen, the intense pride in the traditions, Spanish and pre-Spanish, of the country, and above all the extraordinary impression created in my mind by the visit to Guadalupe: the atmosphere of the place was so fundamentally similar to that of a great Hindu temple that I could not doubt that there was more of Tonantzin than Our Lady present. One could also understand, in a place like that, the terrific power of Rome, and the deep hatred and fear of Rome which goes with that power. One could also understand the deep revulsion of many Evangelicals when they hear that the World Council hobnobs with the Roman Catholic Church. I am sure that one of our biggest ecumenical tasks in Latin America is simply to explore and explain the meaning of the christological basis of the World Council in relation to our confrontation with the power of Rome in this continent.

This is the end of my last tape and I cannot begin to talk about the situation of the Church, except to say again how staggered one is by the infinitely fragmented and splintered character of the evangelical witness here. Yet quite evidently it has power, and it has elements of strength which the Ecumenical Movement itself needs take account of with the greatest seriousness.

The following note in my report did not, at the time, seem very important: 'On Sunday morning I was driven right across the city to a little Anglican church in a downtown industrial quarter where I assisted at a sung Eucharist and preached. The service was of a rather florid Anglo-Catholic variety which I am told was not typical of Mexican Anglicanism, but the coffee and buns afterwards were great fun.' Only many years later did I learn from my friend Jorge Lara Braud that he had persuaded his mother to come with him to that service, and that it was the point at which, as a good Roman Catholic, she had been brought for the first time to think that Protestants could be believers.

The last five days of the journey were spent in Cuba. It was two and a half years since the revolution, but everything still seemed to be in ferment. There was much to praise but also much evidence of blundering. The Churches had lost a high proportion of their leadership. Half of the Methodist pastors had fled to the United States, and while other Churches were not so badly hit, there was an alarmingly large proportion of pastors and lay leaders who, unable to accept the present, lived in the past and hoped for its return. I was glad to be able to spend these days helping, as far as I was able, those who recognized the necessity to face reality and find a way of bearing Christian witness in a Marxist state. I saw that the European Churches could play a role at this point and made proposals for the supply of literature in Spanish and for visits by European theologians and for the strengthening of the staff of the Theological Seminary at Matanzas.

It proved more difficult to get out of Cuba than to get in, but I returned home via Jamaica in time to celebrate our silver wedding with the whole family. These long absences from home made the days with the family more precious. The heaviest burden fell on Helen, and it was her love and wisdom that kept the family so closely united. There was always a wonderful welcome when I came home, and perhaps the very fact that we had these long separations helped to make the times together more precious. John was already developing his gifts as a cartoonist, and the illustrated letters he sent me during my travels or prepared for my homecomings are among the things I treasure.

Margaret's engagement to David Beetham was now settled, and she was to leave for a year in New York, combining study at Union Theological Seminary with work in the East Harlem parish. Alison was in the midst of her nursing training. Janet and John were still at school. I had to go back briefly to the States for a meeting of the TEF Committee to plan the second mandate for the Fund, and thereafter we all had a splendid family holiday in the manse at Harbottle, ten miles up the Coquet from Rothbury at the foot of the Cheviot hills. For a month I was the minister of the little congregation there and in the surrounding villages and hills.

There followed two months when I was mainly at home and then, early in November, I was off to India for the Third Assembly of the WCC and the final acts of integration. The first engagement was for meetings of the East Asia Christian Council at Bangalore. Early on the first morning we had the CSI liturgy in St Mark's Cathedral. I wrote in my diary: 'I felt that I had come home. The joy and thanksgiving could hardly be contained.' Following the IMC staff's new proposals about 'Joint Action for Mission', we planned a series of three 'Situation Conferences' in three Asian countries where we would try to pool needs and resources for mission in a compassable area. As always, D. T. Niles was the motivator and the strategist. From Bangalore I moved to New Delhi for the pre-Assembly meetings and the final meeting of the IMC Assembly which took the necessary actions to enable integration to be accomplished. Only one member council, that of Norway, finally declined to accompany the rest into the integrated Council. And so to the Assembly itself.

The opening worship on the Sunday morning brought together a crowd of several thousand in a gaily decorated *shamiana* and in the afternoon the opening business session was held in the great hall of the Vigyan Bhaavan. To quote from my letter home: 'Wim and I made our speeches. Then there was the formal act of integration. In the end nobody voted against it and as far as I could see there were hardly any abstentions. Wim jumped up and got hold of me with something between a handshake and a Latin-American embrace, and we then had a very simple and moving service of thanksgiving.'

As the discussions developed in the section on 'Witness' it was clear that new questions were being raised and that the church-centric model which had dominated missionary thinking since Tambaram was breaking down. The report contained many signals pointing the way. It spoke of God's rule over the whole created world and said, 'We have but little understanding of the wisdom, love and power which God has given to men of other faiths and of no faith',[8] and in my own diary at the time I wrote: 'It is clear that a Trinitarian, rather than a purely christological understanding of the missionary task is more and more necessary.'

At the administrative level, the entry of the Church of Russia brought unfamiliar problems. The filling of places on IMC committees had hitherto been rather a quiet affair, but Russia had strategic interests in the Middle East which (apparently) had a bearing on the choice of their nominee for the new committee. I had no experience of this kind of game. In my letter to Helen I wrote:

I've been having a terrific battle with Archbishop Nikodim, the leader of the Russian delegation (head of the foreign relations department of the Russian Church). He has been trying to insist on nominating a man to our divisional committee who is (as far as I can make out) quite unsuitable. I've been fighting a sort of running battle about it for five days, and last night I got the Russians in a sort of official way and told them I would not accept the name. It was quite a battle, but in the end he very graciously backed down and substituted another name. I expect we shall have quite a lot of problems of this sort, but – as Wim said – it is all an important part of their education.

I was being educated too.

I was now to be a member of the WCC staff and normal rules dictated a five-year stint. However, as my period of leave from CSI would expire in summer 1964 I was unable to make any commitment beyond that date, and this was accepted.

After ten days in and around Madurai I came home in time for a family Christmas. Immediately afterwards Mother became seriously ill and on a very cold day, the last day of 1961, we brought her by ambulance to a nursing home close to Newcastle where she could have the best possible care. It was to be the last time that I stayed in the Rothbury home which had been so precious for the past forty years. Leaving Mother in the care of my sister Frances I returned to London to prepare for the move to Geneva and the start of a new chapter. But it was not long before I was summoned back to be with Mother at the end. Her last words were only of concern for her children; there was never a murmur of complaint about herself. We buried her beside Daddy. The lovely garden which he had created out of a rocky hillside has gone back to the wild as their bodies have gone back to the dust. But if I read aright what the New Testament says about new heavens and a new earth I cannot doubt that in some sense the reunion with Daddy and Mother to which I look forward will include also that garden renewed and glorified.

16
Geneva: The World Council of Churches

The move to Geneva meant, once again, a separation for the family. I had raised the question whether the integration necessarily required this move. I valued the decentralized style of IMC operations and was conscious of the disadvantages of a large concentration of staff in one office. Helen and I were also very anxious to keep a home for our family in England so that we could be together as much as possible. Margaret was in New York for a year, but Alison was still in the midst of her training as a health visitor which combined a course at Southampton University with a full SRN course at St Thomas's Hospital. Janet and John were still at school. We had been so much separated that we very much wanted to stay in Bromley as long as possible.

But the contrary view prevailed and I was required to move to Geneva. Helen therefore stayed behind, kept the house at Bromley and did some RE teaching in a local High school, while I moved to Geneva and – at the kind suggestion of Stephen Neill – occupied his vacant flat in the village of Chambesy. With the help of a 'Velosolex' I could get back and forward quickly through the Geneva rush-hour to the old WCC headquarters in route de Malagnou. As Stephen had left behind a considerable part of his vast collection of books I had no lack of reading matter for evenings at home.

These, however, were not many. I was still to spend a big proportion of time in travel. The new Division of World Mission and Evangelism now had three offices – in Geneva, London and New York – and I had to be in effective touch with all three, with triplicate filing of all correspondence. Air travel was now becoming so fast that I would, for example, do a full morning's work at the Geneva desk and be in the New York office by 4 p.m. in time for a series of evening meetings. And I was still involved in visits to all parts of the world, usually for consultation with the national church and mission leaders following the pattern of basic Bible study and, on that basis, discussion of priorities for mission. It was important to make integration a reality by bringing the ecclesiastical leaders and the leaders of missionary agencies together and it was a real help that I was a bishop of the Church of South India as well as a secretary of the World Council of Churches. Both roles were important for the work that had to be done in opening up new relationships. There was an extended visit to various countries in the Caribbean (where the first foundations were laid for a Caribbean Council of Churches), to Kampala for the launching of the All-Africa Conference of Churches, to Bangkok for the East Asia Christian Conference, and a meeting of Asian missionaries serving abroad, to Nepal for a week with the United Mission and to many parts of Europe and North America. In many places I tried to meet with political leaders, both to help my own understanding and to help the local churches. I was also frequently involved in speaking to students both in SCM conferences and in university missions. Of special importance were the three 'Situation Conferences' in Madras, Singapore and Japan, sponsored jointly with the EACC, in which we tried to apply to these areas the concept of 'Joint Action for Mission'. The idea was to break out of the traditional one-track relation between an Asian Church and a western mission board, to bring together churches and missions in an area, to look together at possibilities for fresh evangelism, and to mobilize resources in a common plan. These meetings did not achieve all we hoped, but I think they helped to shake the immobility of which I had often complained. Especially memorable for me was the meeting at Amagi Sanso in Japan, a lovely place in the hills where we gathered church leaders from Korea, Taiwan, the Philippines, Hong Kong and Japan itself. The proceedings were in Japanese and English and for me they were a revelation of the profundity of much of the thinking of the young Japanese theologians. On the last night of the conference there was a heavy fall of snow and we had to walk down for some miles to reach our bus. In the brilliant morning sun we turned a corner in the road and had a quite unforgettable view of Mount Fuji, dazzling white against a clear blue sky. It remains my most vivid memory of ten days in Japan.

The days in Geneva were more difficult and perplexing. I was, to begin with, the only staff representative of the new division at the WCC headquarters. The others were in London and New York. The other divisions were, naturally, having consultations about programmes, projects and emergencies in all parts of the world. To almost all of them I was invited because all of them were, in some sense, part of the mission of the Church. At least, I was expected to be interested in what was happening in the countries where missions had long been at work. It seemed as if one had to be informed about everything that was going on at any time anywhere in the world. As editor of the *International Review of Missions* I took it as my job to compile the annual survey of missionary developments. This meant ploughing through vast quantities of material from all the six continents. It was demanding but profitable. But it was a constant strain to try to keep abreast of all that was going on so as to be able to share intelligently in discussions. It was simply impossible for me to be effectively involved in all the vast range of programmes which were being developed all over the Third World by the Division of Inter-Church Aid, the Departments on the Laity, on Co-operation of Men and Women, and on Church and Society. And yet these were all matters in which the missionary agencies were deeply involved and I could hardly absent myself from the discussion and formulation of plans. The difficulty was that, in the traditional areas of missions, anything going on in the Third World was the concern of missions; but integration must mean that all of this is the concern of churches while missions concentrate on the specifically missionary intention of bringing the Gospel to those who have not heard it and this must be directed to all six continents. The need was for the new division to provide a focus of concern for evangelism among all the multifarious and fruitful operations in which the WCC was involved all over the world. But how was this to be done? I found it, probably because of my own weakness, impossibly difficult. Exciting programes were being pushed forward everywhere to help the Churches in the newly independent nations to shake themselves free of the old missionary paternalism and to become constructively engaged in 'nation building'. This, and not the old-fashioned missionary preaching, was seen as the way to make the Gospel 'relevant' to these 'areas of Rapid Social Change'. I have painful memories of such planning sessions in which I interjected a question about the unfinished evangelistic task in the area and was looked at, even by the representatives of the mission boards, as though I was speaking a foreign language. My wrestlings and self-questionings about this were reflected on a scrap of paper where I jotted down my private thoughts during one of the days of retreat which I took from time to time in order to keep 'on course' during this difficult period. It is dated 9 August 1962 and reads as follows:

Convictions

1   That it matters supremely to bring more people to know Jesus as Saviour.

2   That our responsibility in the political order arises out of the love command.

3   That it does not arise out of the expectation of being able to anticipate the establishment of any particular social or political order.

4   That the New Testament teaches us (a) not to expect success in our cause; (b) to expect the sharpening of the issues and the coming of antichrist; (c) that there is no hope apart from Christ.

5   That 'Rapid Social Change' thinking has not developed any coherent theology and is in danger of identifying the movement of revolution with the work of redemption.

6   That in so far as it distinguishes these two things, it fails to show a clear understanding of the sense in which being in Christ is different from and transcends involvement in 'Rapid Social Change'.

It was one of my many failures during this period that in spite of strenuous efforts I was not able to attract to the Geneva staff a younger churchman who would be able to make evangelism his central concern and who would be able to project an image of the primary missionary 'intention' free from the traditional paternalistic elements. With my own missionary background I was aware of these paternalistic feelings in myself as I watched my colleagues in other departments coming back from their travels in the Third World with glowing accounts of the brilliant young churchmen and women they had 'discovered', and as I saw more and more of their 'discoveries' being plucked like ripe fruit from their native bushes to be brought into the ecumenical salad. I was as acutely conscious as my colleagues were blithely unaware of the long years of paternal devotion on the part of missionaries which had gone into the spiritual and intellectual formation of these splendid leaders from the churches of Asia and Africa. I was torn between rival feelings: concern about the 'brain-drain' from the younger churches to the relatively lucrative positions in the ecumenical organisations, against concern that their voices should be heard clearly in the ecumenical forum; and concern that in a proper rejection of paternalism the fact and the requirements of paternity might be forgotten.

Behind these personal tensions and dilemmas were the much larger changes which were taking place in the thinking of the Churches. The kind of Christian statements which were accepted in the 1950s and which arose out of the understanding of the Gospel to which I had come, were no longer accepted. We were into the decade of the secular. The world, not the Church, was the place where God was at work. It was far more important to get people involved in action for justice and development than to have them converted, baptized and brought into the Church. The world of the secular was not only the most important object of attention: it was, perhaps, the only world there is. 'Honest to God', published early in 1962, caught the mood of those who wanted to remain Christians but for whom God was no longer a reality. Later that year I was invited by the BBC to join from London with Hans Küng in Rome and Frank Fry in New York in the first inter-continental debate about religious matters carried by the newly developed satellite transmission. I found that my sponsors in London regarded 'Honest to God' as a new revelation of ultimate truth and were obviously disappointed that their electronic wizardry was being wasted on my old-fashioned theology. I was being challenged at every point to re-examine my most basic Christian beliefs. It was not easy.

Already at New Delhi I had recognized that the missiology of *One Body, One Gospel, One World* was not adequate. It was too exclusively church-centred in its understanding of mission. Only a fully Trinitarian doctrine would be adequate, setting the work of Christ in the Church in the context of the over-ruling pro- vidence of the Father in all the life of the world and the sovereign freedom of the Spirit who is the Lord and not the auxiliary of the Church. In the weeks following New Delhi I wrote for my colleagues a paper with the appalling title: 'The Relevance of Trinitarian Doctrine for Today's Mission'. My hope was that it would provide the basis for a post-integration sequel to *One Body* – a manifesto, in fact, for the new Division of World Mission and Evangelism. But this was not to be. Wim disapproved of its theology, and my colleagues in the Division were not sufficiently persuaded to support me. It was published as a study paper in Britain and the United States and was also translated and published in German, but its impact was limited. It was nearly twenty years later that I had the opportunity to develop its argument in a full-length book, *The Open Secret*.

But the theological earthquake which was shaking the world of English-speaking Christians was a much more serious affair than the debate about missiology. Much as I loved and respected John Robinson (and I had been, at his request, one of the bishops who shared in his consecration) I believed that his book was an attack on the very centre of the Christian faith. It left no room for a truly personal God. I knew that the reading of it had caused not a few ministers of the Gospel to forsake their calling. Yet the debate about it often seemed to generate more heat than light. I felt in myself the thrust of the argument and yet I could not accept the conclusion and I was grieved by the damage it was doing. An invitation to give the Firth Lectures in Nottingham University gave me the incentive to attempt a contribution to the debate. The result was eventually published under the title *Honest Religion for Secular Man*. It was written in the interstices of a very full programme, much of it in airport waiting rooms. The SCM Press, the most helpful and faithful of publishers, had grave doubts about it and would have liked to have much of it changed. But it proved to be, as far as I can judge, the most 'successful' of anything that I have written. It was translated into a great many languages and I was even told by the head of the Holy Office in Rome that he was promoting it among the wavering faithful. Very few experiences have given me more cause for thankfulness than the things that have been said to me in subsequent years by Christian ministers who were enabled by that small and halting effort of communication to recover their faith in God, and to continue their ministry in the Church.

This fundamental theological work, whether in debate with Christians in the West, or whether in Bible study with groups of churchmen in the Third World, seemed to me to be absolutely central to any kind of leadership in world mission. But there was clearly also a huge sector of my job which concerned the development and administration of programmes. There was, first of all, the still unsolved problem of relating to the traditional missionary programmes the new programmes of inter-church aid which were burgeoning at an enormous rate. The Division of Inter-Church Aid had developed a staff more than twenty times the size of the whole IMC operation, with specialists for each major area of the world and each specialized function. Its Director, Leslie Cooke, was under constant pressure from big donor agencies to expand his programme. The committee on 'Specialized Assistance for Social Projects' had teams of expert consultants able to advise on different kinds of development projects. But Leslie Cooke had a sensitive awareness of the importance of those elements in the missionary tradition which could not be replaced by the new inter-church relationships.

Now that we were working together in one organization we were able – not without strain – to hammer out a stable relationship. The dilemma with which I constantly wrestled was how to achieve a permeation of all the activities of the Council with a missionary concern, and at the same time to preserve and sharpen a specific concern for missions as enterprises explicitly intended to cross the frontier between faith and no-faith. Many of the most influential leaders in the mission boards wanted to eliminate the narrow category of missions and to speak only of the total mission of the Church. I resisted the pressure and, in the face of considerable opposition, retained the 's' in the title of our Journal, *The International Review of Missions*. It was only after I left Geneva that the 's' was removed.

The critical point in practice was our relationship with the Division of Inter-Church Aid. To start with, the latter was precluded by the 'Herrenalb Categories' from trespassing into what mission boards regarded as their territory, but this artificial boundary could not remain. It was a great liberation for both divisions when it was agreed that we would abandon the attempt to define which projects were 'missionary' and which were not, and that the Projects List of the Division of Inter-Church Aid should be open to projects of all kinds provided that they were of a short-term character, while the Division of World Mission would open an 'International Fund for Mission' which would seek support for longer-term programmes of evangelistic advance. This made it possible to gather international support for new enterprises designed for the furtherance of the Gospel. This meant, of course, a break with the old IMC tradition, ceasing to be a purely advisory body and entering the field of operations.

The way had been prepared for this by the Theological Education Fund. It had brilliantly achieved the objectives of its first mandate. Ministerial training in the Churches of the Third World had been brought from the margin of missionary concern to the centre, and a score of theological colleges around the world were on the way to becoming the equals or the superiors of anything in the West. One of my first preoccupations was with the designing of a 'Second Mandate' for the Fund. For this purpose we assembled one of the finest teams that I have ever worked with, including Shoki Coe of Taiwan, Erik Nielsen of Denmark, and Nathan Pusey of Harvard. Their report, accepted by the WCC, proposed a concentration on the effort to relate the training of the ministry more fully to the cultural contexts in which the Churches of the Third World have their being. Twenty years later we are reaping the rich fruit of this decision in the growing volume of genuinely fresh 'third-world theology'.

Another matter calling for international action was the production and distribution of Christian literature. Efforts by different agencies were unco-ordinated and the immense evangelistic opportunity offered by the growing number of literate people all over the world was not being effectively seized. The launching of the Christian Literature Fund, on lines similar to the TEF, was an obvious answer. But it caused me some of the most painful experiences of my period in Geneva. I was concerned that the leadership of such a fund must be in the hands of someone whose training and experience was in the world of commercial publishing and not of those whose only experience was of church committees deciding what kind of literature people ought to read. This meant that I had to resist pressure to appoint an obvious candidate and it was the only time in my period as director that relations with colleagues were strained.

But I am sure that it was right to call Charles Richards to be the Fund's first director and it was a joy to watch the whole work of Christian literature move forward under his leadership.

An analogous effort was needed in the field of boradcasting. The US boards had a joint agency working in this field and in Europe there was an Association of Christian Broadcasters. The Lutheran World Federation had secured permission to start a powerful broadcasting service ('Radio Voice of the Gospel') in Addis Ababa, but needed the co-operation of Churches in Africa, India and the Middle East if it was to be effective. It was a complicated business to bring all these interests together, so that there could be an effective World Association of Christian Broadcasters, and an ecumenical agency to support the programme at Addis Ababa so that the churches in the target areas could really recognize the 'Radio Voice of the Gospel' as their own means of sharing the Gospel with their neighbours. I had to give a lead in this matter but the main burden of detailed implementation fell on my colleague George Carpenter in the New York office.

Most of the traditional work of missions in Asia and Africa had been among rural peoples, but during the decade following the end of the war multi-national companies were reaching out into all parts of the world and more and more people throughout Asia and Africa were being drawn into industry and into the sprawling shanty towns that surrounded the new mines and factories. Missions were faced with a new kind of problem, and local pastors trained in the old rural ways were ill-equipped to deal with it. Here was a task which challenged us as a group dedicated to helping the Church in its worldwide mission. But how could we help? As we discussed this problem in staff meetings we were reminded of an example close at hand which could help us. A few years earlier the IMC had launched the 'Islam in Africa Project' in response to the cry of many African churches that they needed help in meeting the challenge of Islam. It was a very low-key but very effective project, making available to the churches which asked for it the service of experts in Moslem faith and practice to train pastors and others in the understanding of Islam. My beloved friend Pierre Benignus had been the inspirer and leader. After his tragic death in an air crash in 1963 the leadership passed to Wim Bijlefeld with a team of three colleagues. Their work had proved enormously effective. Could this be the model for a response to the challenge of industrialization?

We began in East Africa with what was called the 'Urban Africa Programme', but this was soon extended to West Africa with specialists working in Abidjan, Côte d'Ivoire and Nigeria. Meanwhile we had appointed Paul Löffler to our staff with a remit to develop this work. We sent him first to India where he made his centre in Bangalore and worked with my old friend Harry Daniel in developing a vigorous programme of industrial mission. The programmes thus begun on a modest scale were to develop greatly, and in a new direction, after I left Geneva.

In some ways the most exciting of all these new ventures in the internationalizing of missions was in the field of healing. The ministry of healing had been an integral part of modern missions almost from the beginning. All over the world there were thousands of mission hospitals, some large teaching institutions, but most of them simple rural hospitals staffed by doctors of modest training and using simple techniques. In the booming years following the war, they were faced with overwhelming problems. Governments in the newly independent countries were building up health services on a high level of sophistication with the help of large injections of foreign funds. No hospital could now carry on in the old way. New funds were needed for high-technology equipment and for advanced training of staff. Mission boards could not cope with the vast new demands on their resources.

It began to dawn on the people struggling to run these mission hospitals that the WCC's Division of Inter-Church Aid, of which they were beginning to hear rumours, was an apparently inexhaustible source of dollars (pounds sterling were not often heard of and Deutschmarks were still to come). They began sending appeals to Geneva. The trickle became a flood. Soon Leslie Cooke had on his desk medical projects totalling scores of millions of dollars. There was no possibility of meeting such demands. But, surely, this was 'missions' and therefore the proper place for these appeals was on my desk and not on his. And so the problem came to me! What could be done in face of this real but absolutely impossible problem?

God sent the answer in the person of a beloved Nigerian doctor, Ademola, in whose home I had stayed during my visit to Lagos in 1960. He was visiting Geneva as the delegate of his Government to a meeting of the WHO and he came to pay me a visit. As we talked I poured out my problem to him. He was silent for a time and then he said: 'But, you know, the basic unit of healing is not the hospital, it is the Christian congregation.'

For me at that moment it was a completely new idea. It took me a long time to think out its full implications. The result of that thinking was a meeting in Tübingen in May 1964, sponsored jointly by ourselves and the Lutheran World Federation. At the opening session of the conference I said that we were at such an early stage of exploration that we must refuse the temptation to make any kind of public statement. But the outcome was far otherwise. In that meeting God gave us a word about the Church as a healing community which, to my astonishment, echoed round the Christian world and started a profound revolution in the thinking of medical missions. At first we made no attempt to publish the statement which the conference prepared, but as more and more people wrote to Geneva asking for copies we had to print and publish the document entitled 'The Healing Church'. At its heart there was a fresh definition of what we meant by healing; for the writing of this I was responsible:

The Christian understanding of healing begins from its place in the ministry of Jesus. There it was a sign of the breaking into human life of the powers of the Kingdom of God, and of the dethroning of the powers of evil. The health which was its fruit was not something static, a restored equilibrium; it was an involvement with Jesus in the victorious encounter of the Kingdom of God with the powers of evil.

A concept of health which is merely that of a restored balance, a static 'wholeness', has no answer to the problem of human guilt or death, nor to the anxiety and the threat of meaninglessness which are the projection upon human life of the shadow of death. Health, in the Christian understanding, is a continuous and victorious encounter with the powers that deny the existence and goodness of God. It is a participation in an invasion of the realm of evil, in which final victory lies beyond death, but the power of that victory is known now in the gift of the life-giving Spirit. It is a kind of life which has overcome death and the anxiety which is the shadow of death. Whether in the desperate squalor of over-populated and under-developed areas, or in the spiritual wasteland of affluent societies, it is a sign of God's victory and a summons to his service. The Church's ministry of healing is thus an integral part of its witness to the Gospel.

I was myself astonished at the reverberations of this statement. We were in the middle of the 'secular' decade. Medical work was seen as a technical matter to which the Christian or other beliefs of the doctor were irrelevant. At a recent meeting of our divisional committee Bishop Ted Wickham had said that it was as nonsensical to talk of a 'Christian' hospital as it would be to talk of a 'Christian' atomic power station. Christianity had nothing to do with the techniques of modern medicine. Hospitals could better be run by the State just as power-stations were. That seemed to be the 'modern' view in the middle of the 1960s. But the repercussions of the Tübingen report proved that a purely secular view of healing was breaking down. The following years would show how profound was the real crisis of secular medicine. We were inundated with requests for copies of the report and it now became clear that the Division would have to follow it up. As a first step, a 'Medical Panel' was set up under the auspices of SASP, and this soon became a fully developed Christian Medical Commission under the leadership of James McGilvray who had earlier served on the staff of the Vellore Hospital. These developments came at the very end of my time in Geneva. It has been a joy to see how the Commission has developed, and what new hope and direction it has given to Christian medical work all over the world, and how greatly it has influenced the work of the World Health Organization. The tiny seed sown at Tübingen has become a tree in whose branches not a few birds have found shelter.

There were important areas, however, where I have to confess that I failed to achieve what I had hoped for as the result of integration. I hoped that we would be able to use the resources of a world organization to identify and direct resources to places where there were great opportunities for evangelism. I had been much impressed by what I had learned from Pastor Jean Kotto of the Cameroun about evangelism in French-speaking West Africa. In 1965 we organized a survey of evangelistic opportunities in twenty-one counries of West Africa leading up to a very representative bilingual consultation jointly chaired by Jean Kotto and Kenneth Grubb which sought to develop plans for more effective evangelism. I would have liked to see such consultations held in many other areas, but it had to be admitted that there was much less enthusiasm for the direct preaching of . the Gospel and the building-up of the Church than for technical assistance and political action.

I had also hoped that integration might provide the opportunity to bring into the thinking of ordinary church people new models of ministry and congregational life directed more to mission than to mere maintenance. The study programme on 'The Missionary Structure of the Congregation' was intended (at least in my mind) to stimulate new thinking among the older churches about mission and ministry as essentially charismatic realities – gifts of the sovereign Spirit. But other spirits were abroad. The *zeitgeist* was too strong. The study process was carried into the powerful currents of the 'secular' decade and for many people the only fruit of its labour which is remembered is the slogan 'The world provides the agenda',[1] a phrase which pointed to an important truth but could be, and was, very easily misunderstood. Combined with the theology of *Honest to God* it could and did help to persuade many Christians that both Church and ministry were irrelevancies.

An important opportunity to face the issues raised by the secular enthusiasm of the decade was provided at the full meeting of the Commission on World Mission and Evangelism held in Mexico City at the very end of 1963. I had been eager that we should meet there not only because none of the world missionary meetings had so far been held in Latin America, but also because Mexico City seemed to me to embody and express the immense confidence in a secular future which was the mark of the time. The conference was noted for a magnificent restatement of the call to missions by Wim, but I do not think it accomplished very much in the way of fresh clarity for the missionary movement as a whole. In the section on 'The Witness of Christians to Men in the Secular World', however, there was a debate between M. M. Thomas and Hendrikus Berkhof which did seem to me to go to the heart of the matter. At my request Paul Löffler encouraged them to continue the debate on paper and the result was published as a booklet which did, I think, point the way forward.[2]

The Mexico Conference was the first of such world missionary meetings in which the Orthodox took a full part. (I found it entertaining at one moment to hear the Bishop of Carthage remark: 'One of my predecessors, Cyprian, used to say "*Extra ecclesiam nulla salus*". I don't agree, but he had a point.') I was anxious to draw them more fully in and to help to reactivate the great missionary traditions of the Eastern Churches. A young deacon of the Church of Greece, Anastasios Yannoulatos, had gathered round him a group of young people eager to become missionaries in East Africa. Knowing (through Leslie Brown) something of the lights and shades of the story of the Orthodox in Uganda I nevertheless wanted to encourage this group and I spent a very happy weekend with them in Athens. One of them, an iconographer, painted and gave me an icon of Jesus and Mary in what he imagined to be an African scene and I still treasure it. Later I arranged a full meeting with senior Orthodox leaders to discuss the possibilities of their involvement in world mission. When the WCC Executive met in Russia I had the unforgettable experience of worshipping in the cathedral there and of visiting the Patriarch at Zagorsk, and of many long discussions with young men who, after a complete training in the official Marxist ideology, had been brought to faith and baptism and were now part of the Church. Among the senior churchmen whom we met I was delighted to find that several had read *The Household of God* in a Russian typewritten translation and were eager to discuss it. During our meetings in Odessa I was asked to celebrate the CSI liturgy in the bedroom of the Intourist Hotel where we were staying. Sixteen Orthodox clergy came and I noted in my diary that the hotel servants were eager in helping to arrange the room for the service.

Part of the excitement of working in Geneva was the news coming from Rome. The call to the Second Vatican Council had taken the whole world by surprise and for us at the WCC headquarters it meant the possibility that the whole shape of the ecumenical scene would change. The establishment of the Secretariat for Promoting Christian Unity and the appointment of Jan Willebrands as its head meant that there was a point of official contact with the Vatican. He and Wim had an excellent rapport from the beginning and we on the staff liked to think that the future of the Church was being fixed up between them in a Dutch dialogue of their own. Willebrands came to Geneva to discuss the arrangements for observers from the 'separated brethren' and immediately impressed us all by his quiet friendliness and understanding. I noted in my diary: 'He carries a New Testament in his wallet.' When the sessions of the Council began, Lukas Vischer was our observer and sent back a continuous stream of brilliant reports which enabled us to follow with breathless excitement the ebb and flow of debate between the conservatives and the protagonists of renewal. As it became clear how far-reaching were the changes – at least in style and spirit – from what we had been accustomed to, Lukas urged us to arrange a residential meeting between our own missionary leadership and our counterparts in the Roman Catholic Church. This took place at Crêt Berard in April 1965 and I described it in my diary as 'a wonderful experience of good fellowship and good thinking together'. We had seen, and drastically criticized the first draft of the statement on missionary matters prepared for the Council and I believe that the much more acceptable character of *Ad Gentes* as it was finally adopted, owed at least something to our meeting.

I was not now, of course, involved deeply in Faith and Order work, though I was recruited to serve as secretary to the section on the ministry at the Montreal Faith and Order Conference of 1963. It was one of the most frustrating assignments I have ever been given because the reigning ideology which located God (if anywhere) firmly outside the walls of the Church made it almost impossible to discuss the role of the ordained ministry at all. But one event in the field of inter-church relations brought me an experience of pure joy. On 30 October 1961 George Macleod wrote to me about his desire to celebrate the fourteenth centenary of the landing of St Columba on Iona. In a hilariously funny letter he described the various ideas that had been mooted for making it a fully ecumenical occasion in view of the fact that the Churches which ought to be involved were not in communion with each other. According to George, after various proposals for a united celebration were put forward, the idea of archimandrites uniting us led to the kind of ecumenical confusion of discussion dear to the devil himself. The concept of con-celebration led to a discussion so learned that I had to summon all my facial capabilities to create a superficial impression that I understood them.

SO

the Holy Spirit intervened, through the agency of Alec Boyd, and conveyed *simpliciter* that a bishop of the Church of South India was all that was required. Moderators and bishops, of Scotland and Northern Ireland, could all meet together and be rejoiced that if you cast your bread upon western waters in the sixth century it would come back to you after many days: 14 × 365 × 100 precisely. Of course it was not put as well as that, but there is the idea well put.

UNUM PORRO NECESSARIUM

Can you, God willing and weather permitting, be in Iona for the weekend of June 2nd 1963? If so, can I tentatively approach the Primus, the Bishop of 'Derry, the 1963 Moderator of the Presbyterian Church in Ireland, ditto Moderator of the Presbyterian Church of England, ditto the General Assembly of C. of S. 1962?

I replied that I would joyfully launch my catamaran to meet his coracle, and so on the festival of Pentecost, 2 June 1963, on a bright and windy day with a glory of colour that only Iona can display, we gathered in the abbey and I celebrated the CSI liturgy with ministers of the Scottish and English Churches who could not otherwise share communion. Two much-loved friends stood on either side of me at the holy table: James S. Stewart, the reigning Moderator; and Kenneth Carey, Bishop of Edinburgh. With them were Neville Davidson and the Bishop of Durham. As I gave the chalice to each of them I felt overwhelmed by the significance of what was happening against the background of the quarrel between bishop and presbytery which has rent history for so long.

That evening the Stewarts and I were brought back to Oban in a small motor launch and I have never seen the islands, the mountains and the sea so beautiful as they were in the westering sun of that June evening. Next morning I was back in Geneva refreshed by the assurance that, after all, things do move.

In November 1962 we closed the home in Bromley and moved into a flat in a partly finished block of apartments in Grand Lancy, a village on the edge of Geneva. To begin with there were no nearby shops and there was a lot of building work still going on. When the work was finished there were 450 families of at least fifty different languages and nationalities, each living in its little box, communicating with the rest of the world by telephone and rarely meeting each other because the lifts were too small to take more than three or four people. Down in the village of Grand Lancy was the Reformed Church to which, as far as we could discover, few or none of the denizens of our concrete jungle except ourselves repaired on a Sunday morning. The congregation was of a high average age. The pastor was said to be 'un tout petit peu libéral'; he did not believe in the divinity of Christ, but he was a kind man and a thoughtful preacher. Helen and I nourished our souls by going to the eight a.m. communion in the English church on the rue de Mont Blanc and then to the eleven o'clock *culte* at Grand Lancy.

But what kind of Christian witness was possible and appropriate in our concrete jungle where, though the top flats did not quite reach heaven, there was certainly a Babel of tongues? How could I pretend to be a leader in world mission if I could not do anything about mission where I lived? There were several WCC staff families in the complex and we met often to discuss the matter. We started a small 'house church' and the services were blessedly refreshing but the participation was small. In the end, true to the missiology of the time, the world provided the agenda. We formed a 'Tenants' Association' which proved to be an immense success. Under its auspices all kinds of activities began to flourish which brought the separate families together to serve each other, to teach each other's languages, to learn new skills and to resist the more outrageous extortions of the landlord. 'The Palettes' began to be something of a human community and that was surely pleasing in God's sight. But the number who gathered to acknowledge the Source of all blessing was small!. Yet I treasure a beautiful book, given to us when we left by one of our neighbours, with the inscription: 'We asked for language teaching; you gave us friendship.'

We were indeed much blessed in our friendships with Geneva people. The real natives of Geneva are such a small minority, among the hosts of foreign diplomats, civil servants and employees of multi-national companies, that they have an understandable tendency to close ranks, while the foreigners have plenty of their own kind to mix with. The fact that we identified ourselves with the local church opened for us doors into Genevese homes and gave us rich rewards in friendship. When we left I was quite astonished to receive a parting gift and a warm expression of affection from the famous 'Compagnie des Pasteurs' of the Église Nationale de Genève.

In the spring of 1963 I acquired a secondhand car and Helen and I began to explore some of the country. At first we were rather unambitious but later we had many wonderful trips for thirty-six or forty-eight hours into the mountains, climbing in places unfrequented by tourists and enjoying the hospitality of the small village inns which are not on the international circuit. Janet and John came to us for all their holidays and Alison when she could. Margaret and David were married in 1962 and for one of our summer holidays they joined us in Kenthal for ten days of splendid mountaineering. By the time my five-year contract reached its end we were beginning really to enjoy and love our life in Geneva.

The CSI had given me five years' leave of absence from July 1959. I was pressed by the World Council to enter into a further five-year contract. It was only two and a half years from New Delhi, too short a time for integration to become firm and full. It did not seem right to leave when so much remained to be done, especially since the relation between mission and inter-church aid was still the subject of so much confusion and uncertainty. Finally I requested and the CSI sanctioned an extension of two years to the summer of 1966. By that time Wim would also retire.

But in November 1964 I received an official letter from Madras asking me to allow my name to be proposed for the see of Madras left vacant by the death of David Chellappa. I replied that I was willing to serve if elected but that I was not free until the summer of 1966 unless the Central Committee agreed to release me from my contract. The CSI made it clear that the post could not be left vacant for another eighteen months. My own mind was painfully divided. I longed to return to the CSI and to the

211

ordinary work of a local pastor. But I knew that the work of integration had hardly begun and that if I left abruptly I would be putting very heavy burdens on loyal and devoted colleagues. In the view of some of those whom I greatly respected and trusted, to leave Geneva at this point would be a betrayal of trust. And – quite apart from these arguments – it was hard for us, for Helen and for the children, to contemplate another disruption of our family life.

While I was wrestling with these dilemmas the WCC as a whole was plunged into a deep crisis over the appointment of a successor to Wim. The Executive Committee had nominated Pat Rodger and I was very happy with this nomination. It pointed to the style of leadership which I believed was needed at that stage in the ecumenical story. It soon became clear, however, that a powerful movement was being created to oppose this choice. I considered that it was our duty as staff to refrain from being involved in such a movement and to accept the decision of the responsible governing body. Others did not take this view and the Central Committee meetings in Enugu in January 1965 were darkened by a kind of confusion which was unworthy of the cause and of the people. I wrote in my diary at the end of the meeting that I felt that 'the heart had gone out of the business'. That was unfaithful. Like every human organisation the WCC has its failures. But God does not fail, and in the years since 1965 I have had many reasons to be sure that he has not abandoned the World Council.

In the confusion created by the Central Committee's rejection of the Executive's nomination the members had turned to John Sadiq, Bishop of Nagpur, to be the chairman of a fresh nominating committee. It was a tribute to the stature of this quiet, humble Christian pastor. John was also the chairman of my Division and I felt that I must rely largely on his judgement regarding the call to Madras. He was emphatic that I should go. All my Indian friends pressed this view on me. D. T. and Dulcie Niles came and spent an evening in our home. I was very eager that, if I were to leave the post in Geneva, D. T. should be my successor. On that question he was evasive but about my future he was clear. Over and over again he repeated (in Tamil), 'You must go to Madras'. The next day was Sunday 31 January. Helen and I went to early communion and afterwards walked up 'Le

Môle' in deep snow. For the rest I must quote my diary: 'It was an opportunity for making up our minds on the call to Madras, and during the walk we decided to accept, subject to clearing with our children and specially consulting Margaret and David about being able to get a bigger place where Janet and John could go on holidays. I shall never be able to be thankful enough for Helen's willingness to make this decision which I know is a much harder one for her than for me. That evening we went to the service at Lukas Vischer's (flat). Niko Slotemaker (de Bruin) took the service and preached on Philippians 3:12–14. He spoke about how Christ lays hold of us and sends us forward. For Helen and me it was God's word of confirmation.'

On the Monday morning at the weekly service in the Ecumenical Centre, D. T. Niles preached on exactly the same text with the same application. It was a second confirmation. In the following days we were able to consult with our children. They were magnificent in their understanding and support. With the assurance that we would try somehow or other to see them at least once a year either in India or in England I sent a cable to the CSI Moderator to say that I would be available from 1 October 1965 and at the end of March I learned that I had been appointed.

For the remainder of 1965 I had a heavy travelling schedule. I had planned a long visit to Korea, Taiwan, the Philippines and Indonesia for the latter part of the year but this had to be cancelled and I have therefore never had the chance of first-hand contact with these dynamic Churches. At the end of August I handed over charge to Robbins Strong as acting director and we closed our home in Grand Lancy. For John especially there was much sadness in the ending of that chapter in his life and for Helen and me there were many farewells it was hard to say. We finished with a brief but blessed time of retreat at Bossey in preparation for the next stage of our lives and on the evening of 30 September, with a touching farewell from our beloved colleagues who came to the airport to see us off, we left by the night plane for India.

17

Madras: Mission in Metropolis

On the following morning – 1 October 1965 – Helen and I came down the steps from the plane at Madras airport to be received by a select party of fifty on the tarmac and an immense crowd in the airport building. It was a marvellous homecoming and we were overwhelmed by the warmth of the welcome. Many of those present were, of course, old friends from Kanchi days and missionary colleagues from the Church of Scotland mission. The nicest written welcome was a postcard from J. R. Macphail of the Christian College: 'I promise to pray for you and to be respectful to you in public.' We were soon established in the house beside the cathedral which had been built in the time of Bishop Chellappa and in a day or two the Geneva years had vanished and I felt that I was back where I belonged.

But it was a very different kind of job from the one that had confronted me in Madurai eighteen years ago. To start with, it was a very much bigger diocese, with nearly a thousand congregations and over a hundred presbyters and a conurbation growing rapidly towards the three-million mark. It was not the beginning of a new diocese but the continuing of a tradition which was already very long and firm. Madras had had an Anglican bishop since 1835. The Bishop of Madras had been – under the British Raj – the third dignitary of the Presidency after the Governor and the Chief Justice. The church of St Mary in the Fort dated from 1680 and St George's Cathedral, with a history of 150 years, was an accepted place for public acts of prayer and thanksgiving. Moreover, there were Christians, most of them members of the CSI, in a great many of the leading positions in government, the professions and the business world. Apart from any wishes of my own, I was stepping into a tradition which would bring me much more fully into public affairs than I had been in Madurai.

And my own point of view had changed. The years on the WCC staff had accustomed me to thinking all the time about public issues and about the witness of the Church in the political and social order. No one could work for any length of time under the leadership of Wim Visser 't Hooft and then revert to a cosy ecclesiastical domesticity. Looking back in 1965 upon my earlier ministries in Kanchi and Madurai I felt that I had been too narrowly ecclesiastical in my concerns, and I resolved that I would try to challenge the strong churches of Madras City to think less of their own growth and welfare and more of God's purpose for the whole of the vast and growing city. The installation service a few days after we arrived gave me the opportunity to state as clearly as possible how I understood my duty. I preached from Ephesians 4:11-12, reminded the congregation that 'Christ is not just the Lord of Christians; he is Lord of all, absolutely and without qualification'; that the entire membership of the Church in their secular occupations are called to be signs of this lordship in every area of public life; and that the task of the bishop is to help them in this ministry. The Church, I said, is 'the Church for the nation – not withdrawing into the sheltered existence of a minority community, but playing its full part in every aspect of national life, in its mental and spiritual wrestlings as well as its labours of social and economic developments, its politics, its art and music and drama – because all these things belong to Christ and because the Church has been set in the nation as the sign and instrument of Christ's plan for its perfecting'. In the context of the contemporary crisis over Kashmir I stressed the duty of the Church to uphold the ideal of a secular state.

I was happy to find that these words evoked a real response. Eighteen years of life together in a united Church under the wise leadership of Michael Hollis and David Chellappa had made the members more ready to look beyond their separate struggles for existence towards their common responsibility for the whole life of the city. I was to spend much of my time in the next nine years helping them to shoulder these responsibilities.

Services in St George's Cathedral had always been in English, as it was the temple of the old English establishment. I thought it was important to give the central part of my sermon in Tamil and the point of this was not lost, as the very full newspaper coverage next morning showed. Tamil came back easily, but I found that the movement led by C. N. Annadurai for the elimination of Sanskrit words in favour of pure Tamil and for a new style of sentence construction made my Tamil seem very old-fashioned. I therefore got the help of a teacher to steer me, in daily lessons, into a more acceptable style.

Another change of which I quickly became aware was the fading-away of the memory of Gandhi. During the twelve years in Madurai I had always been conscious of, and grateful for, the memory of Gandhi as the one who had so brilliantly demonstrated the way of simplicity in life and non-violence in politics. Now, nearly twenty years after his assassination, that memory no longer seemed to be present. New spirits were in control: the determination to achieve the material goals of 'development', and a nationalism that was in danger of becoming chauvinism. Our arrival in Madras was during the Indo-Pakistan clash over Kashmir. Patriotic feeling was very high. There was fierce resentment against the misinterpretation of the issue in the British media as a conflict between Hindus and Moslems, and the failure to recognize the deep commitment of India to the ideal of a secular state. I completely sympathized with the feeling, but regretted that some of my Indian Christian friends were so unready to consider possibilities of compromise and reconciliation. I wrote privately to a number of people and was delighted that M. M. Thomas welcomed my initiative in spite of the delicacy of the involvement of an Englishman in the dispute. I also took part in an all-party conference called by the Madras Government. I appealed to D. T. Niles as Secretary of the EACC to find an opportunity of bringing together Christian leaders from India and Pakistan to talk and pray together about the conflict. A meeting at Kandy early in December provided the opportunity for such a meeting and I was able to get the agreement of both sides to a joint statement which was issued by the EACC Working Committee and which included the following paragraphs:

The dispute between these two neighbouring countries is occasioned by conflicting claims regarding Kashmir, but it has an especially intractable character because it arises from the deeply held convictions upon which these two nations have based their existence as independent republics. Pakistan came into being because of a conviction that the areas of sub-continent where Moslems were in a majority should form a single Islamic state. India rejected the concept of a state founded on a particular religion and chose to be a secular state. The dispute over Kashmir touches each nation at its central point of conviction. Though a territorial question is the occasion of the dispute, the issue is not primarily territorial but ideological. This makes a compromise exceedingly difficult.

Recognizing these facts, we must nevertheless insist that to look at the dispute solely as a clash between two ideologies will lead to disaster. It can only harden self-righteousness on both sides and make a settlement impossible. Christians have a duty to testify that no ideology can be made into an absolute of policy, and that this dispute, like other political issues, must eventually be settled by negotiation involving political compromise on both sides.

The meeting which has been announced to take place at Tashkent early in the new year provides an opportunity for the leaders of the two nations to seek an honourable settlement by negotiation. We earnestly call upon Christians throughout Asia to unite in prayer that God may give to the statesmen who take part in the meeting the wisdom which He alone can give to find a solution acceptable to both nations and consistent with their national honour and integrity.

The Tashkent meeting did bring about a settlement but the tragic death of Lal Bahadur Shastri, the Indian Prime Minister, within a few hours of the signing of the agreement, brought a deep note of sorrow into the thanksgiving of the whole nation. We held a service of memorial and thanksgiving in the Cathedral at which the Governor, Chief Minister and members of the Cabinet participated. It was my first experience of the kind of public role in which I was now to be involved. A Congress Government was still in power as it had been since 1947, but the election of May 1967 replaced this by a government of the Dravida Munetra Kazhagam (DMK) led by C. N. Annadurai of Kanchi. We had known each other during the war years when we had served as air raid wardens. His party was held together not by a political programme but by devotion to the Tamil language and culture. Their approach to government was pragmatic and populist and I found it congenial. For his part Annadurai was always friendly and ready to listen. Some of my Christian friends who were deeply loyal to Congress looked askance at the DMK because of its official commitment to atheism. I found this rather an asset than a liability, since the gods whose existence they denied were, in my Christian understanding, no gods. Annadurai's real beliefs were well expressed when, at my invitation, he addressed a big congregation in the cathedral during a memorial service for Martin Luther King and spoke of him as 'truly a servant of God'.

One of the first acts of the new DMK government was to organize an international festival to celebrate the glories of Tamil culture. As part of the celebration a series of bronze statues, more than life-size, was to be erected along the two-mile length of the Marina, the splendid stretch of seafront which is one of the glories of Madras. While these plans were being made I received a telephone call from the Secretariat. An anonymous voice informed me that if Pope and Caldwell were not included among the half-dozen statues a grave historical injustice would have occurred. These two nineteenth-century English mission-aries had laid the foundations for the Tamil Lexicon and for the comparative grammar of the Dravidian languages. I asked the unknown caller what he supposed that I could do about this historical injustice. 'You can write to the Chief Minister', came the reply, 'and offer him two statues.' 'And where', I asked, 'do you think I can find 50,000 rupees to put up two statues?' 'That', said the caller, 'is your problem', and rang off.

I was in a dilemma: should I simply forget this anonymous call, or should I take it seriously? I consulted a few friends and they encouraged me to take it seriously. The time was very short if anything was to be done. I found a sculptor who undertook to do the work for Rs. 25,000. I wrote a circular letter to all the Christian churches and schools and colleges in Tamilnadu saying that I wanted Rs. 25,000 to put up statues of Pope and Caldwell on the Marina. Within a few weeks the whole sum had come in small contributions from every part of the country. I wrote to the Chief Minister and offered the statues. He replied accepting the offer and inviting me to dedicate one of them. And so on an evening in January 1968 I stood before an audience of 250,000 people on the Madras beach, with the Chief Minister and his entire Cabinet, and delivered an oration in Tamil in praise of Dr G. U. Pope, the Methodist missionary who had translated some of the Tamil classics into English and laid the foundation of the Tamil Lexicon. And to this day the eight statues which commemorate the makers of Tamil culture include three foreign missionaries – the two whom I have named and the eighteenth-century Italian Jesuit Beschi. It is a nice commentary on the popular view that the only work of missionaries has been to destory native cultures.

It was a great blow for Tamilnadu when Annadurai fell ill with cancer and after long suffering died on 3 February 1969. I visited him in his last illness and walked for two miles behind his body through vast crowds of sobbing people. It was said that a million people streamed into Madras to pay their homage. For me it was an unforgettable experience to walk through those weeping crowds and feel their emotion. As his body was lowered into the grave and I was standing at the side, one of the mourners said: 'There is the Bishop. Should he not say a prayer?' But Nedunchezhian, the next in line for the leadership of the Party, curtly forbade it. The DMK's official ideology remained intact and I said my prayer in silence, but – I am sure – not alone.

My experience in Kanchi and Madurai had been mainly of villages. Now I was living in a city whose population was said to be growing by 100,000 a year. All over the sprawling city, scattered among the fine houses and public buildings, were hundreds of 'slums' – clusters of huts made of mud and thatch and old kerosene tins, huddled together on some patch of unused land, without water, sanitation or light. From one point of view they were a token of the extraordinary courage and resilience of their inhabitants. Groups of families who had migrated from their villages in search of a better life would start as pavement dwellers, living, cooking and sleeping in the open street. From this starting-point they would explore the city till they found a vacant spot. Over a period of time they would collect odd bits of building material and then, on a moonless night, move in together and work all through the night to put up their flimsy huts. At first light they would call at the house of some aspiring political leader, inform him that the new village was named after him and invite him to come and hoist a flag with the promise that they would all vote for him at the next election. By the time the police arrived, the new residents would have a secure political base! The place may be a squalid sight, yet behind the squalor there is an amazing resourcefulness and fortitude. But for the city administration it is a nightmare. How to provide water, sanitation, lighting, roads, schools, health services and transport for 100,000 additional people every year on a desperately tight budget?

Before my arrival in Madras steps had been taken to form a Christian Council for Social Service, including Roman Catholics, the CSI and most of the other Churches. I suggested that we invite the head of the city administration to come and talk to us about his problems. It seemed clear that these slums formed the most acute challenge to the Christian conscience. We had a big map made with signs to show the location of each Christian congregation and each slum. The former were clustered in little huddles at various points on the map – a visible sign of the ridiculous rivalry of our Churches in the past, more anxious to compete with each other than to minister to the whole city. The slums were evenly spread over the whole map. We divided up the 600 or more slums among the 200 congregations, allotted three or four to each congregation, and sent a letter signed by the Roman Catholic Archbishop and me to the incumbent of each, with the challenge to undertake responsibility for the care of the allocated slums, and the offer of training for relevant action. Many gave no visible sign of response, but some were moved to action. The idea began to take root, at least here and there, that a Christian congregation must be seen as a community which cares for its neighbours. From small beginnings this led to bigger programmes of action in the emergencies caused by flood and fire. After one especially disastrous flood in which thousands were made homeless, the Chief Minister invited us to undertake some long-term constructive programme. After much debate we decided that we would try to equip thirty-six of the slums with modern sanitation as a pilot project which the Government might follow up. We had the support of Christian Aid, and the help of a retired engineer. The important thing was to have the backing of the whole slum community and this meant becoming very much involved in their politics. It took several years to complete the first dozen projects and then, to our great delight, the Madras Government announced its intention to create a new agency with a strong political leader at its head, to devote itself entirely to the problem of the slums.

The populist approach of the DMK Government was a great asset at this point. The man in charge of the Slum Clearance Board, A. N. Arungannel, was himself from a poor home, understood the feelings of slum people, and was most ready to welcome our co-operation. The programme for rehousing the slum communities was worked out in close consultation with the residents themselves. They were assured places in the new buildings and were able to stay on the sites in temporary huts while the new homes were being built. Our main contribution was given through an agency called the New Residents Welfare Trust. This was the brain-child of a very creative group of citizens brought together by a young Scots missionary, Murdoch Mackenzie. The idea was to provide a trained social worker for each of the newly housed communities to assist them in making the difficult transition from a mud hut on the ground to a flat in a three-storey building, and to give them a strong voice in making their needs known. Arangannel himself insisted that this should be a non-governmental organization so that it would have freedom in dealing with Government. At his suggestion I became chairman, he was vice-chairman, a very able and devoted Hindu was the executive secretary and a Moslem was treasurer. The social workers employed were given special training at our Community Service Centre and did a marvellous job in helping these newly housed communities to become really human communities with a sense of shared responsibility for their own welfare.

These various programmes were not without their difficulties. There were conflicts between young pastors who opened the churches to children from the slums as day-care centres, and elders who resented the resulting deterioration of their treasured sanctuaries. There were those who felt that these programmes did not have a sufficiently clear evangelistic purpose. The engineer in charge of the sanitation programme was a devoted evangelical and wanted to insist that a text from Scripture be provided for each latrine! I was also eager to find effective ways of evangelism for this bustling city, but it seemed to me essential that the Church which preached the Gospel should be recognizable as a body which cared for its neighbours. With some justification Hindu officials had often regarded Christian interventions in social affairs with suspicion lest they should really be a cover for proselytizing. We tried to make it plain that we were concerned about conversion, but that conversion should mean more and not less concern about one's neighbours. I was happy that our contribution was so warmly welcomed.

The danger, of course, was that it was too paternalistic. I was beginning to become aware of words like 'conscientization' and 'community organization'. We learned of training programmes being conducted in the Philippines for community organization along the lines developed by Saul Alinsky in Chicago. We sent two men, one a young pastor and one a Hindu, for this training. They returned with both appreciation and criticism. The course seemed to be designed to maximize conflict. They had been taught that the first essential is to identify 'the enemy'. The approved answer to the question 'Who is the enemy?' was 'the Government'. But they had learned to regard the Madras Government as an ally whose help could be enlisted. We decided that, with the training they had received, they should begin work in some of the most squalid slums on the north side of the City. Their work soon began to show results. The most acute problem was water, and bureaucratic delays were preventing the provision of a proper supply. The residents marched with their water-pots to the City centre, massed in front of the Corporation offices and demanded to see the concerned authority. The campaign was successful and they got their water. We hoped that we were on the right lines.

But this deviation was not approved in Manila. A body called the Asian Council for People's Organization (ACPO) deputed an American to Madras to train some of our people in the proper methods. I ventured to suggest that some knowledge of the language and culture would help in understanding the issues, but the American trainer bluntly told me that this was typical missionary paternalism. The candidates were to be trained in the techniques of arousing anger and creating conflict. An excellent case was discovered in a village where the diocese had sold some land which had been, as far as we knew, left for a long time without proper cultivation. One afternoon, without any warning, I suddenly found myself visited by a deputation including an Australian whom I had previously met at a conference, who told me that they had unearthed all the facts about this scandal and that unless I took immediate action to restore the land to the villagers of Cheyyar, my name was going to be splashed across the headlines of the press throughout India. A photographer was present to ensure that my photograph would accompany the revelations of ecclesiastical corruption.

There followed a period of several weeks which were, I think, the only really unhappy time in my Indian experience. The American organizer, who seemed to have unlimited funds, brought the villagers to my house in taxis and organized them into what in India is called a *gherao* – a sort of mob action in which the victim is imprisoned until he has given way to the demand of the petitioners. He did not permit me to talk with them in Tamil, because he did not understand. And he did not permit me to explain to him in English what I was saying, because my business was to talk to them and not to him. Whenever we were nearing understanding, he would drive them to reopen the attack. The climax came when he organized an absurd meeting in the village, for which he had hired a whole lot of chairs and a public address system, refusing to allow any face-to-face discussion but insisting that we sit at a distance and shout at each other. One of the young trainees was deputed to hover round with a camera (in which there was no film), pretending to photograph every gesture, a technique which (as he afterwards explained) was guaranteed to arouse anger. In this case it succeeded. The people of the neighbouring village (and this was really an inter-village dispute) lost their tempers and seized the camera. The American owner of the camera then lost his and attacked the villagers. They then seized him bodily and threw him out of the village. Finally, as we made our way home in the darkness, we were attacked with knives in an attempt to kill, and only with difficulty persuaded the attacker to calm down.

I tell this sad story because it caused me to think very hard about the Christian approach to social justice. The American organizer was a Christian sent and funded by an organization which was the direct derivative of the 'Urban Industrial Mission' which I had been involved in launching during my days with the IMC. I had occasion to read and ponder what was being published about Christian action for social justice. I think it is true that my approach hitherto had been too paternalistic. But it was also clear that the methods developed and put into practice in this case were not likely to result in more justice. I had the strong impression that they were the outworkings of a guilty middle-class conscience and that the villagers of Cheyyar were instruments but not beneficiaries. This certainly did not mean that I was converted back to pacifism. I am sure that coercion is an inevitable element in the securing of justice. But I am sure that a Christian must always be seeking for the reconciliation that lies on the other side of successful coercion, and that the requirement that one begins by designating 'the enemy' and goes on to force his unconditional surrender is not the way to achieve lasting justice.

Another typical urban problem which occupied a lot of my time, and for which (perhaps) the solution I found was a trifle paternalistic, was that of the many victims of leprosy crowded into the most squalid of all the slums. Leprosy is now not a medical but a social problem; it can be cured, but many people (apparently) cannot lose their fear of even a cured sufferer. The Madras Government had opened homes for the victims of leprosy, but these were rather places of segregation than of care and freedom. Many refused to enter them. One particularly robust group had formed themselves into 'The Lepers' Union of St Anthony', had established themselves on a piece of waste land beside the suburban railway line, and were living by begging. Officially they did not exist, were not included in the census, and did not have ration cards. From time to time they were arrested, imprisoned, kept for a few weeks and then released to begin the old routine. They were not passive about their lot; on one occasion they paraded in force outside the Chief Minister's office to demand their human rights. If St Anthony was their patron, it appeared – for reasons unknown to me – that I was deputy patron. They would come again and again and squat in front of the house. Their demand was simple: 'We want to be free to be human beings, live our own life and earn our own living.' For a long time I could think of nothing except to sympathize with them, visit their huts and pray with them. In the end the solution came through my good friend Joseph John, a remarkable Indian pastor who had developed a farm colony with all kinds of experimental projects for rural advance. He told me that he could get hold of an area of wild jungle, about eighty acres in extent, near his centre. With his equipment he was able to do some preliminary clearing and ploughing. I raised money in small gifts in Scotland to build houses. And in due course we transported the entire Lepers' Union of St Anthony in lorries to begin their new life as independent farmers. It was an enormously hard transition for them, though we provided them with rubber shoes and gloves to protect their stunted limbs from injury by sharp stones and thorns. But they had immense courage and stamina and, little by little, they have made good and have been accepted by the neighbouring villagers who were at first horrified by their arrival. A few have been unable to face the difficulties and have drifted back to the city. The rest are carrying on – another shining example of sheer human courage.

The challenge of the city was so great that I was always in danger of giving less than due attention to the rural areas. Village congregations were out of sight and could easily slip out of mind. I did try to keep up a steady round of visitation. There were (as always in India) disasters which hit the villages with staggering force. In 1966 there was a cyclone which destroyed thousands of homes, churches and schools and a huge rebuilding programme had to be launched. In 1969 there was a long drought, and some of the village people were reduced to walking up to five miles for drinking-water. Our response to this was a programme for deepening wells (about 2500 in all) and providing electric pump sets on a mortgage basis organized through the banks and the manufacturers. The village elementary schools were a source of great anxiety. For the past thirty years the received wisdom among missionaries had been that Government would take them over. Mission boards had lost interest in supporting them. The CSI Synod had (a few years earlier) gone on record in favour of handing them over to Government. In the northernmost part of Madras diocese, which was part of the Andhra State, the Government had moved to take over the schools. The Roman Catholics had refused, and our people had wanted to do the same, but – under missionary pressure – had submitted. The result was predictable. In spite of promises, the mission schools, which were in the Harijan quarters, were closed and the children told to attend the schools in the caste village. There they could, of course, attend – but only by sitting outside in the street. Effectively the Harijans were denied education and a new generation of illiterate Christians was growing up. The diocese would never again submit to missionary pressure on this point, and since the boards made it clear that they wished to reduce grants for these schools, we had to struggle to sustain them. When the Indian rupee was devalued, we used this windfall to create funds which could be drawn upon by village pastorates for part grants towards new school, church and parsonage buildings.

Shortly before I came to Madras, the diocese had appointed a survey team to identify the unevangelized areas of the diocese and this reported at the first meeting of the Diocesan Council after my arrival. Surprisingly we found that there were three large areas within the diocese where there was effectively no Christian presence. We were able to mobilize funds and to find workers to go into these areas, and before long we had flourishing Christian congregations in each of them as centres for further outreach. Throughout my time in Madras I was constantly being called to the dedication of newly erected churches, most in the expanding industrial suburbs of Madras, but many also in the rural areas. In order to avoid repeating the mistakes of the previous century I suggested to the Lutheran and Mar Thoma Churches that we should create an interdenomin-ational trust body to purchase sites for churches in the areas likely to develop in the near future, and then to allot sites to each church as required. In this way we hoped to ensure that for the future no part of the City would be without a Christian presence, and no wasteful competition would take place in the newly developing industrial suburbs. It was the application of the old principle of comity to an urban situation. It was not easy to subordinate denominational ambitions to the common task, but the Madras Churches' Development Trust did achieve much of its purpose and continues to function.

The rapid growth of industry in the City presented an obvious challenge to the Church. Following upon the visit of Paul Löffler in 1961, and the work of Harry Daniel at the cathedral in Bangalore, an impressive 'Industrial Mission' had been developed in that city. Its general approach was that of Wickham and the Sheffield Industrial Mission, that is to say that 'industry' is seen as an unevangelized mission field into which missionaries must enter with, of course, a relevant message. I was convinced that this was not the right approach, at least in Madras, for the reason that 'industry' was not in fact a vacant field as far as the Church was concerned. I estimated that probably 10 per cent of the workers in the Madras factories were Christians. They might not be very 'relevant' in their understanding of industry and its problems, but they were Christians, and therefore mission to industry must start with them and not with someone sent in (from another culture!) from outside. Moreover, many of the people in managerial positions (though not many owners) were members of the Church. I suggested that our approach should be through those congregations which had industry in their parishes, and that we should take as a base of operations those – whether worker or manager – who already professed to be Christians. I did not have any direct responsibility for the carrying out of these ideas, but I did have the chance of participating in some of the meetings of workers and managers (sometimes together, sometimes separately) to discuss their concerns and commitments as Christians, and I found them most impressive and illuminating. We also arranged, at the Community Service Centre, day conferences of people engaged in the same secular occupation (such as Government officials) where, sometimes with the help of role-play, they thrashed out the ethical dilemmas which they were facing in their daily work.

Obviously my main job, as always, was to help sustain the ministers and other workers in their faith through Bible study and prayer with them. As there were about fifty presbyters in the City alone, we had a monthly meeting beginning with Holy Communion and breakfast, at which I opened up for discussion some aspect of our common ministry. A few of these talks were later published as *The Good Shepherd*. In the rural areas we had monthly meetings for a full day which were devoted to 'corporate sermon preparation'. The morning would be spent in exegetical study of the Bible passages appointed for the Sundays of the following month. In the afternoon there would be four or five groups to prepare sermon outlines for the Sundays of the month, and then a plenary session for mutual criticism. For the teachers in the elementary schools we had residential meetings for Bible study, and for the teachers in High schools (of which we had about twenty-five) an annual 'holiday conference' in the cool climate of Bangalore for Bible study and relaxation. I also did a whole series of public Bible studies in Madras on the Epistles of Paul and was delighted to find that so many people were eager for just such spiritual food. At the Community Service Centre we organized periodical conferences about the big public issues, and some of these took the form of inter-faith meetings at which representatives of the major faiths and ideologies shared together their insights about the problems which faced us all in the public life of the nation. I found these, on the whole, more fruitful than the purely religious discussions which I had had with Ramakrishna monks in Kanchi. In these latter we were always inclined to defend well-known and well-prepared positions; in the Madras discussions we were all – Christians, Hindus or whatever – reaching beyond our standard formulas to seek answers to the problems with which God was confronting us all. These discussions really stretched the mind and forced the participants to think fresh thoughts.

Throughout this period I was also carrying heavy responsibilities for the CSI as a whole. I was Deputy Moderator, and – being in Madras – often had to act in emergencies, or to take the place of the Moderator when he was away. For most of this period Bishop Solomon of Dornakal was Moderator and on his many necessary visits to Madras he always stayed with us and we became very much attached to him. I was also Convener of the Synod Ministerial Committee, and had much to do with getting the new seminary at Arasaradi finally launched. After much persuasion Dr Sam Amirtham had agreed to leave the college in Bangalore to become the first principal of the new seminary. We wanted to involve the churches fully in the planning of the curriculum and style of the seminary, and for this purpose convened a conference of bishops and others with Shoki Coe and Erik Nielsen of the Theological Education Fund. The result, under Sam Amirtham's inspired leadership, was a kind of ministerial training which was more truly appropriate to a missionary Church than anything I have known before or since. The final achievement of this goal, almost thirty years after I had been asked to convene the first committee for the purpose, was one of the most joyful experiences of my life.

A less happy experience was the convenership of a committee to advise on the future of Serampore, the famous college on the banks of the Ganges, founded at the end of the eighteenth century by William Carey and, since early in this century, the donor and arbiter of theological degrees for the whole of India. The committee was a splendid team, and we worked very hard in consultation with all concerned to formulate proposals which were radical but, we believed, appropriate. The 'Newbigin Report' was, however, too radical for the people most concerned. In good Bengali style a bomb was placed in the college premises as a mark of disfavour. Fortunately it failed to explode, but this is the only time when I have had a bomb dedicated to my personal account! Like the bomb, the report was a failure, and the college authorities were so diligent in destroying all known copies that I doubt if any survive.

In the autumn of 1968 Dr Frank Lake was invited to spend about two months in South India giving teaching to clergy in all the dioceses about counselling. The response was such that the bishops and the Synod Executive were convinced that there was need for a centre of training in counselling to serve, if possible, the whole of India. I was given the responsibility of getting such a centre established. Vellore seemed an ideal place, since the hospital there drew patients and their families from every part of India and there would be possibilities for supervised practical experience for students from all areas in their own mother tongues. The seminary buildings of the Arcot Mission were generously made available, with adequate ground for expansion, and the Christian Counselling Centre was opened in 1971. Until I left India I chaired its governing council and it has been a joy to see how rapidly it has developed under the leadership of its young director, Dr Prashantham.

Because Madras has a large Christian population with a high proportion of English knowledge, it was a prime target for the purveyors of instant revival. There was a constant stream of such brethren, mostly from the United States and always assuring me that they would guarantee spiritual revival if given a free hand for ten days of meetings. One of the by-products of these exercises was usually the re-baptism of a few people (often very good and devout people) who felt that their Christian life up to that moment had been invalid, and that they must start again with a new baptism by the evangelist. There was also the powerful witness of the local Pentecostals who regarded speaking in tongues as the only valid sign of 'baptism in the Spirit' and who told those willing to listen that membership in the CSI was a sure road to everlasting perdition. Because it was the best and most sensitive of church members who were shaken by this teaching I felt that a big campaign was needed throughout the Churches to help people to understand the meaning of baptism and the relation of baptism to the work of the Holy Spirit. I therefore spent much time in holding one-day congregational 'teach-ins' on these matters and these evoked a great response. The young people in the city organized a series of meetings on the subject at which the attendance was nearly 3000 and I wrote a small series of Bible studies which was published in Tamil and English.

The young people of the diocese were taking an increasingly active part. We had altered the constitution so as to require that 30 per cent of the membership of all church committees at local and diocesan level should be under thirty-five years of age and this had a real effect on the whole life of the diocese. There was a series of excellent youth assemblies organized both for the diocese and for the Church as a whole. I was also much involved in speaking at student conferences and in teaching missions in the Christian Medical College and elsewhere. Two of these series were published as *Christ our Eternal Contemporary* and *Journey into Joy*.

During the whole of the nine-year period I was involved in the continuing struggle for unity between the CSI and the Lutheran Churches. A doctrinal consensus had been reached after about twenty years of discussion and this, on Lutheran principles, should have been enough. We went on to prepare a basis of union and constitution for a united Church to be called 'The Church of Christ in South India'. The CSI Synod expressed its readiness to unite on this basis subject to a few minor changes. No action, however, was taken from the Lutheran side. It was a great disappointment.

At the same time I was convener of the NCC's Committee on Faith and Order. With the full-time help of a young Syrian Orthodox priest I headed up an all-India study programme involving the Orthodox, Roman Catholic, Mar Thoma and Protestant Churches, culminating in a residential conference at Nasrapur in August 1972. This was a very blessed occasion on which we found a deep unity of spirit even when we tackled very controversial issues. As far as I know there was no formal action for follow-up but I cannot believe that that work was without fruit.

Inevitably I was still involved in meetings outside of India, some of which I had undertaken to attend before I knew of my appointment to Madras. I was brought back on to the Working Committee of Faith and Order and took part as far as I could in all its meetings, to my great happiness and reward. In 1966 I gave the Beecher Lectures at Yale Divinity School, later given in Cambridge and published as *The Finality of Christ*. The subject was chosen because I was dissatisfied with what seemed to me a confused kind of 'ecumenism', namely the inclusion of the 'inter-faith' dimension in the ecumenical idea. I believed that the whole integrity of the Ecumenical Movement depended upon the acceptance of the centrality and finality of Christ, and that to move from this was not a legitimate extension of the Ecumenical Movement but a reversal. The argument around this issue was to become much more sharp as time went on. Since Elihu Yale was a member of St Mary's church in Madras before he gave the money which created 'Yale College', I was happy to tell my audience in Newhaven that the 'mother church' would always watch the progress of her distinguished daughter with a benevolent eye! (By way of return, we had a delightful occasion when Chester Bowles, an alumnus of Yale, was the US Ambassador in Delhi. With some of his classmates he raised a fund to make some much-needed renovations in St Mary's and visited Madras to open a permanent exhibition depicting the early history of the Church.)

In 1968 I was invited as a consultant to the Lambeth Conference and shared in the work of the committee on the ministry of bishops. I was a delegate of the CSI at the Uppsala Assembly in the same summer. At the end of 1969 I was in Uganda for a mission to Makerere University along with John Gatu and others. In 1970 I was in Alaska and various parts of the USA and took part in the COCU meetings at St Louis. In 1971 I was again in East Africa for the first meeting of the Anglican Consultative Council, and in the following year at Bangkok for the WCC meeting on 'Salvation Today'.

Among these many meetings three stand out in my memory as being important for the development of my own thinking. Uppsala was in many ways a shattering experience. The plenary sessions were dominated by the realities of economic and racial injustice. The mood was one of anger. The well-drilled phalanx of students in the gallery ensured that the emotional temperature was kept high. It was a terrifying enunciation of the law, with all its (proper) accompaniments of threat and wrath. We were corporately shaken over the pit of hell. The word of the Gospel was hardly heard except, in a muted way, when a little band of Salvationists sang to us. More characteristic was the evening when Peter Seeger sang the well-known mockery of the Christian Gospel which affirms that 'there'll be pie in the sky when you die', and the assembly sat in rapt silence and then applauded as though it were a new revelation of truth. How, I couldn't help wondering, could such a group be so easily brainwashed?

At Uppsala I was involved in Section 2 which dealt with the missionary theme. It had been prepared not only by well-reasoned documents from Geneva and from the German and Norwegian mission councils, but also by a deafening barrage from Donald McGavran about the unevangelized millions of the world. This was in effect counter-productive, for it put those of us who wanted to include a strong word about the unfinished evangelistic task into a position where we seemed to be aligned with the high-pressure propaganda of the 'Church Growth' school. John Taylor did a masterly job in drafting the first part of the report which sought to develop from a biblical base the theme of mission as humanization. The later sections, however, seemed to reduce mission to nothing but a desperate struggle to solve insoluble problems. Obviously the Church itself was the major problem, and there was no enthusiasm for enlarging the membership of this dubious institution. Perhaps the best thing that could be said about the report was that it honestly reflected the profound confusion in the Churches about what mission is. The saddest thing was that we were not able seriously to listen to each other.

The Bangkok meeting has been much criticized but I felt that, painful though it sometimes was, it represented a move in the right direction. There was a real search for a new kind of spirituality which was best expressed in Kosuke Koyama's phrase: 'Not crusading minds but crucified minds'. Prayer and waiting upon God had a much more central place than at the meetings of the recent past. The brief, sung refrain 'Out of the depths I cry unto thee, O Lord' truly expressed the central mood of the meeting. There was, however, too much easy division of the world into oppressors and oppressed, the speakers being usually confident that they were oppressed except for some of the western delegates who, if they did not remain silent, were

tempted to beat their breasts and confess their sins of oppression
– an exercise described by the Brazilian Reuben Alves as 'a sado-
masochistic ritual which leaves reality unchanged'. But, to quote
the report I wrote at the time:

> Our concern about power led us again and again to the vision
> of the powerlessness of the Lamb. We did clash and hurt one
> another, but there was no pitched battle in which one side
> defeated the other. Rather, we were humbled, and because we
> saw that the powerlessness of Jesus is a more profound reality
> than our powers, we were helped to accept one another in our
> need of mutual help and understanding . . . I think that the
> personal reality of Jesus himself – not as a theological concept
> but as a living and encountered reality – laid hold on us as
> persons and not just as minds.

In my own private diary I wrote: 'There was more emotion than
thought. But it was right to have a meeting of this kind at which
the old dominance of the Western Churches was completely
broken and we were together as one family depending on the
suffering of the cross. But the old kind of language just could not
be used any more.' Perhaps it was perverse of me to add in my
diary: 'I think this must be the last of this kind of meeting that I
attend.' In fact it was not to be the last, and at the Fifth Assembly
in Nairobi three years later I was to see a real recovery of joy and
confidence in the Gospel.

At Louvain in 1971 I shared in the full meeting of the
Commission on Faith and Order and was asked by Lukas Vischer
to chair the section on 'Conciliarity' and draft the report. I had
great hesitation about accepting this, for I was sure that
'conciliarity' would be seized upon as an alternative to organic
union and therefore welcomed by those who wanted at all costs
to preserve denominational identities. Unfortunately my fears
proved to be well-grounded for, in spite of repeated statements
by the WCC to the contrary, bodies like the Lutheran World
Federation have enthusiastically welcomed a concept of conciliarity (further described as 'reconciled diversity') which enables
them to take part in councils of churches but to retain their
separate sovereignty. I therefore regret that I was responsible
for drafting the operative document. But in another respect the
Louvain meeting was a time of great enrichment for me. I shared

in the section on the role of the handicapped in the life of the Church and through the Bible studies in that section, and through the testimony of my friend Jerry Moede, who had been crippled by a sudden onslaught of the rare Barré Syndrome, I came to a quite new realization of the vital role of the incurably handicapped in the life of the Church. I tried to express this in a chapter of the WCC book entitled *Partners in Life*.

Madras was a sufficiently important place to attract many visitors and during these nine years we had a number of distinguished guests. Malcolm Muggeridge, having filmed the work of Mother Teresa in Calcutta, came to spend a few days looking at the CSI. His BBC manager did not think that villages were important but fortunately he was laid low with 'Madras tummy' and I was able to take Muggeridge to a village confirmation and church dedication. He was, as I knew he would be, far more impressed by this than by what the BBC wanted him to see. We had, of course, several heated arguments, but he was a most charming person to have around.

The church at whose dedication he assisted had an interesting history. Two years earlier Donald and Jean Coggan, then at York, honoured us with a visit. On our way along a country road the car was stopped by a large crowd. A man opened the door and said: 'Your Grace, will you kindly dedicate our church?' I knew nothing of the matter, but it appeared that this group of Christians had been trying for a long time to get a site for a church, had heard that I was bringing the Archbishop along that road the next morning, had vowed that at all costs he must dedicate their church, had brow-beaten the local revenue officer into allotting them a small piece of public land, and had worked like beavers all through the night to put up a small shed of bamboo and thatch. Now they had their Archbishop and all was set! He looked at me and said: 'What do I do?' I said: 'Go ahead and dedicate it! York Minster probably began as a shed like that.' So with evident delight he offered prayers of dedication while Jean held the candle which was considered an essential part of the rite. Now, two years later, they had built a substantial brick church with tiled roof, and they had Malcolm Muggeridge and the BBC camera men to help them dedicate it.

In my last year in Madras we had the great joy of a visit from Michael and Joan Ramsey who stayed with us for several days.

To have the Archbishop of Canterbury stand with me behind the Holy Table in Madras Cathedral and to join with him in celebrating the Eucharist according to the CSI order was something that filled me with happiness. As I remembered the battles of the past and the absence of the Church of England from the great act of union twenty-six years earlier, I felt that I could really say *Nunc dimittis*.

Among others whose visits brought us great delight were two very different characters: Hans Küng with his sharp, probing mind, so willing to range afar but so firmly rooted in Christ, and Mother Teresa in whose presence one felt the radiance of an entirely earthy holiness. During these years I had the happiest of relationships with the Roman Catholics in the City and was often asked to speak to their people. One Eastertide the leader of the Newman Society phoned me in great distress to say that many of his members seemed no longer to believe in the resurrection and would I come and convince them that it really happened! Our greatest joint activity was the celebration of the nineteenth centenary of the martyrdom of St Thomas at the place which is still called 'St Thomas's Mount'. That the apostle Thomas came to India, that he was martyred and that his bones lie buried under the Cathedral of Mylapore is, for most Indian Christians, an article of faith almost worthy of inclusion in the Apostles' Creed. Indeed there is an impressive amount of evidence to point to the possibility that it may be so. The Catholic authorities were kind enough to suggest that we should join them in the celebration of the nineteen-hundredth anniversary of the alleged martyrdom. I suggested to our Diocesan Executive that this gracious invitation placed us in a dilemma. 'If we accept we may find ourselves involved in various things of which we do not approve; if we decline we shall be asking the public to think that Thomas was a Roman Catholic and not a good member of the CSI!' The problem was nicely settled by Murdoch Mackenzie who said: 'I propose that we accept the invitation on the basis of the fact that Thomas was a well-known sceptic and that we can share in whatever goes on with our own doubts about whether his bones really lie in Mylapore.' In the event the whole celebration was a great witness to the City. There was a vast public meeting in the Island Ground where several ponderous addresses in English were lost on the audience, but the Chief Minister and I spoke in Tamil and I think something of the meaning of the event was communicated. At any rate one of the Jesuit Fathers ran up to me at the end and embraced me and said: 'I have been converted all over again!'

When we had left Geneva to return to Madras we promised the family that we would try to visit them every year. In fact, with my frequent journeys for World Council and other meetings we were able to keep in close touch and had some wonderful family holidays in Scotland and in the south west of Ireland. Alison went to serve as a VSO in Miri, Sarawak, for a year from 1966 to 1967. Her work in developing health services took her on long journeys by river into the interior of the country where she lived in the village long-houses during her visits. It was a very tough assignment. On her way back she spent three months with us in Madras. Two years later she returned and spent fifteen months with us working in a pioneer programme of village health care under a Hindu doctor. Again the conditions were very tough and she contracted tuberculosis which entailed a period of rest and return to England. Margaret and her husband David Beetham had made their home in Manchester where he was teaching in the university and where their two children, Helen and Katie, were born. Janet, having completed her university course at Durham, took up a teaching post in Birmingham and in July 1968 we celebrated her marriage to Andrew Williamson who was working for the British Council of Churches Housing Trust. They made their home in Lambeth and their first son, Nicholas, was born during our last year in Madras. John finished his schooling after we left Geneva and came out to Madras to spend some months with us before going up to Cambridge. He was much involved in the creation of the Cambridge Students' Union and stayed up an extra year to be its full-time president. During his Cambridge days he came out to spend a vacation with us in Madras, making the journey overland by various orthodox and unorthodox means. From Cambridge he went to Brixton to make his home there and to serve as a youth worker among the very deprived young people, black and white, of that area.

Apart from family holidays Helen and I were able to have three wonderful spells in the Swiss mountains on our various journeys between India and Britain. We also had one holiday at Darjeeling and did a trek with Sherpa porters along the route to Kancheng-junga – a magnificent experience of some of the greatest mountain scenery in the world. Apart from these major holidays we made it a practice to take twenty-four hours off every three or four months and stay quietly in our old home at Chingleput where we could rest and read and walk the jungle tracks which we had first explored nearly forty years earlier. They were always times of deep refreshment.

The rules of the CSI provide that a bishop should normally retire at the age of sixty-five but that, in certain circumstances, service may be extended up to the age of seventy. I did not wish to ask for any extension. I thought that it was best for all bishops to retire at that age, and I had seen the harm done when good men had tried to continue beyond that age. Obviously there are many kinds of useful work that a man over sixty-five can do, but the job of a diocesan bishop in the CSI is not one of them. The pressures are so heavy and so unremitting that only a person in the fullness of strength can hope to stand them. Like every other missionary I had often had to ask myself whether the time had come to leave so that an Indian might succeed, but since I had been called to the office by the Indian Church I was sure that I should remain up to, but not beyond, the normal retiring age. That meant leaving in 1974. We therefore announced our intention of leaving near the end of March 1974 after the pastoral stationings for the following year had been arranged.

Once again we were quite overwhelmed by the affection lavished upon us during the last few weeks before leaving. Five years earlier the diocese had celebrated my sixtieth birthday with tributes of affection which so overwhelmed me that I felt quite unable to respond. I knew that my ministry had been marred by many serious faults – by moments of anger and bad temper, by a too dominating style of leadership and by failure to be as fully available for others as a bishop should be. I knew that all who had worked with me were conscious of these faults. And yet we were given such a warmth of affection that I felt both ashamed and comforted. I knew that much of it was because Helen had made up what was lacking in my ministry. She had always insisted that her work was to make a loving home where people were welcome and the words spoken to us at the many farewell meetings showed that she had done just that. It was also something that warmed my heart to find that it was not only the Christian people of the diocese who had taken us to their hearts. A few hours before we

237

left there was a public meeting arranged by the Government with the Governor presiding. Spying the UK Deputy High Commissioner in the audience, the Governor called to him: 'Why don't you get the British Government to bar the Newbigins' re-entry?'

Once again we had to say goodbye to a big gathering on the platform of Madras Central Station and we knew that it was really farewell to India for good. In spite of the sorrow of parting, there could be nothing but thankfulness as we settled down for the long slow journey across the Deccan to Agra and Delhi and beyond.

18
Birmingham: A New Dimension

Helen and I had cherished for a long time two ambitions which we hoped to achieve before finally leaving India. One was to walk up to the Everest base camp; the other (inspired by Dervla Murphy's *Full Tilt*) was to explore in a leisurely way the land route from India to Europe. The first exploit was tentatively scheduled for the spring of 1973, but it had to give place to the joy of welcoming the Archbishop of Canterbury in Madras. The second we were determined to achieve. And we wanted to have an emotional shock-absorber between the strenuous years in Madras and the new and unknown future in England. We decided to do the journey by local transport, travelling short distances each day and hoping to make contact with churches and Christian groups along the way. We wanted to feel free to travel as and when and where we pleased, so that for a couple of months no one would know where we were. So, with two suitcases and a rucksack we set off.

It was to be a wonderful journey, an experience that changed my own perspective in many ways. After a week in Delhi and a visit to the matchless beauty of the Taj Mahal, we had a long weekend in Lahore, a brief stop in Peshawar, and then ten days as guests of Indian friends in Afghanistan, seeing as much of the country as we could. In Meshed we were guests of the tiny evangelical community led by a courageous Moslem convert on the university staff. In Teheran we had meetings with the Presbyterians and with several bishops of the ancient Churches. In the lovely city of Isfahan we stayed in the ever hospitable home of Bishop and Mrs Deqani Tafti and in Shiraz with a missionary of the Church Missionary Society. After that we were on our own, travelling by easy stages through Western Iran by Ahwaz, Hamadah and Kermanshah to Tabriz. We had hoped to go through Iraq to Baghdad and Damascus but could not get permission. From Tabriz we hitch-hiked with a friendly Turkish *gastarbeiter* on his way back to Germany. He took us along a rough country road round the base of Mount Ararat, covered with fresh snow and gleaming in the light of a full moon, to his native village on the Soviet border. From there we travelled along the river which divides Turkey from Russia and looked across to the villages of Soviet Armenia on the other side, and then over high mountainous country to Erzurum, Kesari (the Caesarea of the Bible) and so to Cappadocia for a memorable weekend exploring that extraordinary region.

From there we travelled by the famous 'Cilician Gate' through the Taurus mountains to Tarsus and Mersia and then by the spectacular coast road along the 'Turkish Riviera' to Antalya. On the right were the great ranges of the Taurus mountains plunging steeply down into the sea, pine-clad slopes, sandy bays, turquoise-blue water and a series of great ruined castles reminding one of the wars of Byzantine, Crusader and Ottoman rulers. Antalya (the Attalia of Acts 14:25) was a good centre for following and reflecting on journeys of St Paul, and then we went on to Ephesus, Izmir (Smyrna) and Istanbul. And finally an uneventful journey through Bulgaria, Yugoslavia and Austria, savouring the gradual changes in style of architecture and of cultivation, until at 5.30 a.m. on 10 May we stopped in the centre of Munich and had our real culture shock.

The whole trip had taken two months, but into it had been packed a world of new experience. One could write a whole book in the effort to convey the impressions that the journey left: the rugged wildness of the Khyber Pass and the Kabul Gorge, the splendour of the vast statues of the Buddha cut out of the cliffs that flank the Bamian Valley, the old teahouses (*chaikanas*) which still welcome the traveller along the route from China to Europe as they did during the centuries when rumours of this mysterious beverage were spreading to the West. In Iran there was the matchless beauty of Isfahan, the day spent as guests of the Armenian Christian community in New Jolfa, and above all the visit to Persepolis with its magnificent sculptures preserved so perfectly under the ash that has covered them from the day that Alexander the Great burned down the palace. In Afghanistan we had seen the treasures of the great King Kanishka who, at the end of the first century AD, had in a single room jade from China, ivory from India, glass from Egypt and bronze from Rome. Here at Persepolis, from a period 500 years before Kanishka, we saw the brilliantly portrayed figures of the representatives of twenty-six nations each bringing the distinctive offerings of their peoples to the king of kings. It was a vivid reminder of the fact that, for at least a thousand years before the rise of Islam, the whole region from India to Greece was one living space, and Europe was still essentially a peninsula of the one Eurasian continent.

Throughout our time in Afghanistan we were constantly reminded of the way in which four religions had competed for the allegiance of central Asia: Zoroastrian, Buddhist, Christian and Moslem. In Eastern Turkey we were vividly aware of the way in which one of the greatest centres of Christian life and thought had been completely taken over by Islam. Cappadocia, once the nursery of Christian theology, was the only place in our whole trip where we had to have our Sunday worship by ourselves, for there was no other Christian to be found. We took a picnic lunch and walked over the fresh green turf of the Goreme Valley on a crisp April day, explored the ancient cave churches with their vivid wall paintings and tried to come to terms with the fact that a great living Church can be completely destroyed. It was among the relics of a long-obliterated Christendom that Helen and I made our offering of worship that Sunday morning. I had felt the same burden in preaching to the American community in Kabul on Palm Sunday; how does one interpret the Kingship of Christ in a place where history seems to be just an endless series of wars, conquests and defeats for one 'civilization' after another? Plainly a realistic eschatology has to be free from any triumphalism about the growth of the Church. And plainly also a Christianity which sees history only from the point of view of western Europe and its colonial offshoots is gravely defective.

The two months of our journey were so full of rich new experience that we had no chance to feel nostalgic about India. We were ready for the next chapter. It was wonderful to have time to spend with our children and to get to know our grandchildren – now three in number. For the three summer months we lived in beloved Edinburgh and there was leisure for reading. I decided to do what I had not previously attempted: to read the whole of Barth's *Dogmatics*. It was an immensely rewarding experience. Barth condensed and Barth quoted I had found totally unimpressive. But the real Barth, and especially the famous small-print notes, was enthralling. It was a needed preparation for the much more difficult missionary experience which (as I did not then realize) lay ahead.

In July I had three weeks in Ghana for the meeting of the Faith and Order Commission and for a series of visits to churches in different parts of the country to speak on behalf of the Ghana Church Union Committee. I was able to stay in the home of my old friend Christian Baeta and to visit the immense Volta River Project. But more than anything else I shall remember the visit to the old English fort at Cape Coast where the African slaves were kept chained in a dark dungeon at water-level till the boats took them to the slave ships, while in the chapel immediately above, the English garrison conducted worship, keeping watch through a hole in the floor on the inmates of the dungeon below. I am always amazed that these crimes can be so easily forgotten. Ever since that visit I have wished that some representative English-man – an Archbishop or a Prime Minister – might come to Ghana and go down into that dungeon, kneel down on the floor, and offer a prayer of contrition. I still hope it may happen.

Early in September we moved to Birmingham where I had been invited to join the staff of the Selly Oak colleges. This invitation had come as the result of a suggestion by David Paton and indeed nothing could have been more attractive as a task for a retired missionary. My main work was teach 'The Theology of Mission' and 'Ecumenical Studies' to those who were undergoing mission-ary training. The student body was made up both of men and women preparing to go from England and the European continent as missionaries overseas, and also of those from churches in all parts of the world sent to England for a period of study. There was not only a rich mix of races, nations and denominations, but also a very wide range of academic level – from High-school leavers to Ph.Ds. I had written to various centres to find out what was being taught under the rubric of 'theology of mission' and found that most of it was descriptive studies of various 'third-world theologies'. I wanted to attempt something different, something that would help these people to understand why the Church has to be missionary. It was not easy to do it in a way which was intelligible to those who had no theological training and yet challenging to those who came to us from a full course in theology. The result of these attempts was eventually published as *The Open Secret*.

I also had the responsibility of teaching Hinduism to the students of Westhill College who were taking Religious Education in the B.Ed. course of Birmingham University. This necessitated a substantial amount of reading, both in Indian history and in the Hindu classics which I had almost totally neglected since the days in Kanchi. It was hard work but I was very grateful for the challenge.

For twenty-seven years I had been a bishop in the Church of South India. Thirty years ago we had been innocent enough to hope that three decades would be enough to enable the divided Churches in England to catch up with India. For all these years we had lived in a fellowship where the treasures of the Anglican, Methodist and Reformed traditions were all ours to share. Now we faced the painful necessity of choosing which slot to go into. My old friend of Cambridge days, Laurie Brown, was Bishop of Birmingham. Very graciously he invited me to become an assistant bishop. I was grateful for the invitation but I was sure that it would be wrong to accept it. If we must choose between the three alternatives, the integrity of our commitment to unity in the Church of South India required that we should choose the one from which we had come. This was the more attractive since the Presbyterian and Congregational branches of the Reformed version of the faith had become one in the United Reformed Church. I therefore applied to the URC for admission as a minister and was in due course received. It so happened, however, that there was a vacancy in the local parish church and for a year I helped to fill this by taking the 8.0 a.m. communion each Sunday. We were both very grateful for this. We had come to rely upon the weekly celebration of the Eucharist and the absence of this in the URC was not easy to accept.

As time went on I began to receive invitations to take part in conferences of ministers and lay people. I began to feel very uncomfortable with much that I heard. There seemed to be so much timidity in commending the Gospel to the unconverted people of Britain. There were two aspects of this. One was the feeling that 'the modern scientific world-view' had made it impossible to believe much of traditional Christian teaching. One had therefore to tailor the Gospel to the alleged requirements of 'modern thought'. This was, of course, an old problem, but it seemed to be much more pervasive than before. The other and newer aspect of the problem was the result of the presence of substantial numbers of Hindus, Sikhs and Muslims in the big cities. The fact that the world contains large numbers of people who follow these religions had not, apparently, made any impact on the minds of good church people who had been supporting foreign missions since childhood. Sensitive Christians felt deeply and rightly concerned about the racist attitudes which became horribly visible in the actions of the National Front but were also present not far below the surface among those who repudiated such overt racism. It was an easy move from this proper concern to argue that respect for these minority communities precluded any kind of evangelism. The Gospel was all right for white Europeans, but it was an improper intrusion into the lives of Asians. Early in my time in Birmingham I participated in a meeting of a body called 'All Faiths for One Race'. It was typical that all those present were Christians and that a clergyman among them described missions as 'theological racism'. I was provoked into advising him to beware of theological fornication!

It was also clear that new and very difficult questions were being faced by the schools. Religious education was a compulsory part of the curriculum and this had always been understood as meaning Christian education. But if half the pupils came from homes professing another faith it was wrong that the State should use compulsory education to give Christian instruction to the children of Hindu or Muslim homes. Birmingham had sought to meet the problem with a new syllabus which was directed 'towards developing a critical understanding of the religious and moral dimensions of human experience and away from attempts to foster the claim of particular religious standpoints'.[1] Very specially there seemed to be great anxiety lest any child should become a committed Christian as the result of religious education. Pupils were to study religions 'objectively' as aspects of differing cultures, not to accept any of them as true accounts of how things are. It seemed obvious to me that the alleged 'objectivity' effectively concealed the real commitment of the practitioner of this kind of teaching, a commitment to the accepted values of the consumer society of which he was a part. In a supermarket society, a rich variety of religions was a welcome addition to the shelves. The debate about the syllabus was made more passionate by the inclusion of Marxism as one of the 'stances of living' to be studied. I personally found this one of the redeeming features of the syllabus, since it is plain that Marxism is a living faith about what is really true and can never be relegated to the position of an aspect of culture to be studied dispassionately along with Polynesian *kava* ceremonies and Indian *puranas*. But I did become involved in the critical debate on the syllabus because it seemed to me to rest on altogether false assumptions.

In both these respects I therefore found myself going against the stream, and I was the more astonished when, at the URC Assembly of 1977 I was elected to be Moderator for the year 1978–9. This was something that I had never dreamed of, and I could only accept it as evidence of the large-heartedness and open-mindedness of this Church. I chose as theme for my address to the 1978 Assembly Paul's words: 'I am not ashamed of the Gospel', and during the ensuing year, as I had the privilege of preaching and speaking all over the country, I tried consistently to sound this note. I found the experience immensely encouraging and rewarding. No doubt a visiting Moderator, during his one brief year of glory, is shown the brightest side of what he visits. But even making allowances for this, I found much to encourage. At the end of the year I was constantly thinking of the parable of the vine and of its pruning by the Gardener. The URC, I could report, was a bush which had been hard pruned. It was small and had lost many members. But in very many places I had found the new buds which are to be expected after good pruning, people of all ages coming afresh – in many different ways – to the faith of Christ.

During this period negotiations were proceeding for the union of the URC with the Churches of Christ. One of the issues to be settled arose from the important place occupied in the latter body by 'auxiliary ministers' – men and women serving in local teams as a non-stipendiary ministry of word and sacrament. I was eager that this opportunity should be seized to develop a well-trained non-stipendiary ministry for the whole Church. As I was also convener of the Church's Ministerial Training Committee I was in a good position to press the idea. There was, of course, some opposition – mainly clerical. But there was also strong support and I was able to use my moderatorial visits to the Provincial Synods up and down the country to expound and defend the idea.

After all the necessary deliberations over several years the General Assembly finally adopted the proposals of the Ministerial Training Committee and there is now a large and growing company of dedicated men and women preparing for and serving in the auxiliary ministry.

During the five years of teaching at Selly Oak I still had the opportunity to share in several activities of Faith and Order, but the most exciting and rewarding ecumenical experience was the meeting of the Fifth Assembly of the World Council of Churches at Nairobi during the closing months of 1975. I had accepted the invitation somewhat reluctantly. Uppsala had been an unhappy experience and I feared that the Nairobi meeting might become an ungodly clash between the rich and the poor. The work of the World Council's programme to combat racism had been furiously attacked in Britain, even by many good Christian people, and there was a growing tendency to regard the WCC with hostility and contempt. The *Church Times*, on the eve of the Assembly, regaled its readers with an article entitled 'Why Nairobi will be irrelevant', and the media coverage in the following days was almost uniformly disgraceful.

In fact I came back from Nairobi encouraged. In the report which I wrote, and which was widely circulated, and helped – I believe – to correct false impressions created by the media, I wrote as follows:

The Fifth Assembly was a more realistic testing ground for the Christian claim than any of its predecessors. If I may risk some over-simplification I would say that for the first three assemblies the old establishment (white, western, 'developed') was in unquestioned control; the rest of the world was present, but on the margins. At Uppsala the rest of the world (black, young, poor) forced itself, often stridently, into the consciousness of the Assembly. At Nairobi there had been a clear shift of control. This, more than any of its predecessors, was an Assembly in which control was fully shared, in which no part of the world could impose the agenda upon the rest. It was also more fully representative than previous assemblies of the whole range of the Church's life: there were more lay people, women, young delegates and (very important) ministers of local congregations. The shift in feeling was very obvious.

As compared with previous assemblies there was also a discernible shift in style. It was characteristic of this Assembly that its final word to the churches was not a declaratory message but a prayer which can be used everywhere. It is a prayer that gathers up and expresses the themes of the Assembly. But it also expresses something about the style of the whole meeting – one in which prayer and praise were woven into the texture of the meeting rather than being conducted as separate exercises. The refrains sung during many of the plenary sessions – 'Come Lord Jesus', 'Abba Father, set us free', 'Break down the walls that separate us'; the music which helped so much to give life to the liturgical acts; and the unforgettable closing worship beginning with the rich solemnity of an Orthodox choir and ending with a gay dance down the steps of the Assembly Hall into the great square outside – these are things that I will always remember as expressing the feel of the whole meeting. Above all, the fact that for the first few days we met in eighty small groups for Bible study on the main theme, that we met each other at the level of personal faith, need and experience, gave a texture to the whole meeting which has been missing (in my experience at least) in all of the previous ones.

During the years that have followed I have constantly returned in thought to the great hall of the Kenyatta Conference Centre. My place happened to be at the extreme edge of the semi-circle in which the members were seated, and I was able to see all of them and to sense the way in which the moral and spiritual centre of gravity had shifted from the old 'establishment' of the European and North American Churches to the representatives of Orthodoxy and of the Churches of the 'Third World'. Ever since those days I have tried in my public speaking to hold that scene in my mind and to speak in such a way that I would be willing for all in that conference hall to hear and acknowledge what I was saying as a valid Christian testimony and not just the expression of an Anglo-Saxon culture.

In 1979 I completed the five-year stint of teaching at the Selly Oak colleges. I did not think it right to continue in a salaried position after the age of seventy when there was such a vast and growing number of unemployed. I was very grateful to be able to continue to use the Library and to do occasional teaching. I looked forward to the opportunity of wider reading and to putting into book form the studies in St John's Gospel which I had been developing ever since the weekly Bible studies in Madurai in the early 1950s. But an unexpected call came for another kind of service. At a meeting of the Birmingham District Council of the URC in 1979, in the absence of the Chairman I was asked to preside. One of the items on the agenda concerned a small congregation of about twenty members which worshipped in a building just across the road from the Winson Green prison. It had begun 120 years earlier as a mission from the Handsworth Congregational church to an area which was described as being bounded by the prison, the lunatic asylum, the London North-Western Railway and James Watt's famous foundry. Officially known as 'Mary Hill' it was popularly described as 'Merry Hell'. From the first preaching on a cinder heap the Revd Robert Ann had collected a few children and started a Sunday School. This had grown into a flourishing congregation with vigorous companies of the Boys' and Girls' Brigades. But conditions had changed. The civic authorities had grandiose plans for development. Houses were pulled down and the inhabitants moved to the suburbs. A demolition order had been served on the church building thirty years ago. Some new houses had been built but over large areas weeds and rubbish covered the ground. The new residents were mostly from the Indian sub-continent and the West Indies. For forty years there had been no full-time minister. During the past six years the congregation had enjoyed the devoted service of the Revd Florence Mowat on an honorary and part-time basis. Now she was compelled to leave the district and the suggestion to the Council was that the church should be closed.

I could not reconcile it with my conscience to preside over such a decision. I suggested to the Council that if the Church abandoned such areas in order to settle in the relatively easy circumstances of the suburbs it would forfeit the claim to be a missionary Church. I urged that some other solution should be sought, and the Council agreed to defer a decision. In the following days Helen and I talked and prayed about the matter and the outcome was a call from the congregation to become their pastor with the understanding that it would be on a part-time basis. On 2 January 1980 I was duly installed and since then I have been struggling to fulfil the obligations of this ministry. It is much harder than anything I met in India. There is a cold contempt for the Gospel which is harder to face than opposition. As I visit the Asian homes in the district, most of them Sikhs or Hindus, I find a welcome which is often denied on the doorstep of the natives. I have been forced to recognize that the most difficult missionary frontier in the contemporary world is the one of which the Churches have been – on the whole – so little conscious, the frontier that divides the world of biblical faith from the world whose values and beliefs are ceaselessly fed into every home on the television screen. Like others I had been accustomed, especially in the 1960s, to speak of England as a secular society. I have now come to realize that I was the easy victim of an illusion from which my reading of the Gospels should have saved me. No room remains empty for long. If God is driven out, the gods come trooping in. England is a pagan society and the development of a truly missionary encounter with this very tough form of paganism is the greatest intellectual and practical task facing the Church.

During the 1970s the English Churches had been seeking new approaches to unity following the rejection by the Church of England of the proposals for unity with the Methodist Church. The result of these efforts was the enunciation of ten propositions as the basis for a convenant between the Churches. Five of these – Anglican, Methodist, Moravian, United Reformed, and Churches of Christ – agreed to form a 'Council on Covenanting' with a view to entering into such a covenant. I was appointed a member of the URC team on the Council, and this was to become a major preoccupation for me during the years 1979 to 1982. The URC was deeply divided but its General Assembly did finally accept the proposals by a majority slightly over the needed two-thirds. Once again, however, the move was defeated by a narrow margin in the General Synod of the Church of England. The whole exercise and the character of many of the debates in which I was involved exposed in a painful way the lamentable fading of the ecumenical vision in the minds of English church people. I began to realize how great was the loss which had been inflicted on the Church by the virtual eclipse of the SCM. I belonged to a generation which had been given their formative vision of the

Christian life and received their Christian calling in an ecumenical setting. But now the majority of those in the Churches had been shaped either in a conservative evangelical setting where visible unity was not seen to be important, or in a merely denominational setting which had deprived them of the opportunity to form deep and trustful friendships outside of that setting. With the failure of the Covenant the whole movement which had begun with the Lambeth appeal of 1920 seemed to have come to a dead end, and the united churches of the Indian sub-continent were marginal oddities rather than pioneers. But that was not, of course, the whole picture. Local ecumenical projects made their brave if always vulnerable witness, and prayers for unity in the month of January brought together great gatherings each year. As in the days before 1947 I find myself driven back to the simple fact that Jesus prayed for the unity of his Church, that he still prays for it, and that that prayer cannot be for ever denied. And I remember with gratitude the text on which Visser 't Hooft preached to us in Madras at the Second Synod of the Church of South India more than thirty years ago: 'We are partakers of Christ if only we hold our first confidence firm to the end.'

19
Looking Back and Forward

These memoirs have been written primarily as an act of thanksgiving for having been led along ways that I would never have guessed at the beginning and into a 'larger room' than I had dreamed of. I have been given friends who have enlarged my understanding of the Gospel through the insights of Christian traditions remote from the one in which I began. I have had at least a taste of what the Apostle describes as learning with all the saints the length and breadth and height and depth of the love of God. And at a time when families seem more fragile than ever before I have been given the inestimable blessing of a loving and united family, all in different ways giving themselves in service to the community, and of a partner whose wisdom and love have been the steadying and sustaining factors through all these years.

But the writing of these memoirs has also been an occasion for contrition. As I have looked back I have been compelled to remember the many failures in the simple courage that is needed for faithful witness, and the many ways in which – as a missionary – I failed in the sensitivity that is needed to understand another culture. I know that I have been guilty of the sins which I have so easily seen in other missionaries. Perhaps the reason why missionaries usually feel so much at home in each other's company is that they are guilty of the same sins! Yet , as every missionary could testify, the deepest reason is that they have shared in the joy of bringing the Gospel to others.

With thanksgiving and penitence there is also the need for some sort of assessment. I have to ask how far the causes which I have tried to serve have been the right ones and whether the hopes I invested in them were justified.

From the beginning of my discipleship the SCM taught me to see unity and mission as two sides of a single commitment. I have lived to see them systematically separated and opposed to each other. 'Evangelical' and 'ecumenical' have become mutually opposed rallying calls, and the ecumenical movement has come to be seen by 'evangelicals' as a threat rather than as an invitation to all who confess Jesus as Lord to become one. For the tragic separation I think that both sides have to accept a share of blame. I have to ask myself whether, as the first director of the WCC's Division of World Mission and Evangelism, I should have given more time and effort to the building of a bridge across the gulf. Those were the early years of the fateful decade of the 1960s, the decade which began with Kennedy's promise to put a man on the moon, when 'secular' was the dominant word, when the problem-solving technocrat had replaced God as the source from whom all blessings flow, and when we were invited to stop looking up and instead to find our hope in the ground of our own being. Although I fought against these currents, I realize now that I was partly carried along by them and unable to keep spiritual contact with those who remained entrenched in the old positions. That decade ended in the wild confusion of the student revolution and the 1970s saw a swing to the opposite extreme. 'Spirituality' replaced 'secularity' as the key word. Never, surely, was a best-seller so quickly buried and forgotten as Harvey Cox's 'Secular City'. But the scars left on the body of the Church by that traumatic decade will take a long time to heal.

The mood of the 1970s, with its interest in 'spirituality', did nothing to restore a sense of urgency about the restoration of visible unity to the Church. The new climate created by the Second Vatican Council brought much joy in the mutual discovery by Catholics and Protestants of the spiritual riches hitherto kept separate, but this expressed itself in informal meetings and co-operative projects rather than in the slow and tedious labour of reconciling structures. Visible unity is, for the present at least, far down in the list of agenda, and the CSI and its sister churches are no longer challenging models but only remote oddities. The failure of the English Covenant proposals has seemed to many to mark the final collapse of the whole thrust towards organic unity which was initiated by the 'Appeal to All Christian People' of the 1920 Lambeth Conference. The Anglican communion, it would seem, has decisively adandoned the leadership which it provided, for the decades following 1920, to the movement for reunion among the non-Roman churches. If people still talk about unity, the models now offered are less demanding. They do not call for the disappearance of the 'denominations' as we know them but for a tolerant coexistence which is dignified by the name of 'reconciled diversity'. And because these proposals do not force a radical challenge, they do not evoke a deep response. The question of unity becomes something marginal, unimportant in comparison with the great issues of justice and peace. And in so far as the divided Churches cannot themselves be a sign of peace, they have to become campaigners for peace – which is a very different thing.

For many in the period following the Second World War, the World Council of Churches did provide a sign. Probably it still provides a sign of hope for many in the younger churches, but for the Churches in Britain it is seen now as a threat. With its sustained insistence on justice for the poor, the oppressed and the forgotten it threatens – for many in Britain – the comfortable identification of Christianity with the established order. No doubt, like everything human, the WCC needs criticism and correction. But the hostility which it now evokes among many church people in the rich world is a piercingly clear evidence of the unrepented sin of our society. In this situation the Churches fail to hear the judgement which the existence of the WCC implies upon their still jealously guarded denominational sovereignty.

Yet nothing can remove from the Gospel the absolute imperative of unity. I am sure that, for so long as I have breath, I must continue to confess my belief that God intends his Church to be – in the words of the Lambeth Appeal – 'an outward, visible and united society', and that the unity he wills requires (in the words of the Third Assembly) that 'all in each place who are baptized into Jesus Christ and confess him as Lord and Saviour are brought by the Holy Spirit into one fully committed fellowship' and at the same time are 'united with the whole Christian fellowship in all places and all ages'. And I am sure that, while obedience to this vision calls for immense patience, it does not permit any slackening of prayer and effort. There can be for me no escape from the conviction that the essential contribution of the Church to peace and justice in the world is a fellowship which actually realizes (even if only in foretaste) that peace and justice which Christ has won for all peoples in his atoning death and resurrection.

As I have been writing this concluding chapter I have read the memoirs of my beloved friend John Coventry Smith with the title *From Colonialism to World Community*. Like me, he has lived as a missionary and an ecumenist, through the process of decolonization. Like me he had to struggle to decontaminate missions from their alliance with colonialism. But it is not yet clear to me how the era of European colonial expansion will be seen in the perspective of world history. Is there really emerging a secular 'world community' which will be held together by the science, technology, commerce and political ideas of post-Enlightenment Europe? Twenty years ago I thought so, but now I am not sure. Africa, where the colonial period was shortest, shows signs of a chaos comparable to that of Western Europe after the collapse of Roman power. Will history be repeated? Will it be the task of the Church to preserve what is worth keeping in our disintegrating 'modern' culture and slowly re-create a new society in Africa? India is a different case. The bonds binding India and Britain have been woven over four centuries and are still immensely strong. India's culture is one of the most enduring in the world and just for that reason the deep-going change brought about in these 400 years will not be undone. And who is to say what role the mighty civilization of China will play in the next few centuries? And is Islam at the beginning of a new worldwide expansion?

About all these questions I am much less sure than I was twenty years ago when I was too much impressed by the thesis of Arendt van Leeuwen's *Christianity and World History*. I do not now believe that the 'modern' secular culture of the post-Enlightenment West has an assured future. It seems to me to show all the signs of disintegration. I look back with real penitence on the occasions when, as a missionary in India, I censured some things and commended others on grounds which – I now realize – were not evangelical but merely cultural.

But at the end I return to the beginning, to the vision which was given me during that distressing night in the miners' camp in South Wales. I still see the cross of Jesus as the one place in all the history of human culture where there is a final dealing with the ultimate mysteries of sin and forgiveness, of bondage and freedom, of conflict and peace, of death and life. Although there is so much that is puzzling, so much that I simply do not understand and so much that is unpredictable, I find here – as I have again and again found during the past fifty years – a point from which one can take one's bearings and a light in which one can walk, however stumblingly. I know that that guiding star will remain and that that light will shine till death and in the end. And that is enough.

Notes

Chapter 10 Madurai: New Beginnings

1 *Three Worlds: One World*

Chapter 11 Lambeth, Geneva, Amsterdam: An Ecumenical Excursion

1 *The Long Road to Unity*, p. 220.

Chapter 12 Madurai: Getting Down to the Job

1 See *Ecumenical Review*, January 1952, pp. 122f.

2 See *Ecumenical Review*, October 1951, p. 69.

3 Ibid.

4 *Ecumenical Review*, April 1951, pp. 252–4.

Chapter 13 Madurai: Towards a Responsible Church in an Ecumenical Setting

1 See Goodall: *Missions under the Cross*, pp. 17–18.

2 *Missions under the Cross*, p. 240.

3 *The Ministry of the Church: ordained and unordained, paid and unpaid.* Edinburgh House Press, 1953.

4 *The Journal of Religion*, January 1955, p. 31.

5 *The Missionary Church in East and West*, ed. D. Paton, 1957, pp. 81–90.

6 Op. cit., p. 17.

Chapter 15 London: The International Missionary Council

1 *Missions under the Cross*, p. 40.

2 *The Ghana Assembly of the IMC*, p. 141.

3 The word 'place' here is used both in its primary sense of local neighbourhood and also, under more modern conditions, of other areas in which Christians need to express unity in Christ, e.g., all those engaged in a local industry.

4 *The Student World*, Nos. 1–2, 1961, pp. 20–21.

5 Ibid., pp. 81–2.

6   Ibid., p. 19.

7   *The Ecumenical Advance*, ed. H. E. Fey, p. 90.

8   *The New Delhi Report*, ed. S. M. Calvert, p. 82.

Chapter 16   Geneva: The World Council of Churches

1   *The Church for Others*, WCC 1968, p. 20.

2   *Secular Man and Christian Mission*, ed. P. Löffler, SCM Press 1968.

Chapter 18   Birmingham: A New Dimension

1   *Agreed Syllabus of Religious Education*, City of Birmingham Education Committee, 1975, p. 4.

Index of Names